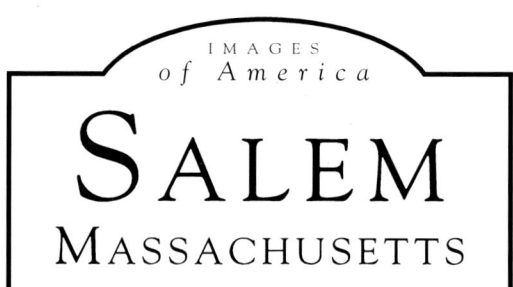

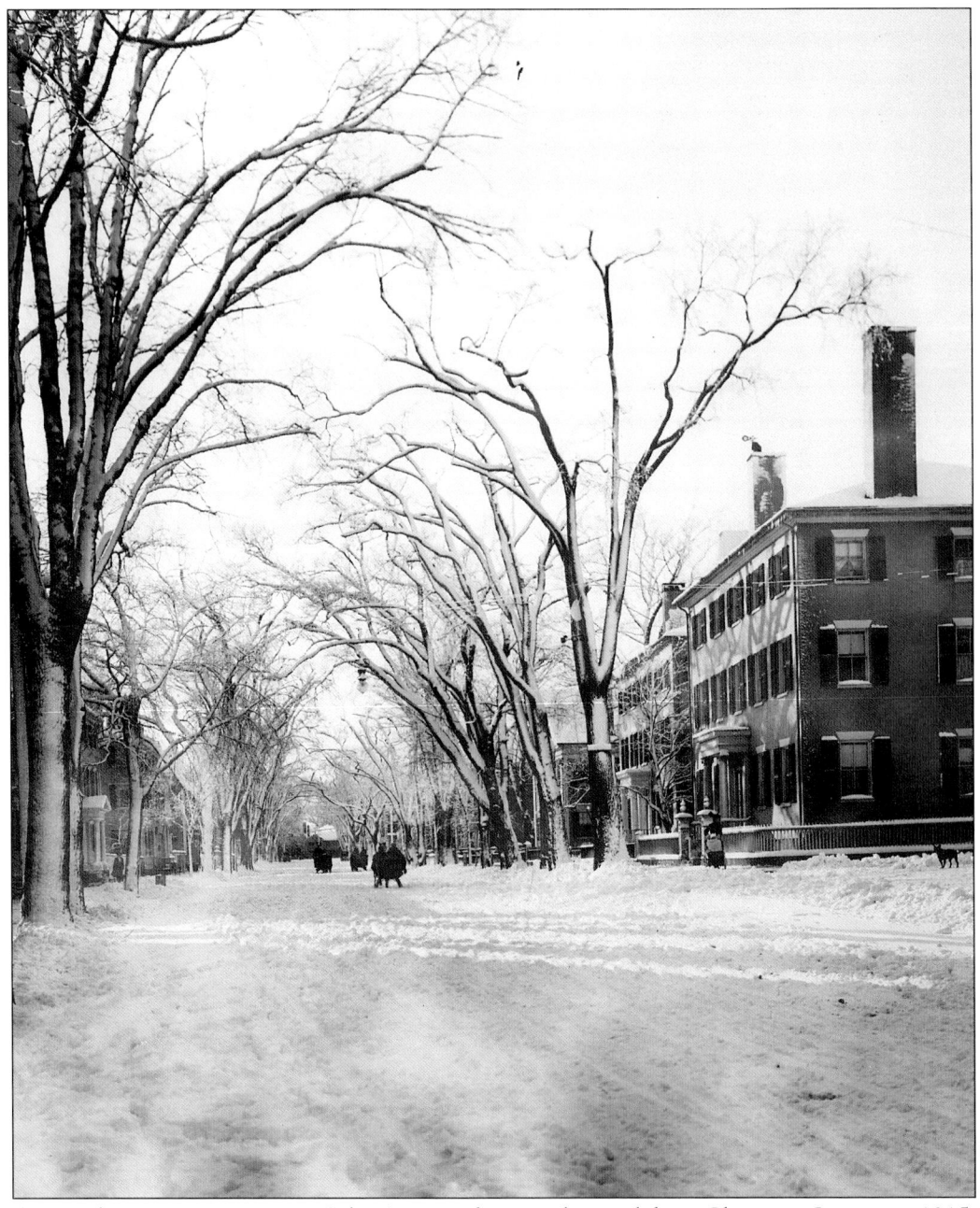

A nostalgic winter scene on Salem's most famous thoroughfare, Chestnut Street, c. 1915. (Courtesy D. Michel Michaud.)

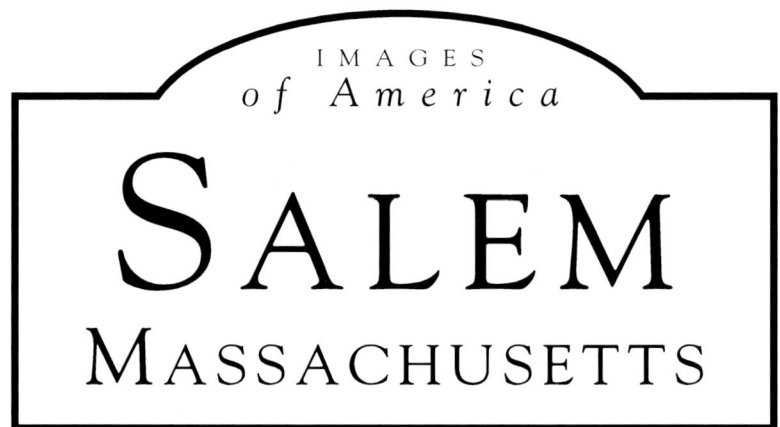

Kenneth C. Turino and Stephen J. Schier

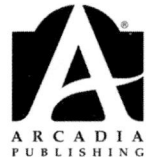

Copyright © 1996 by Kenneth C. Turino and Stephen J. Schier
ISBN 978-0-7385-3540-1

Published by Arcadia Publishing
Charleston, South Carolina

Printed in the United States of America

Library of Congress Catalog Card Number: Applied for

For all general information contact Arcadia Publishing at:
Telephone 843-853-2070
Fax 843-853-0044
E-mail sales@arcadiapublishing.com
For customer service and orders:
Toll-Free 1-888-313-2665

Visit us on the Internet at www.arcadiapublishing.com

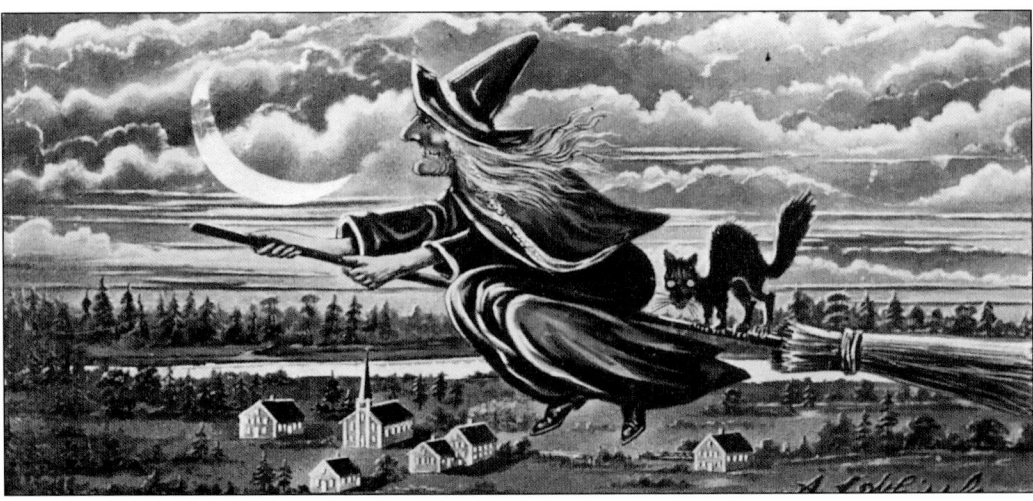

An amusing postcard showing an imaginative scene of a witch flying over Salem Village.

# Contents

| | | |
|---|---|---|
| Introduction | | 7 |
| 1. | Salem Street Scenes | 11 |
| 2. | Doorways and Exterior Views | 27 |
| 3. | Salem Interiors | 43 |
| 4. | Schools and Public Buildings | 55 |
| 5. | Churches | 69 |
| 6. | Salem Businesses | 83 |
| 7. | Fires and Firefighting | 105 |
| 8. | Salem Willows and Surrounding Areas | 115 |
| Acknowledgments | | 128 |

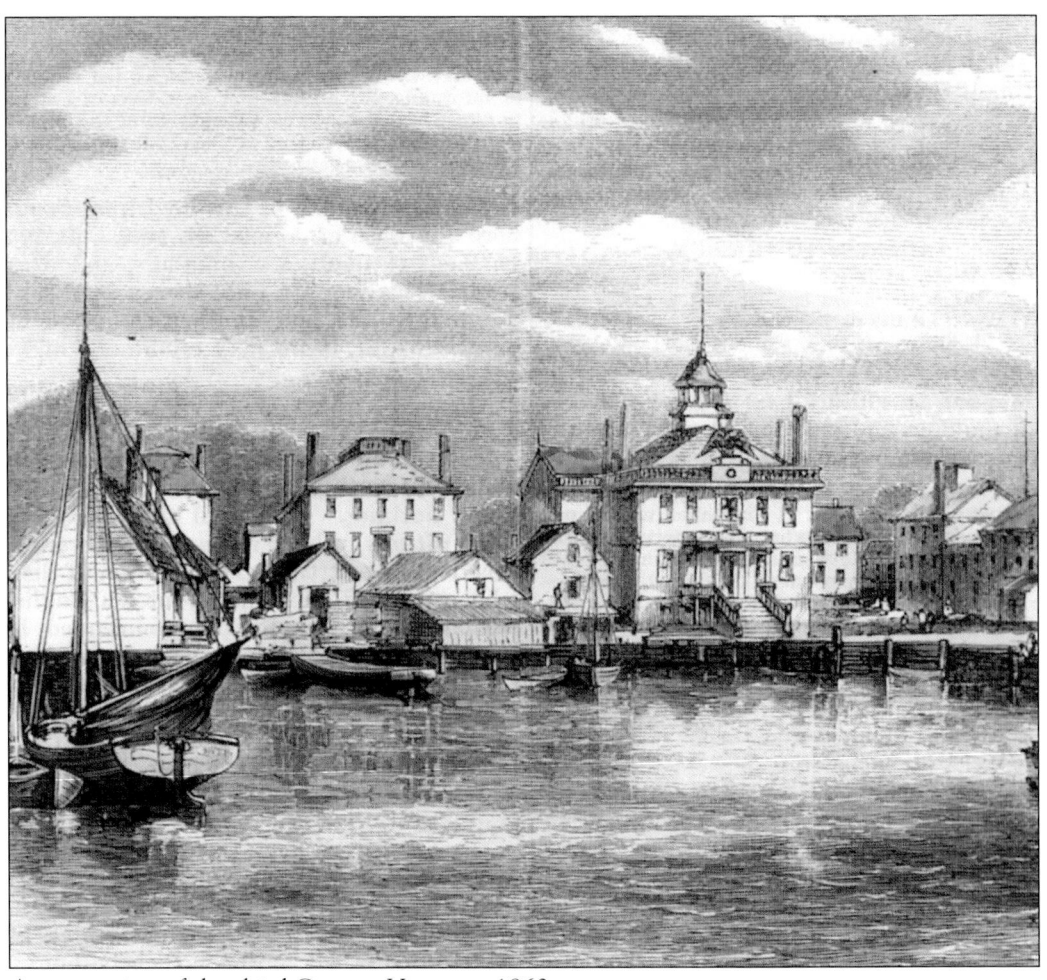
An engraving of the third Custom House, c. 1860.

# INTRODUCTION

Salem, Massachusetts, founded in 1626, is one of the oldest and most historic communities in New England. Salem's history began when Roger Conant (1592–1679) and a group of settlers came to a place, then called Naumkeag, after an unsuccessful attempt at settlement on Cape Ann. Originally the colonists settled along the North River at the foot of what is now Skerry Street. The early colonists, mainly Puritans, suffered through several seasons of much sickness. Although death was common, the population gradually increased with births and the coming of new immigrants. Like most coastal towns of the early period, Salem quickly established farming and fishing as its economic mainstays.

Salem is most often associated with the witchcraft hysteria that began in 1691 in Salem Village—now Danvers, Massachusetts. At that time witchcraft was believed to be a powerful evil force, both in Europe and the New World. The Salem hysteria began with a small group of young girls who met at the parsonage of Reverend Samuel Parris (1653–1720), and spread throughout sections of Essex County. Warrants were issued against people whom the girls proclaimed were witches; trials were held in which the girls acted as if they were possessed by spirits. Hundreds of people were accused and arrested. In 1692, nineteen people were hanged and one man, Giles Corey (1616–1692), was pressed to death before the madness ended. It was not until May of 1693 that Governor William Phipps (1651–1694/95) released from jail the remaining victims, signaling the end of the most notorious chapter in Salem's history.

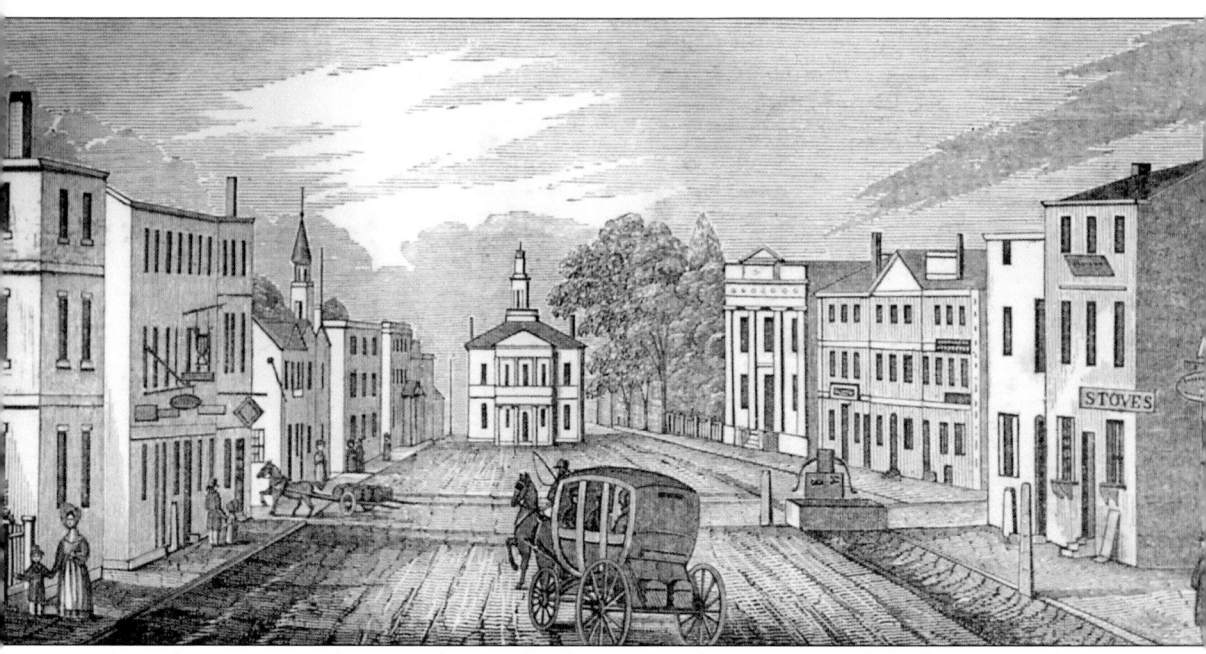

A southern view in the central part of Salem, 1839, showing part of Washington and Court Streets. The courthouse is in the distance, fronting the south, in the central part of the engraving. The city hall is the building with pilasters on the eastern side of Court Street.

With the North River on one side, the South River on the other, and a good harbor, Salem became "a maritime place." Fishing was a staple industry in the early period, but soon shipbuilding and ocean trade grew in importance. From the 1640s, Salem-manned vessels were trading with merchants in such places as Antigua and Barbados, returning with cargoes of exotic spices and goods.

During the Revolutionary War, Salem merchants turned their ships into privateers, private ships commissioned to cruise against the commerce or warships of an enemy. The pace of construction and the size of the ships increased during the war; over 158 vessels carrying 2,000 guns and manned by several thousand seamen cleared Salem harbor from 1775 to 1783.

After the first war with England, Salem's trading reached its peak. New trade routes were opened to Russia, the Cape of Good Hope, China, the East Indies, Java, Japan, and many other markets. Derby Street with its wharves became the town's natural commercial center. Vast fortunes were made including that of the nation's first millionaire, Elias Hasket Derby (1739–1799). Examples of the treasures brought back by the ships and merchants of Salem can be seen at the Peabody Essex Museum.

From 1794 to 1815 Great Britain and France were almost continuously at war, and both powers interfered with United States maritime trade; President Thomas Jefferson passed a comprehensive embargo in 1808 cutting off these countries from shipments of American food and raw materials. War with Great Britain followed in 1812, and this conflict seriously damaged Salem's lucrative maritime trade. Much of this commerce was never recovered, even though forty privateers did their best to impede British shipping. Salem's sea-borne trade continued to decline through the nineteenth century, as noted in the first chapter of Nathaniel Hawthorne's famous *The Scarlet Letter*. Newer, larger ships could not navigate in the harbor and the coming of the railroad in the 1830s helped to hasten the end of Salem's rich maritime history.

In 1836 Salem was granted a city charter, the second charter in Massachusetts after Boston. The new city grew and changed from a maritime economy to a manufacturing and business center. During this time period Salem produced one of the nation's finest authors, Nathaniel Hawthorne (1804–1864), who was born on July Fourth. It was while he lived on Mall Street that he wrote *The Scarlet Letter*.

The following eight chapters are filled with numerous unpublished photographs of Salem from the 1860s to the 1950s. The city's rich architectural heritage, including the work of noted woodcarver and

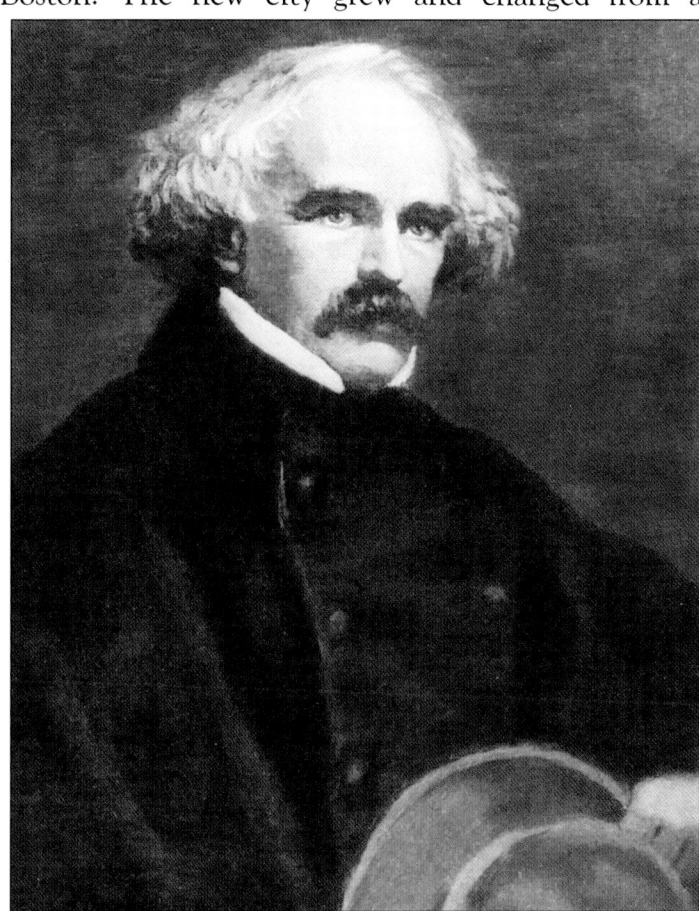

Nathaniel Hawthorne (1804–1864), portrayed here in mid-life, is Salem's most famous author.

architect Samuel McIntire (1757–1811), is revealed. Rare glimpses through elegant doorways offer intimate views of the interiors of many prominent homes. The variety of Salem's business interests is highlighted in an especially interesting chapter about the city's importance as a center of trade and commerce. Both the religious and secular sides of life, including the city's popular resort and amusement center, the Willows, come to life in words and pictures. One of the most devastating events in the life of the city, the Great Salem Fire of 1914, is depicted in detail. The fire consumed 256 acres, destroying 1,792 factories, homes, and buildings.

These images offer a fascinating visual record of the people and life of Salem, Massachusetts, one of our nation's most historic cities.

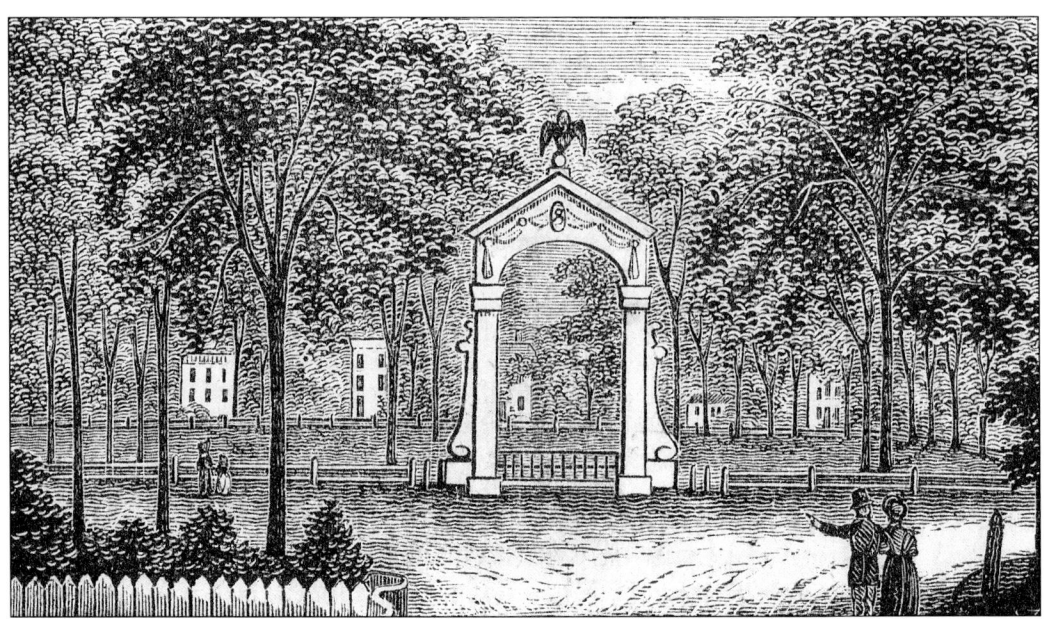
A western view of Washington Square, 1839.

# One
# SALEM STREET SCENES

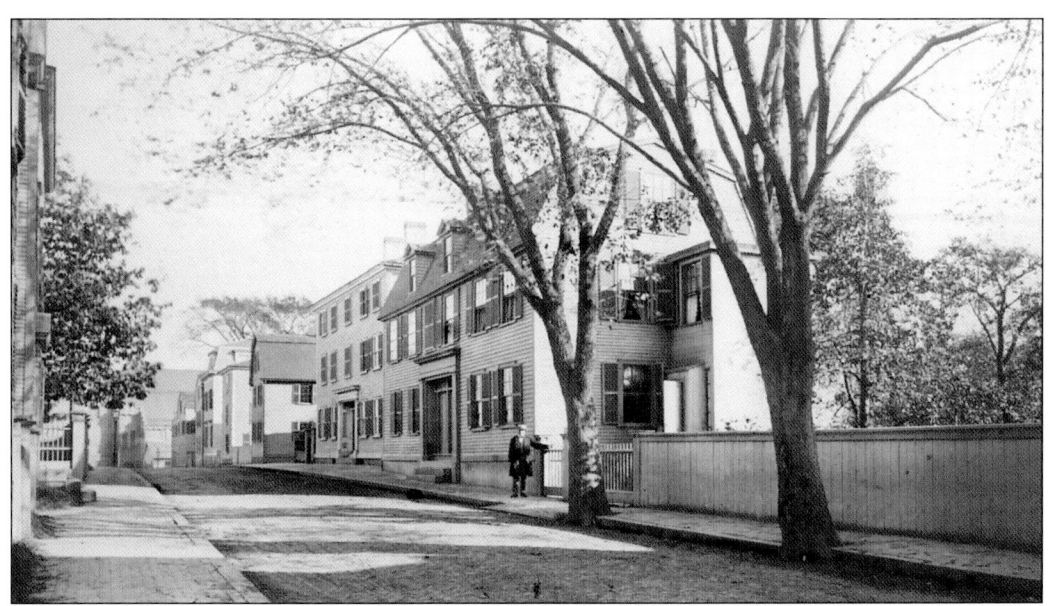

Norman Street, c. 1890, looking toward the train depot. The gambrel-roofed house in the foreground is the Benjamin Cox House (21 Norman Street). Many of these homes were removed prior to 1932 to make way for the United States Post Office building designed in the Colonial Revival style. (Courtesy Pickering Foundation.)

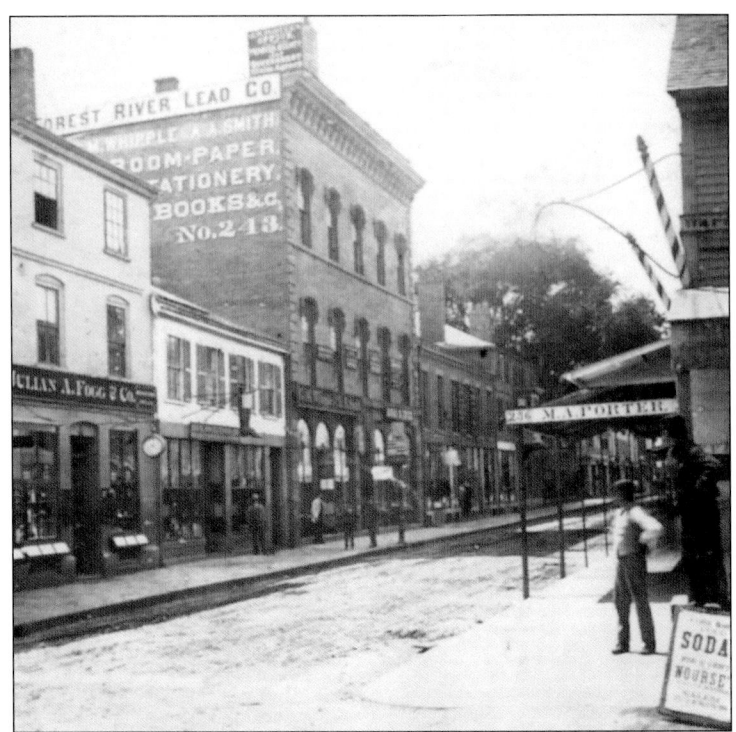

Essex Street (once called "Old Paved Street") in 1874, showing a busy commercial center. On the right, at 236 Essex Street, Miss M.A. Porter's dry goods store is clearly visible. Across the street, at 233 Essex, is Julian A. Fogg & Company, jewelers, and E. Sweetser, a dealer in boots. G.M. Whipple & A.A. Smith, stationers, had set up shop at 234 Essex Street. (Courtesy D. Michel Michaud.)

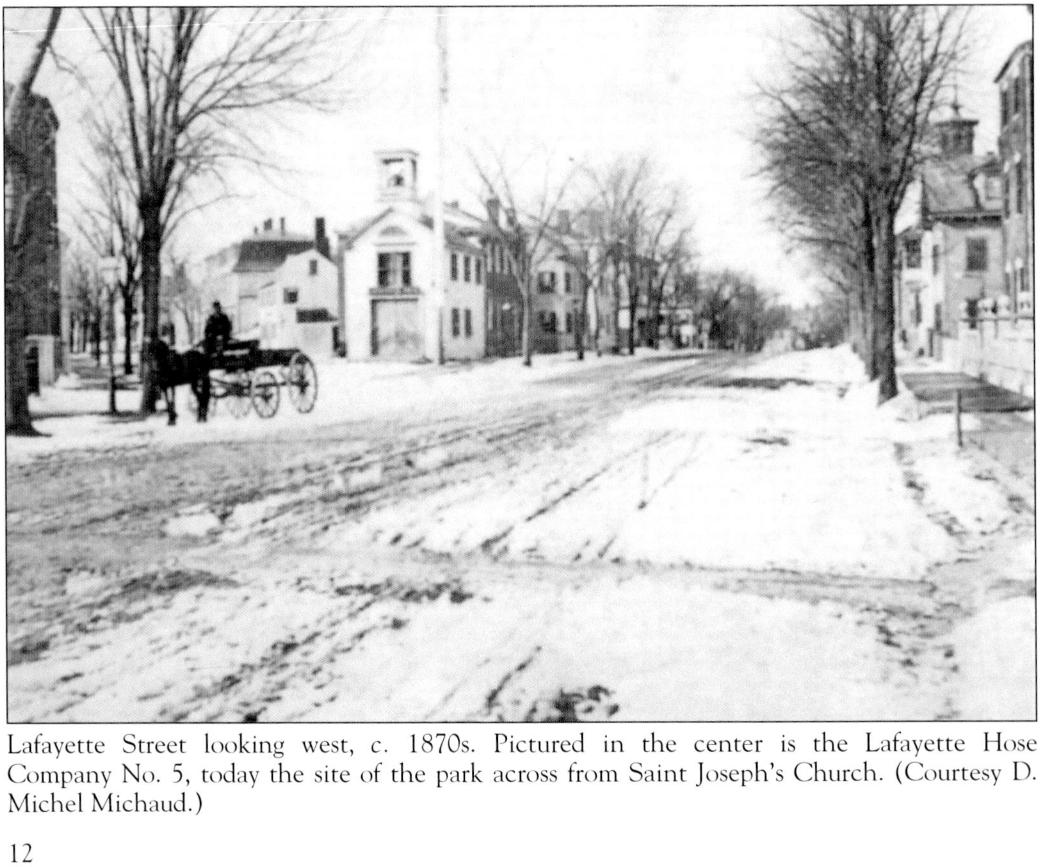

Lafayette Street looking west, c. 1870s. Pictured in the center is the Lafayette Hose Company No. 5, today the site of the park across from Saint Joseph's Church. (Courtesy D. Michel Michaud.)

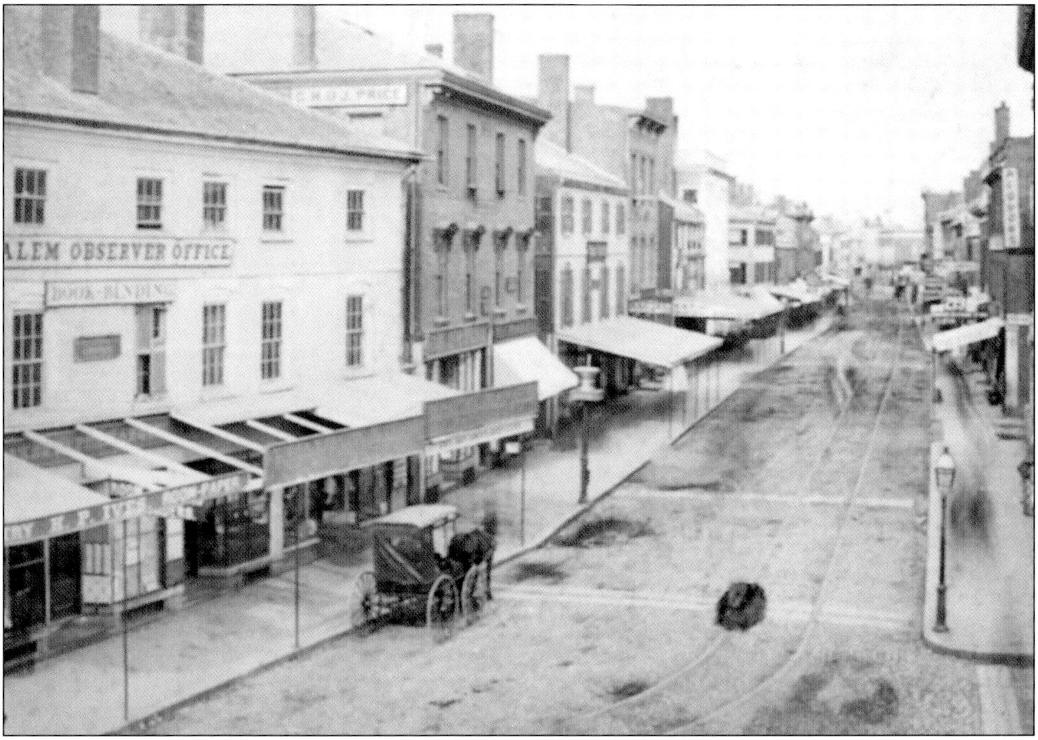

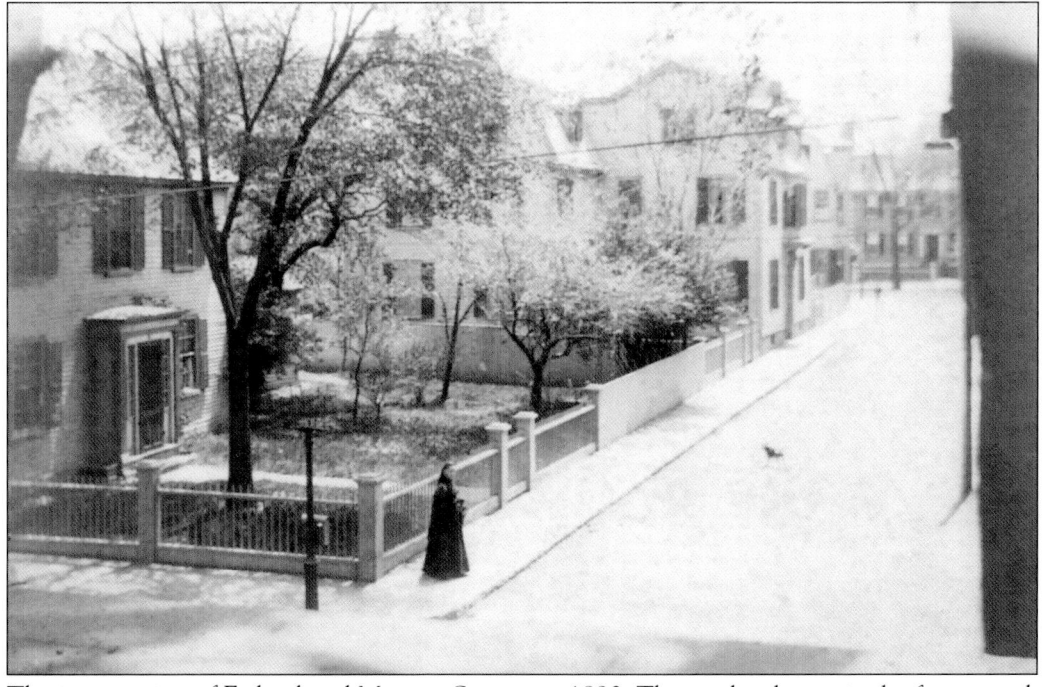

A stereoscope view of Essex Street, from Washington Street, c. 1870. Note the apothecary sign on the lamppost. (Courtesy D. Michel Michaud.)

The intersection of Federal and Monroe Streets, c. 1890. The modest house in the foreground, 10 Monroe Street, was built c. 1782 for Rebecca Gould.

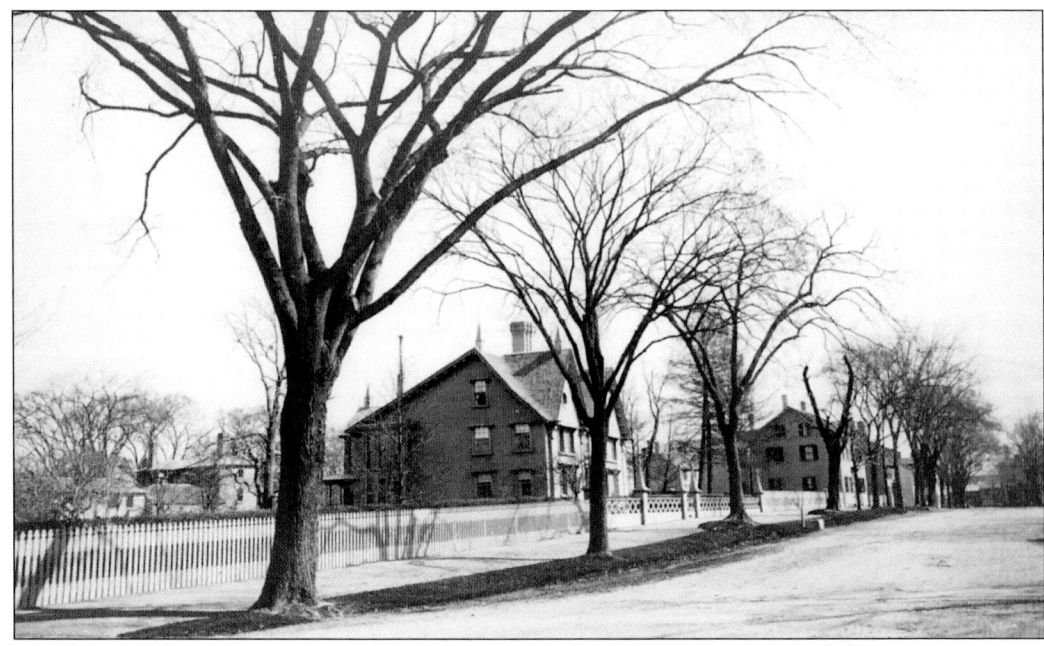

A sweeping view of Broad Street, c. 1890, showing stately old elm trees and the ancestral home of the Pickering family. (Courtesy Pickering Foundation.)

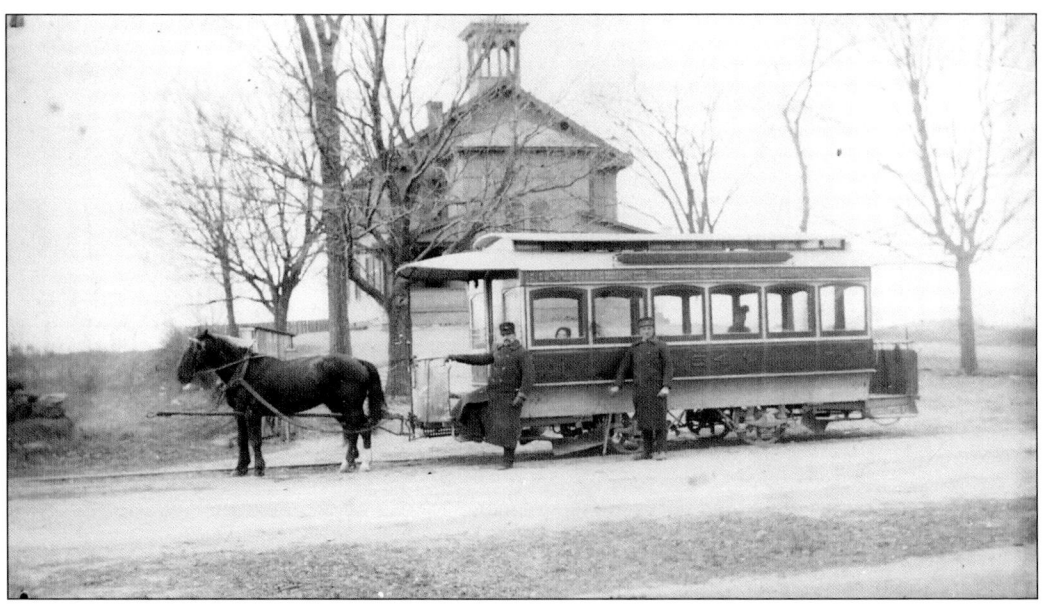

The Naumkeag Street Railroad, one of several street railways in Salem. With offices at 233 Essex Street, this line began in 1874, and ran from Danvers through Salem, out to the Willows and then on to Marblehead. (Courtesy Lynn Historical Society.)

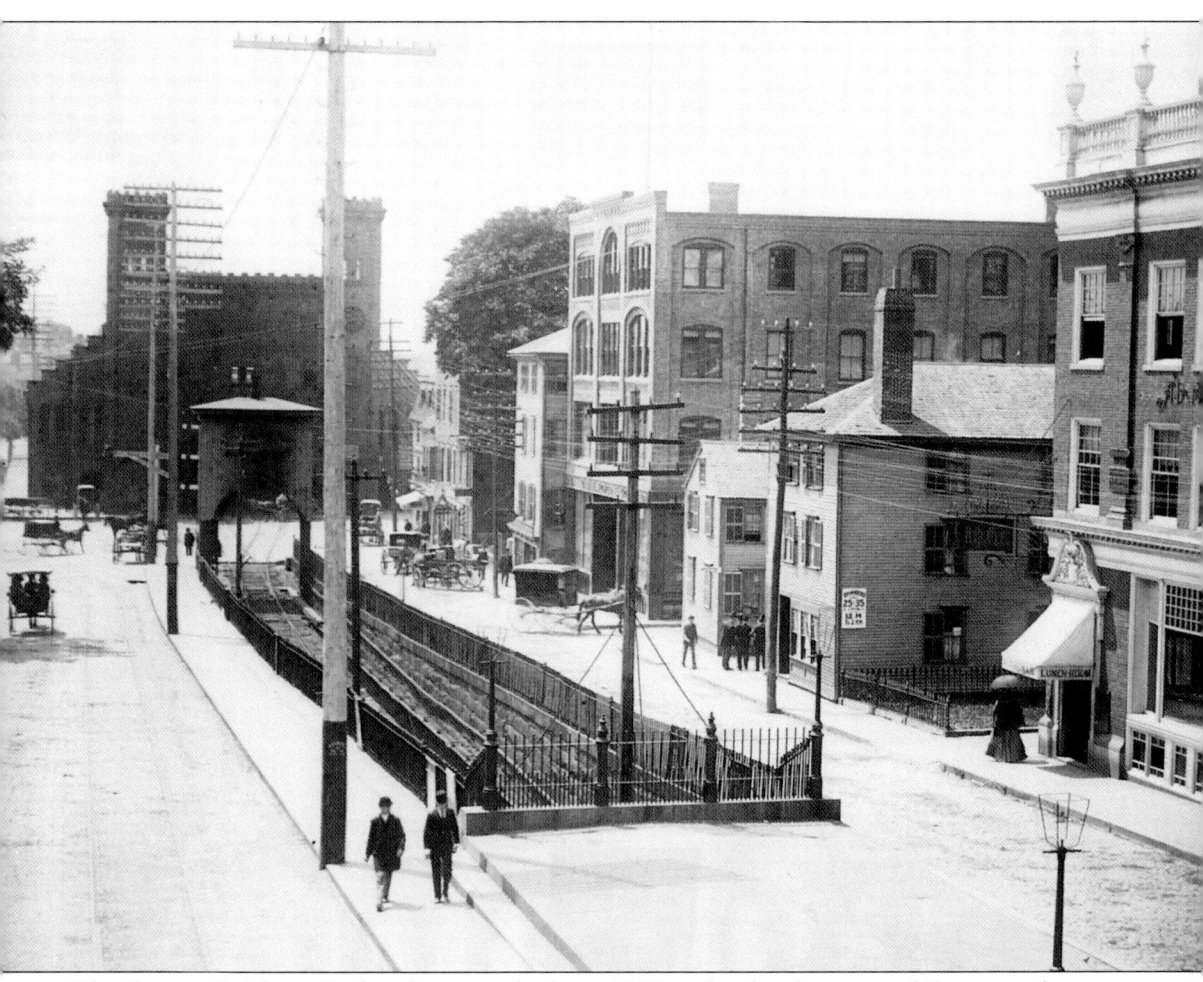

The Boston & Maine Railroad station, built in 1847 under the direction of Boston architect Gridley J.F. Bryant. On April 6, 1882, a fire destroyed the wooden portion of the structure and a new station was built around the original Norman-style granite facade. In 1954, the great superstructure was demolished to make way for Riley Plaza. It is shown here c. 1900. (Courtesy Lynn Historical Society.)

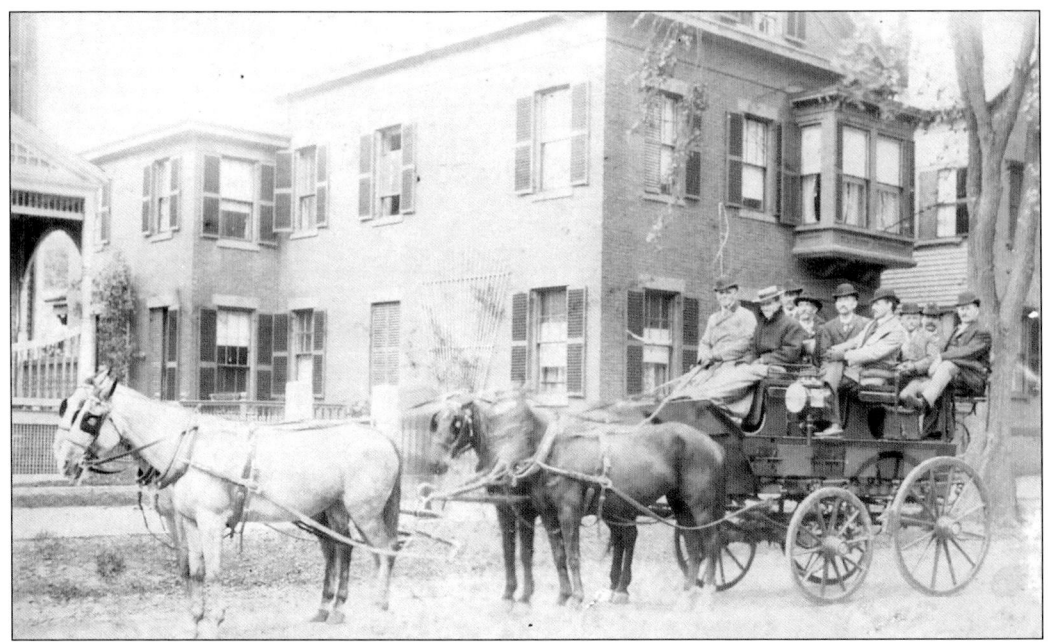

The home of Captain John Bertram (1796–1882) and his family at 24 Winter Street. The Bertrams lived here until 1855, when they moved into a new Italianate brick and brownstone mansion at 370 Essex Street. Winter Street is one of Salem's busiest thoroughfares and is regarded as next in importance to Chestnut Street. Depicted here are several well-dressed individuals enjoying a coach ride in the 1890s.(Courtesy Danvers Historical Society.)

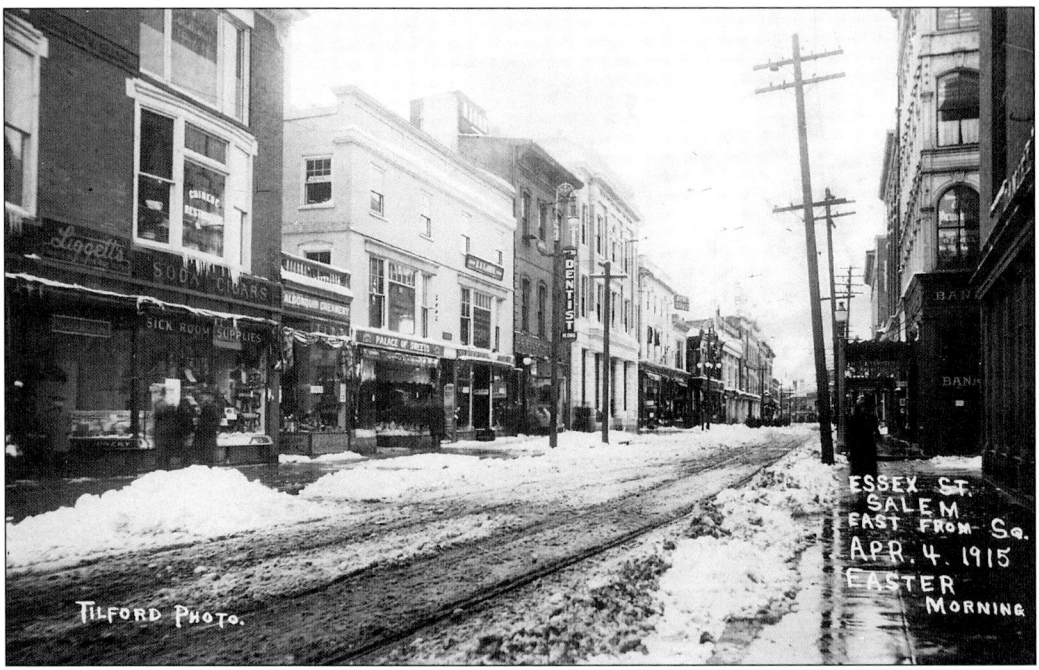

An early spring snowstorm on Easter morning, April 4, 1915. This view from Town House Square shows a quiet Essex Street. At this time Essex Street had a vibrant retail trade. (Courtesy D. Michel Michaud.)

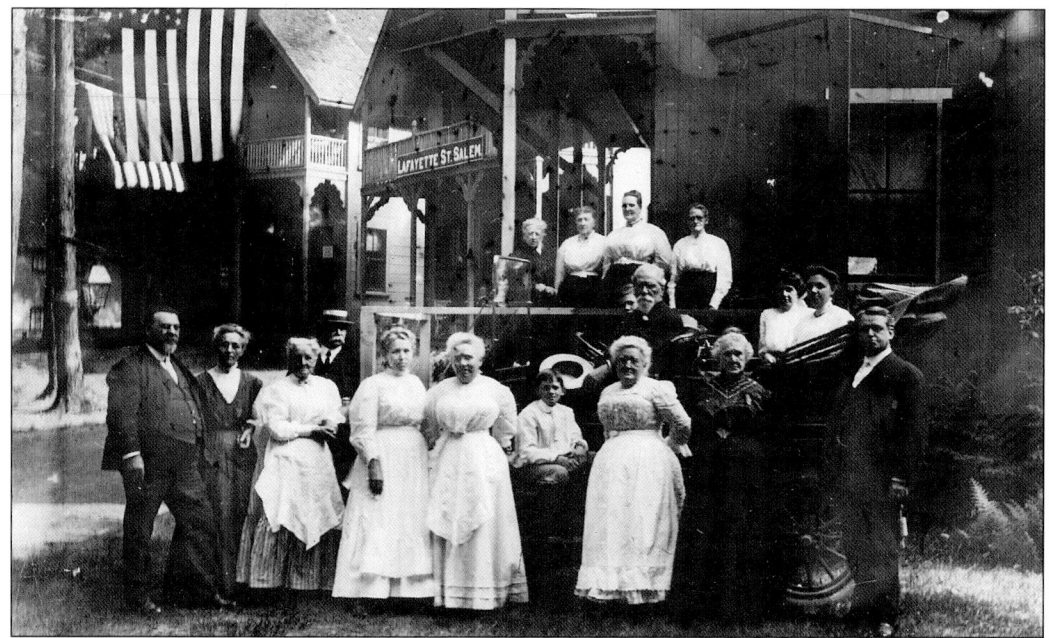

A group portrait of Lafayette Street residents getting ready for a Fourth of July celebration. This photograph was taken before the Great Salem Fire of 1914. (Courtesy D. Michel Michaud.)

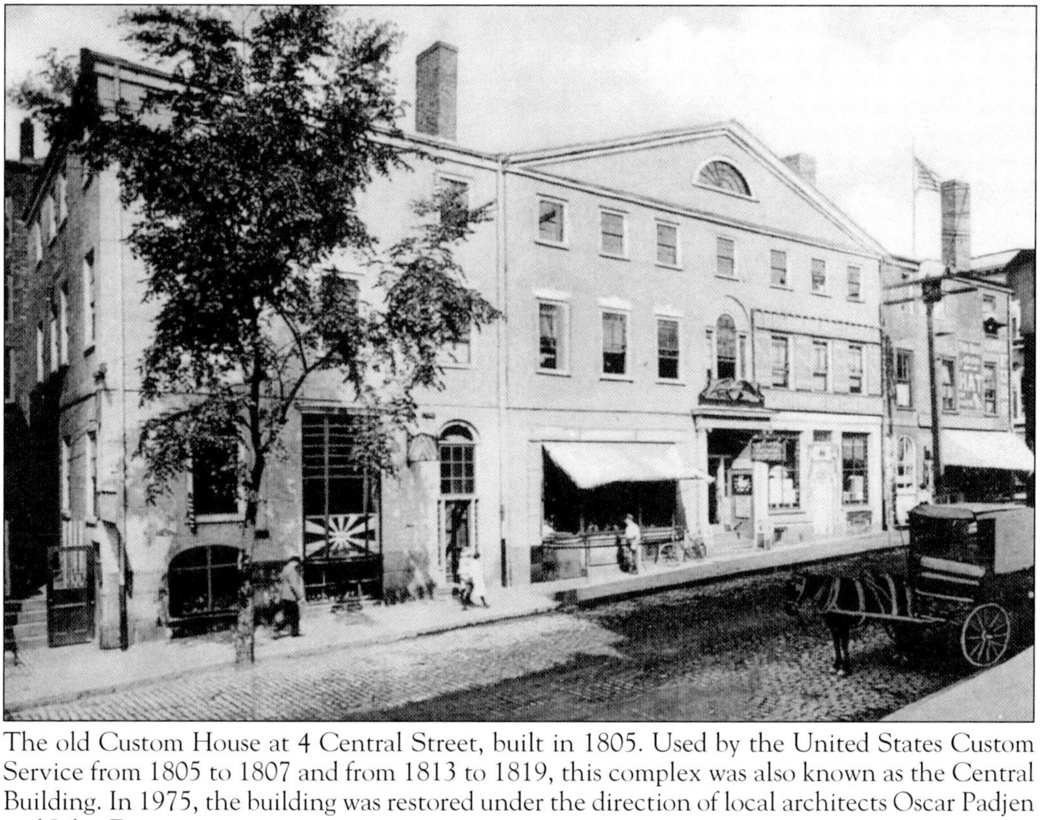

The old Custom House at 4 Central Street, built in 1805. Used by the United States Custom Service from 1805 to 1807 and from 1813 to 1819, this complex was also known as the Central Building. In 1975, the building was restored under the direction of local architects Oscar Padjen and John Emerson.

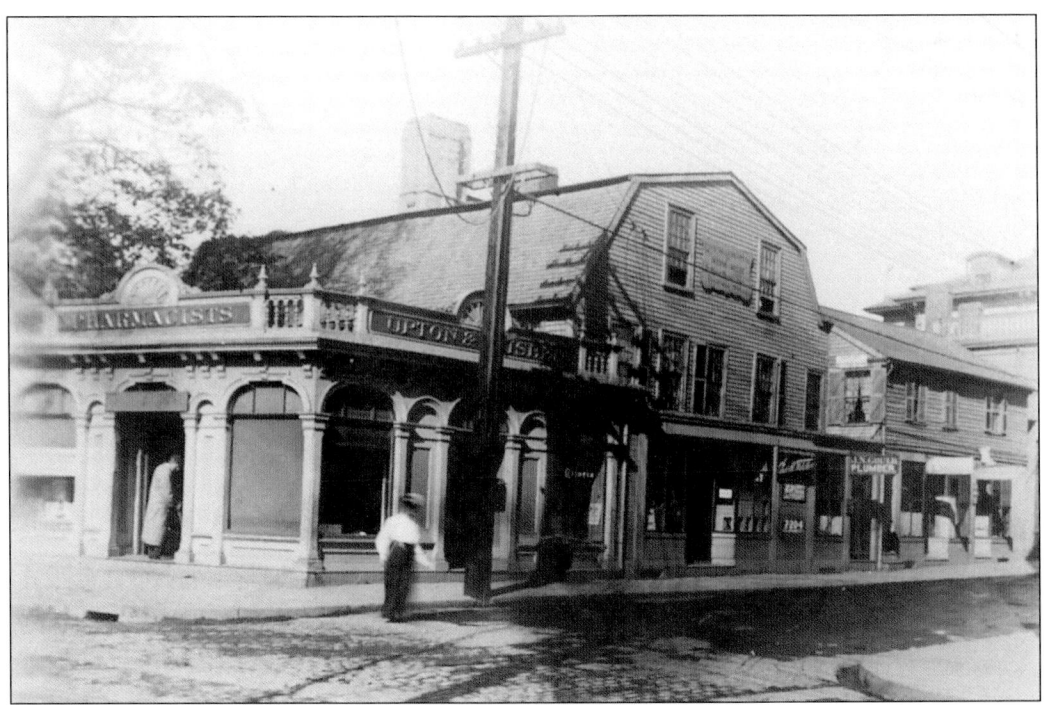

The Witch House at the corner of North and Essex Streets, built c. 1675. This was the home of Jonathan Corwin, who served as a magistrate and justice at the Salem Witch Trials in 1692. Preliminary examinations of the accused witches were held in the upstairs chambers. The storefront was added in 1856 and remodeled in 1885 for use as an apothecary shop. The house was restored in the late 1940s by Historic Salem, Inc. The popular site is maintained and opened to the public by the City of Salem.

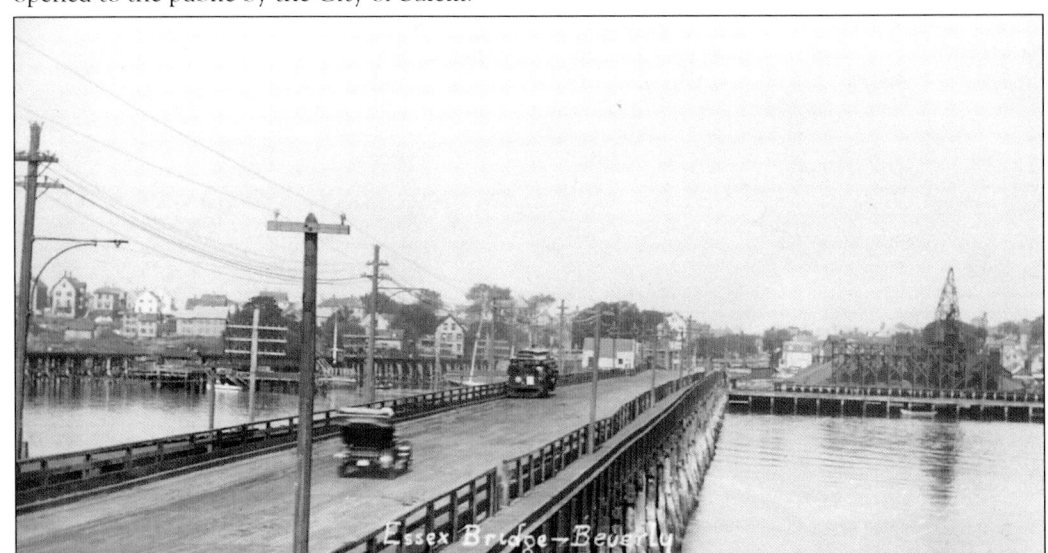

The Essex Bridge connecting Salem to Beverly, first built in 1788. In 1793 George Washington rode across this bridge on the way to Beverly. From its conception to the present day, it has always been a drawbridge. Note the trolley service on the bridge in this c. 1912 photographic postcard. (Courtesy Borinous Schier.)

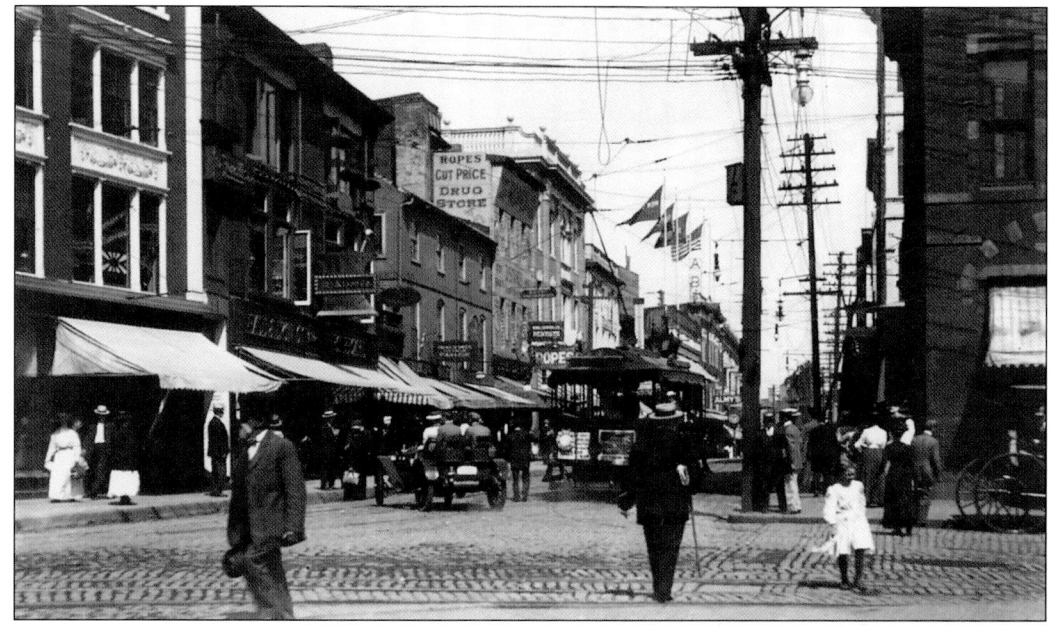

The busy intersection at Washington and Essex Streets, known as Town House Square, c. 1910. The mercantile district is in full swing, crowded with pedestrians and various forms of transportation. (Courtesy D. Michel Michaud.)

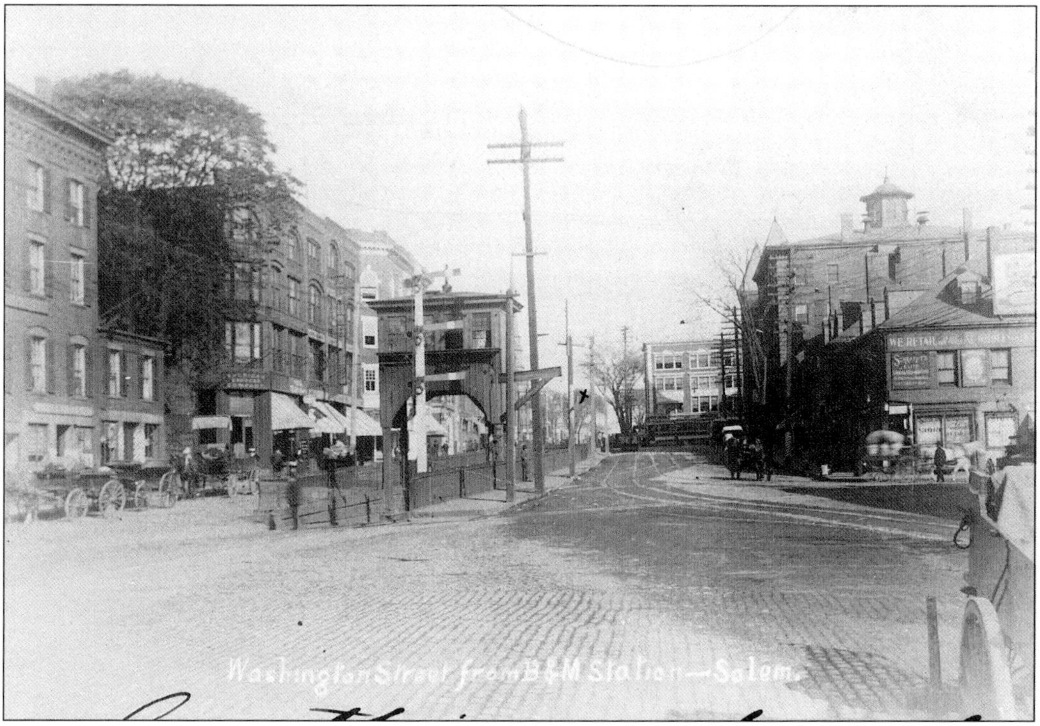

The entrance to the Boston and Maine Railroad tunnel, Washington Street, which runs under Town House Square, c. 1906. The tunnel is about 650 feet long. (Courtesy D. Michel Michaud.)

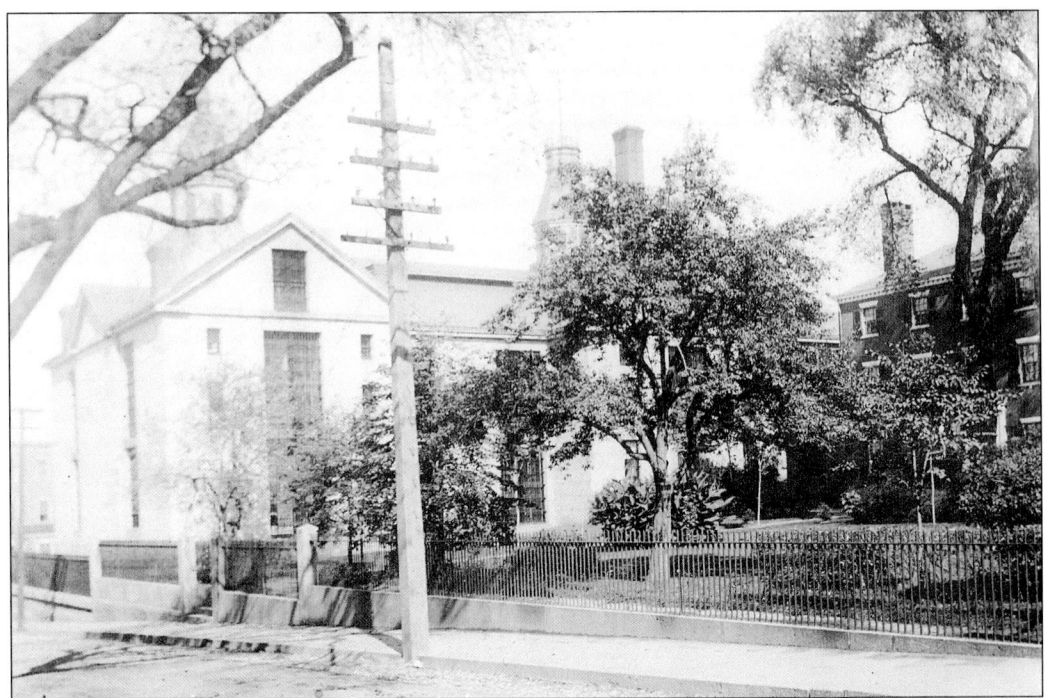

The Salem Jail, 50 Saint Peter Street, c. 1908. This imposing structure was built in 1811–1813 and enlarged in the same style c. 1884. The facade is constructed of Rockport granite. Up until a few years ago this county jail was still in use, holding the ignominious distinction as the oldest continually operating jail in the country. In the nineteenth century, executions by hanging were held here. (Courtesy D. Michel Michaud.)

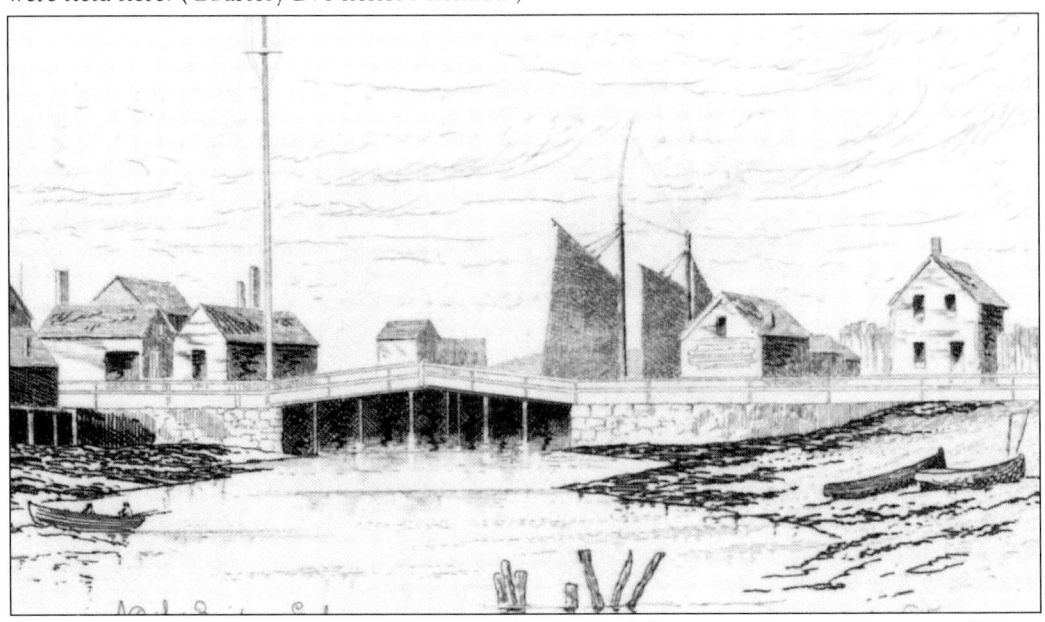

A c. 1887 copper plate engraving of the North Bridge by Salem artist George Merwanjee White (1849–1915). This drawbridge over the North River was the site of Leslie's Retreat on February 26, 1775. (Courtesy John Hardy Wright.)

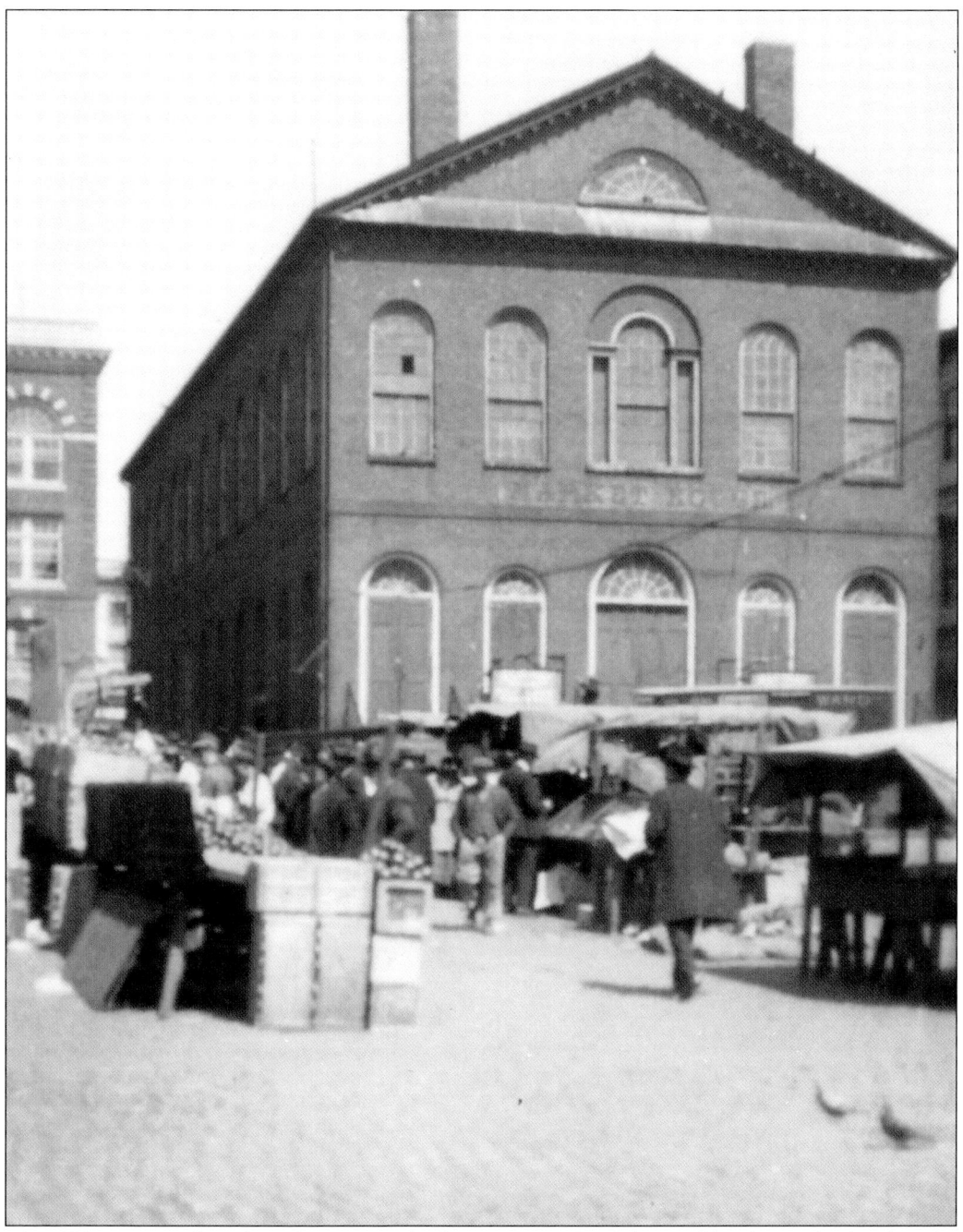

The Old Town Hall and Market House, built in 1816 on land donated by the Derby family. The second story was designed as a hall, while the lower level was used as a market. On July 8, 1817, the hall was opened to the public; President James Monroe was the guest of honor. (Courtesy D. Michel Michaud.)

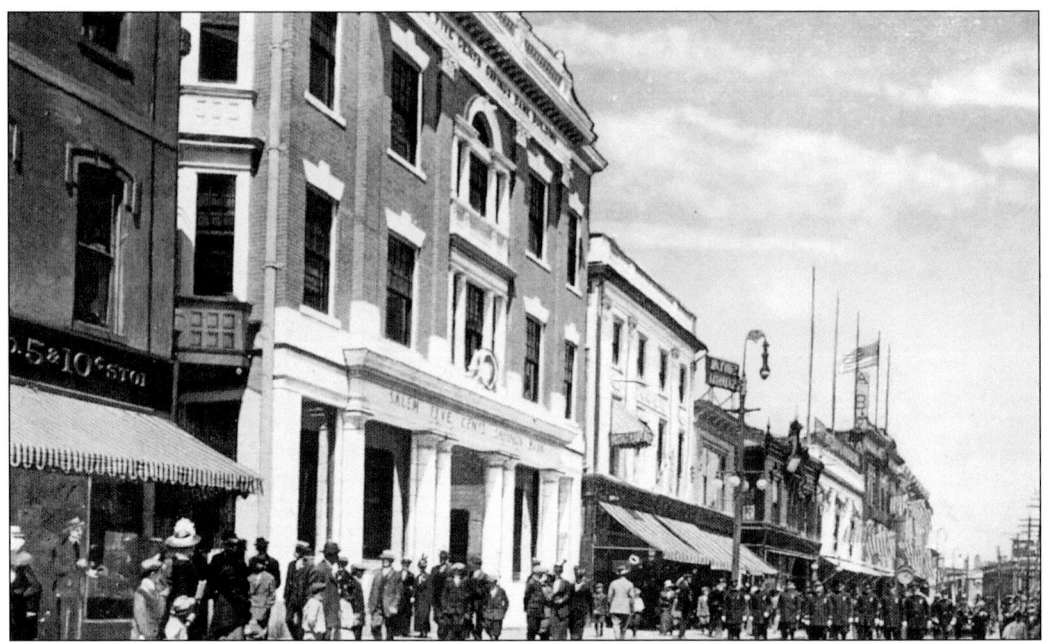
A parade of policemen marching down Essex Street in front of the Salem Five Cents Savings Bank, c. 1915.

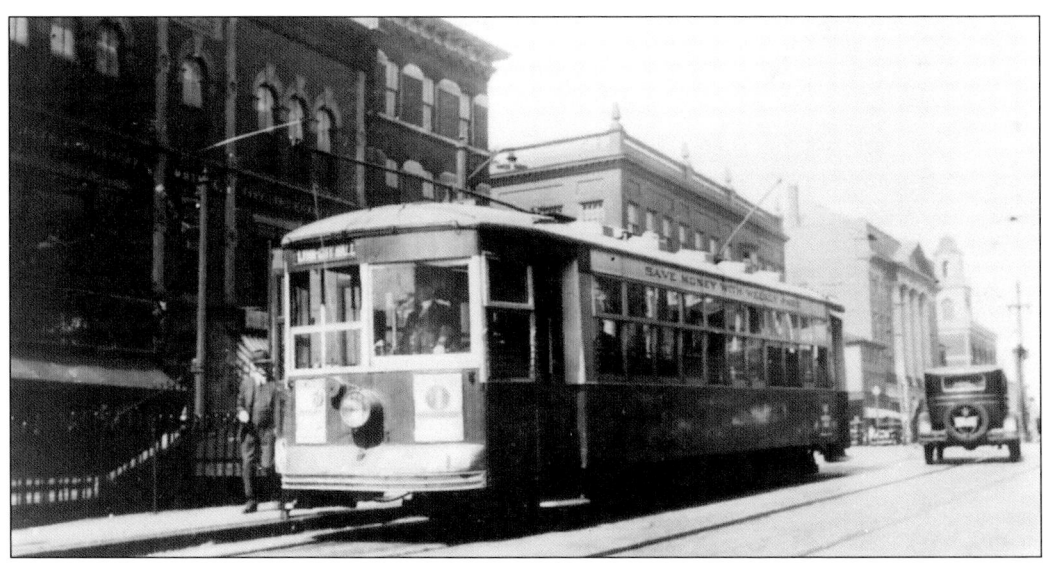
Town House Square at the Boston & Maine Railroad's Salem tunnel entrance in 1924. Car #7036 of the Salem-Lynn line of the Eastern Massachusetts Street Railway is shown here. (Courtesy D. Michel Michaud.)

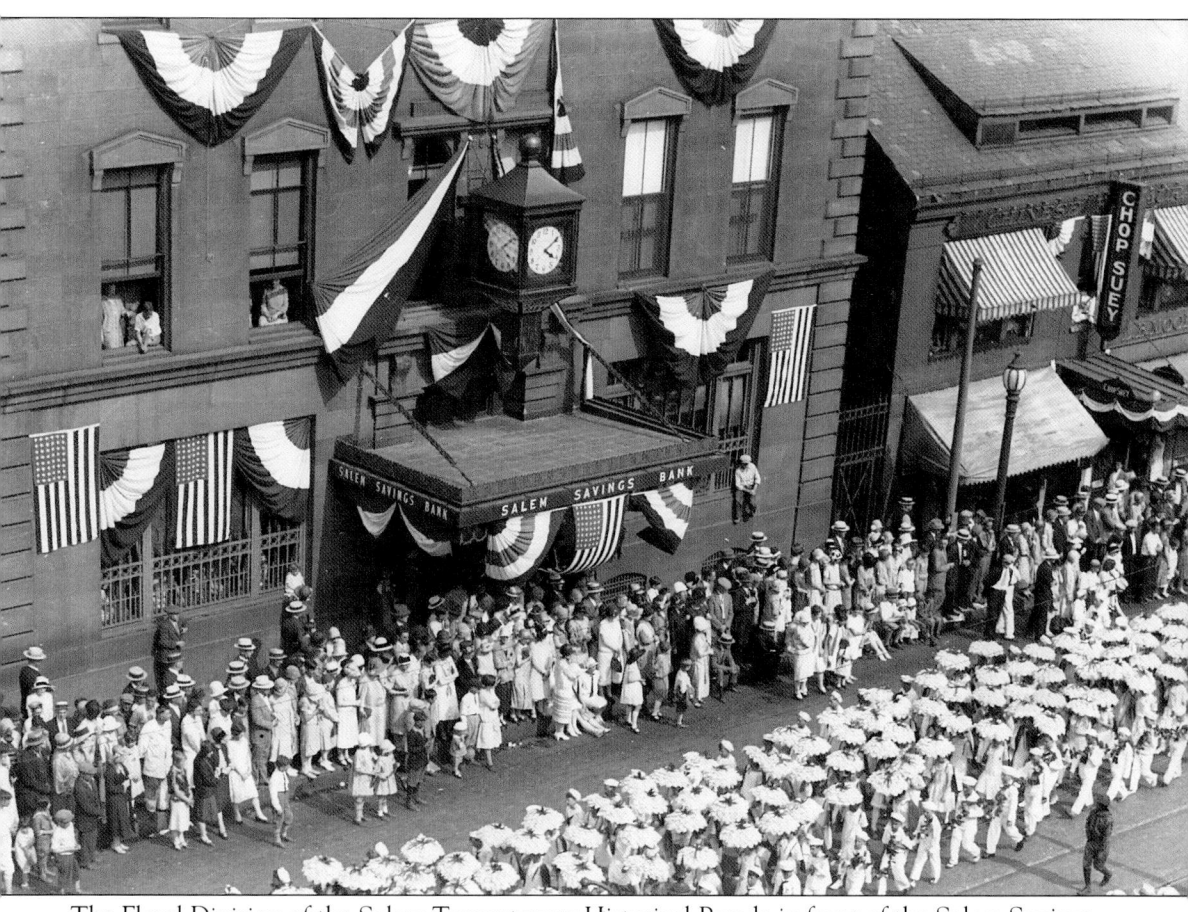
The Floral Division of the Salem Tercentenary Historical Parade in front of the Salem Savings Bank on Washington Street, Friday, July 9, 1926. (Courtesy D. Michel Michaud.)

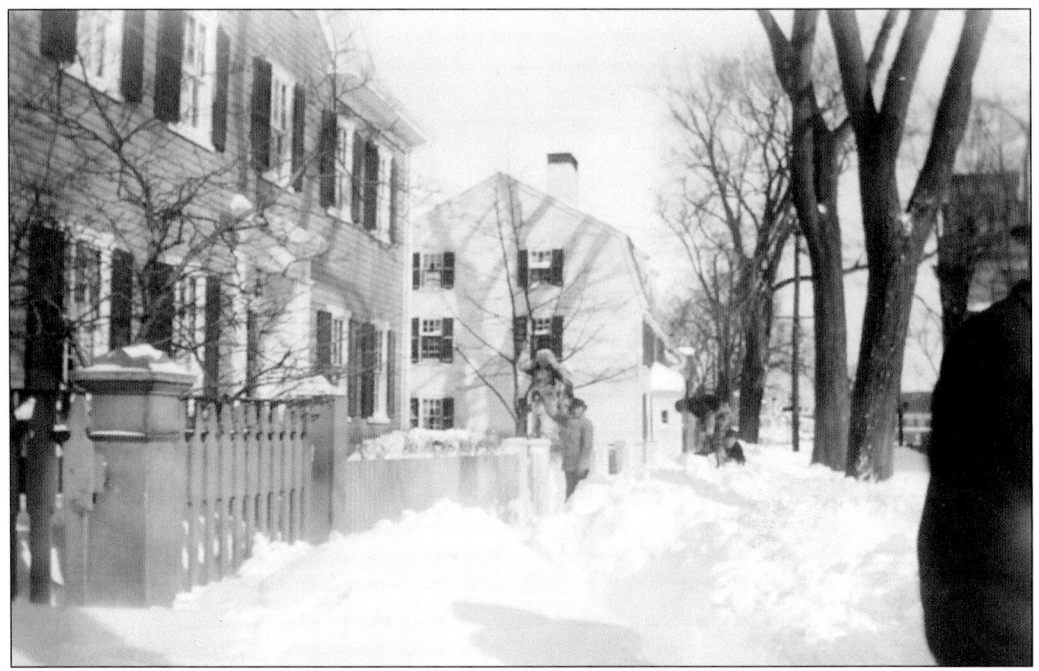

A winter scene on Broad Street, c. 1926, showing the William Stevens House at 14 Broad Street. Built in 1836, the William Stevens House is now the home of Steve Thomas, the celebrated television host of "This Old House." The gambrel-roofed dwelling next door at 12 Broad Street is known as the Jonathan Neal House, built in 1767. (Courtesy Pickering Foundation.)

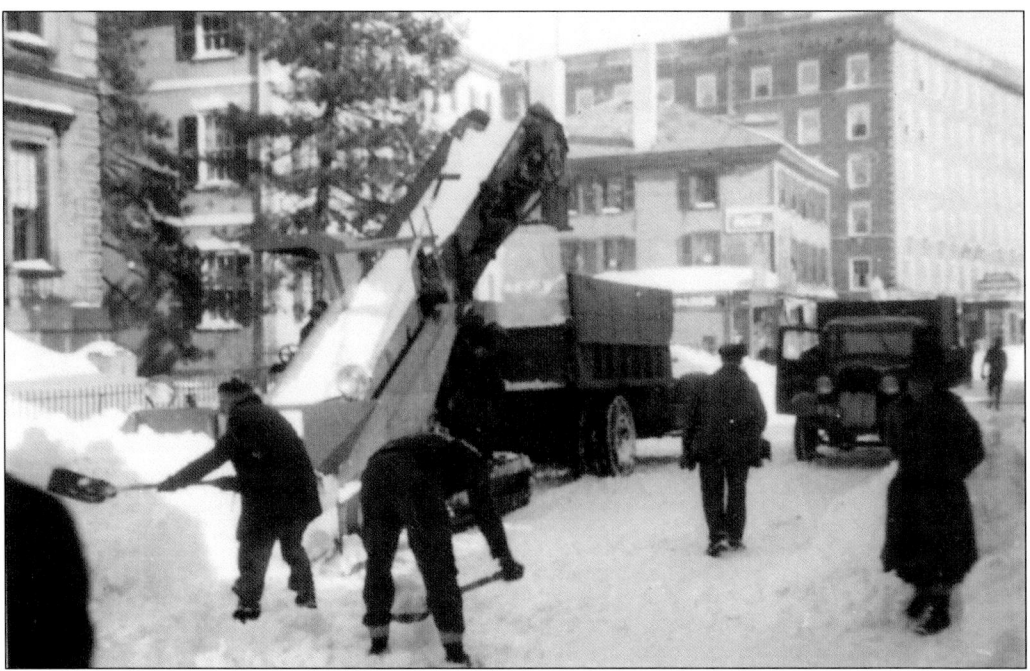

Removing snow on Essex Street after the February 15 storm of 1940. In the background is the Hawthorne Hotel. (Courtesy Henri Michaud.)

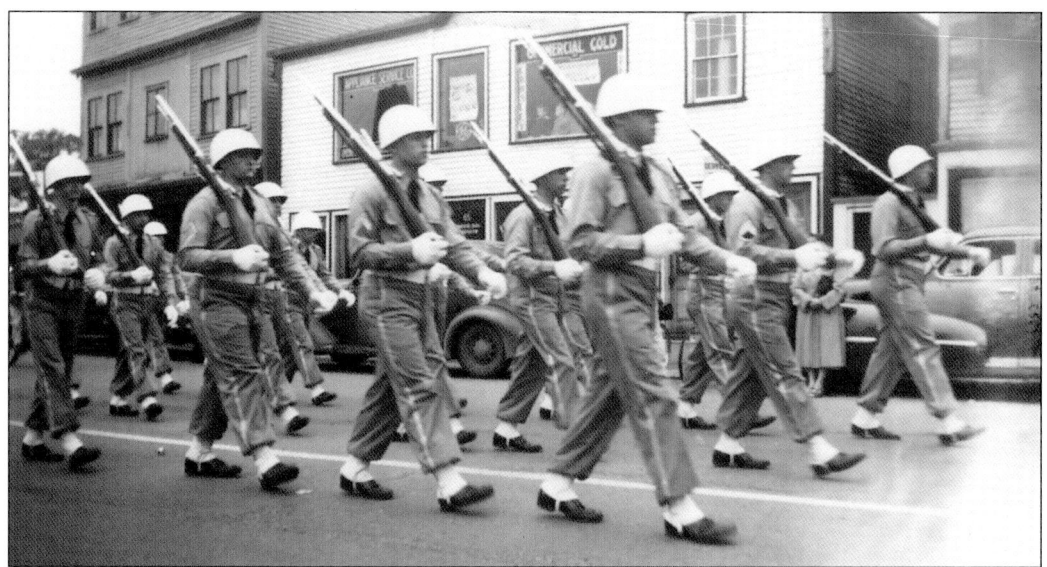

Patriotic celebrations. Parades were a popular form of civic pride in Salem for years, as these two c. 1950 views of North Street demonstrate.

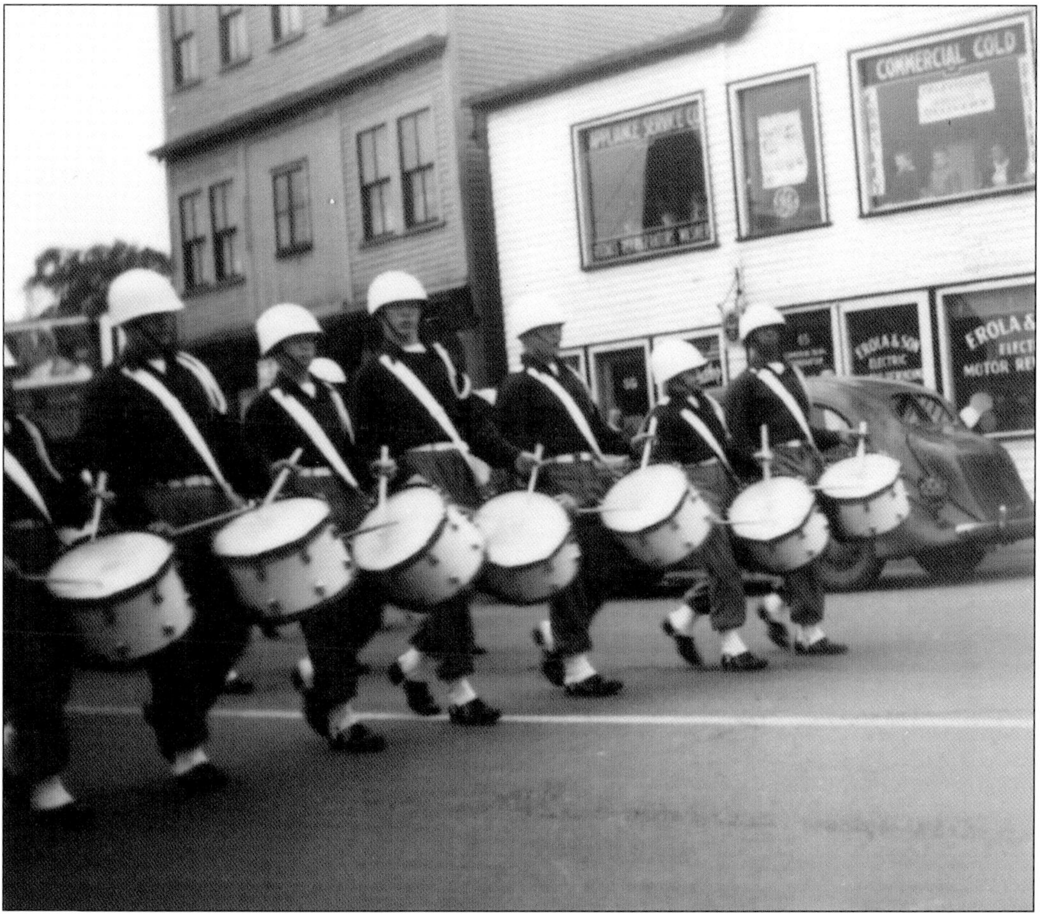

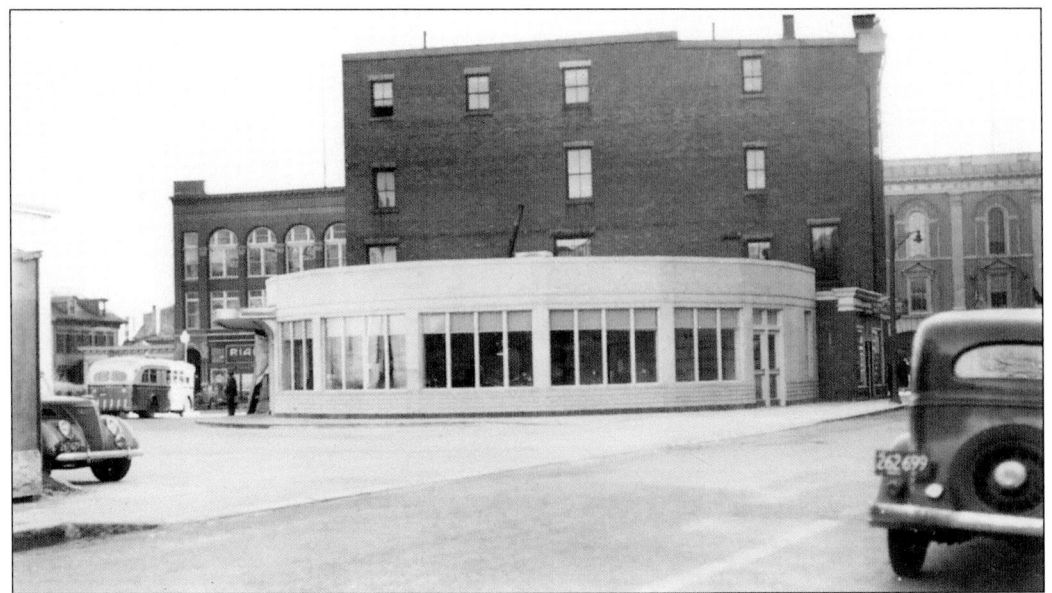

A quiet scene facing Washington Street in 1938. The Art Deco bus terminal on Lynde Street is in the center of the photograph.

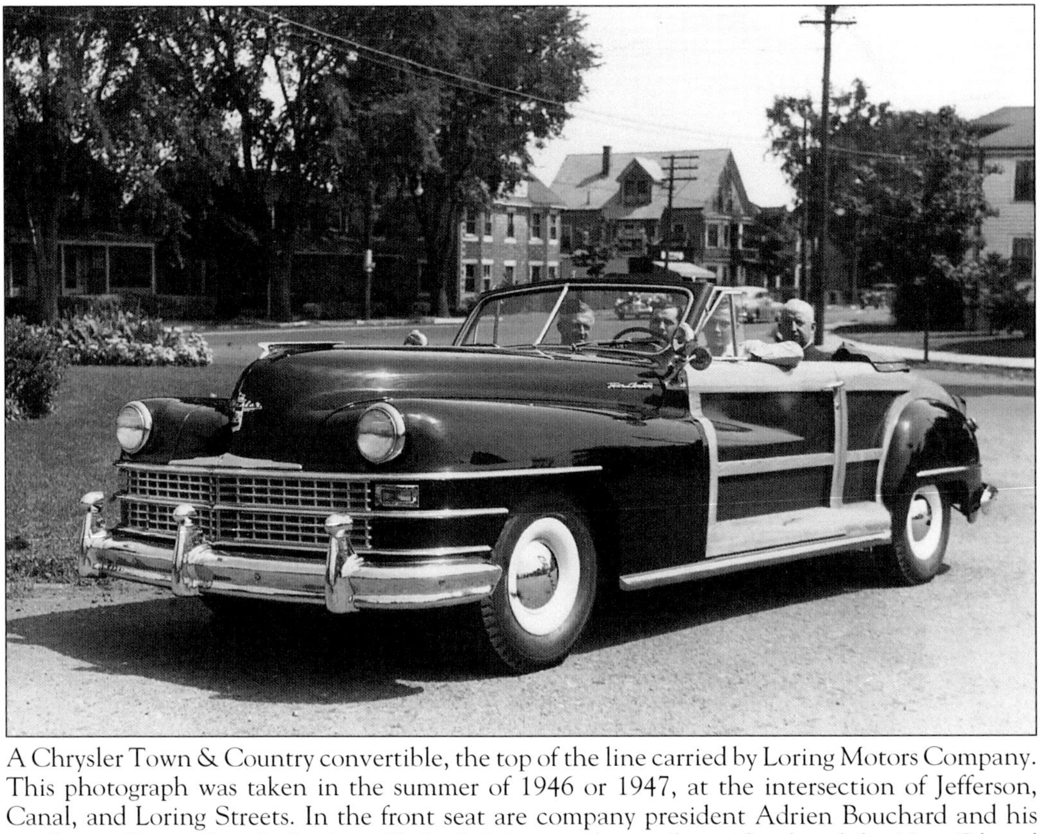

A Chrysler Town & Country convertible, the top of the line carried by Loring Motors Company. This photograph was taken in the summer of 1946 or 1947, at the intersection of Jefferson, Canal, and Loring Streets. In the front seat are company president Adrien Bouchard and his son Roger. Pictured in the back are Philip L. Morency (council president) and the Hon. Edward A. Coffey (mayor of Salem). (Courtesy Henri Michaud.)

# Two
# Doorways and Exterior Views

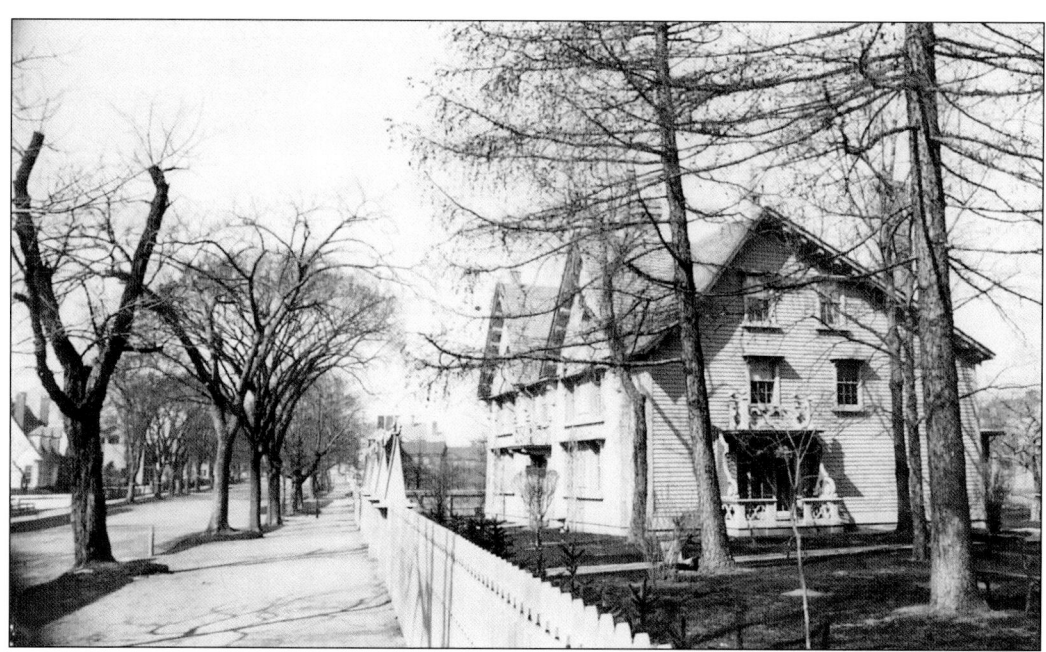

The John Pickering House, 18 Broad Street, built in 1651 and remodeled in the Gothic style in 1841. It has been home to ten generations of Pickerings, and is shown here c. 1890. (Courtesy Pickering Foundation.)

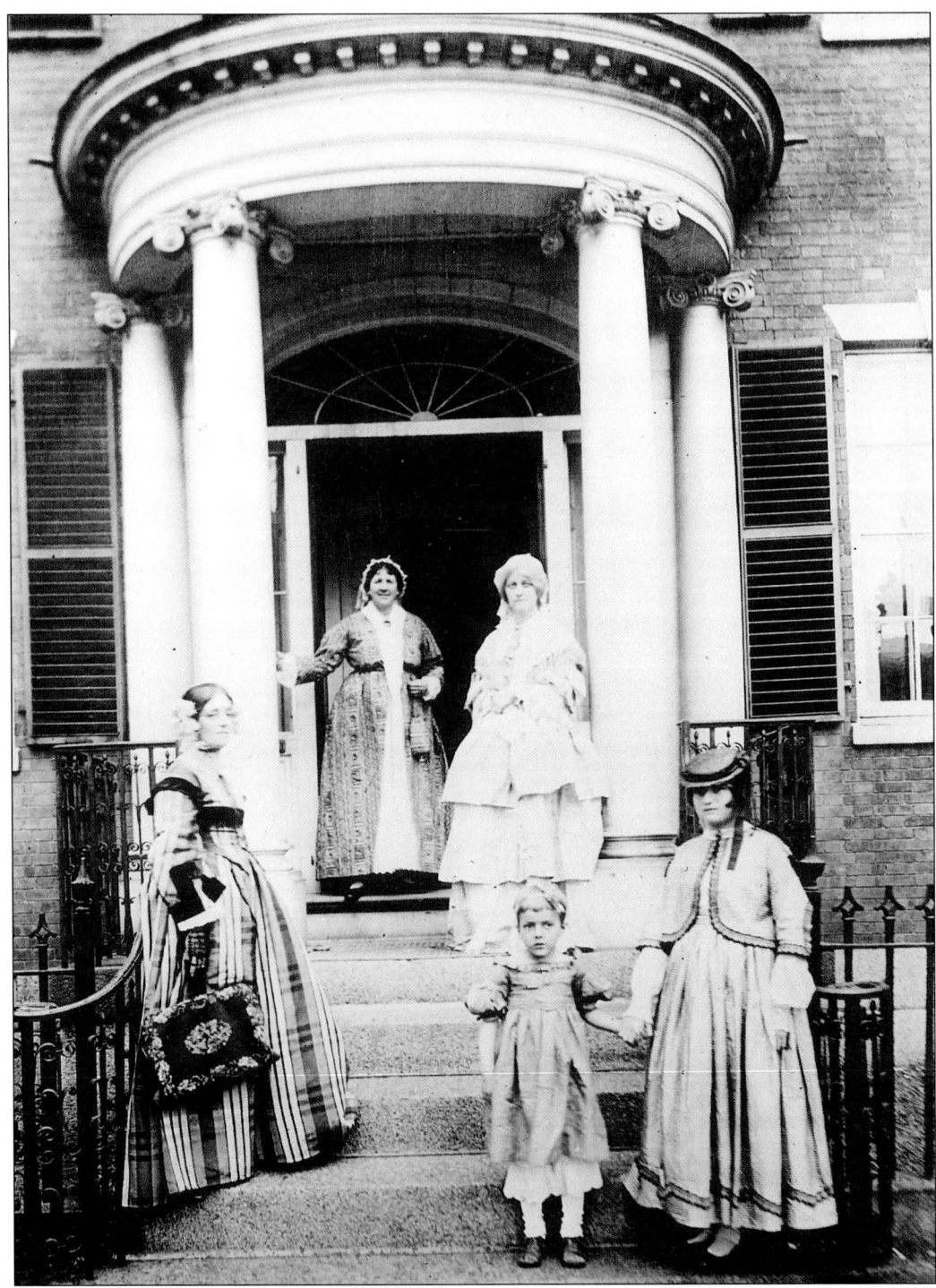

The Pickering-Mack-Stone double House, 23 Chestnut Street. Salem is famous for its beautiful doorways in a variety of architectural styles. Dressed in period-style clothing, probably for a Chestnut Street Day celebration, a group pauses in front of the house built for John Pickering VI in 1814–15. (Courtesy D. Michel Michaud.)

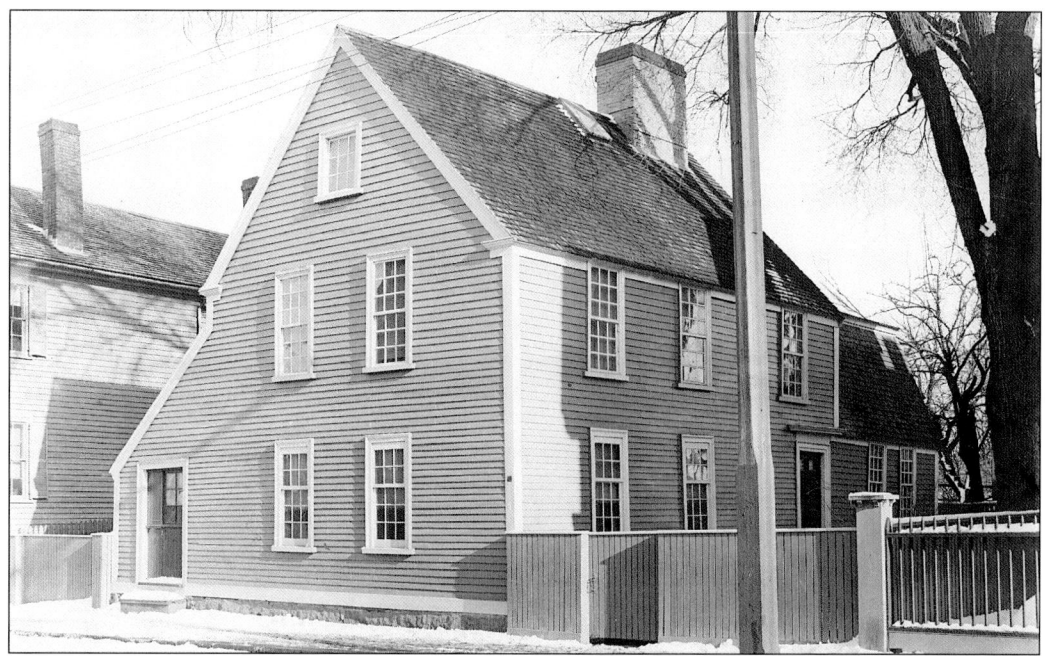

The Narbonne House, Salem Maritime National Historic Site, 71 Essex Street, built in 1672. One of the oldest surviving houses in Salem, the Narbonne House was purchased by the National Park Service in 1964. The building serves as an educational study house for historians, scholars, and students. The half-door at the left in the lean-to addition was the entrance to Mrs. Ives's cent shop, similar to the one in The House of the Seven Gables. (Courtesy D. Michel Michaud.)

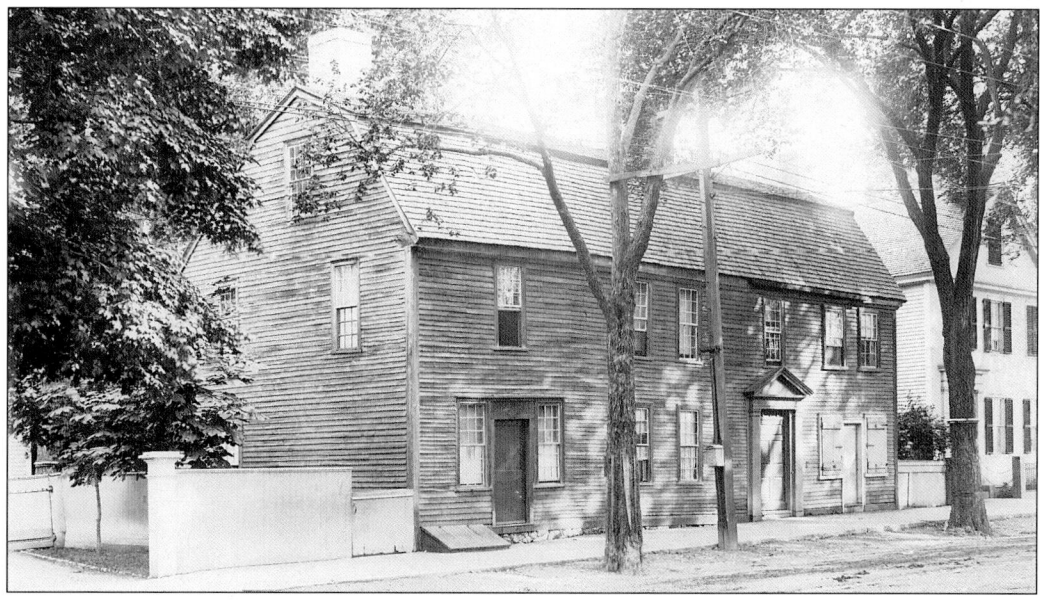

The Jeffrey Lang House, 369 and 371 Essex Street, built c. 1740. The house was razed by the Low family prior to 1919. The dwelling on the right, at 373 Essex Street, was built for Mary Ann Ropes in 1843–44. Miss Ropes later married Captain John Bertram, one of Salem's last great merchants. (Courtesy D. Michel Michaud.)

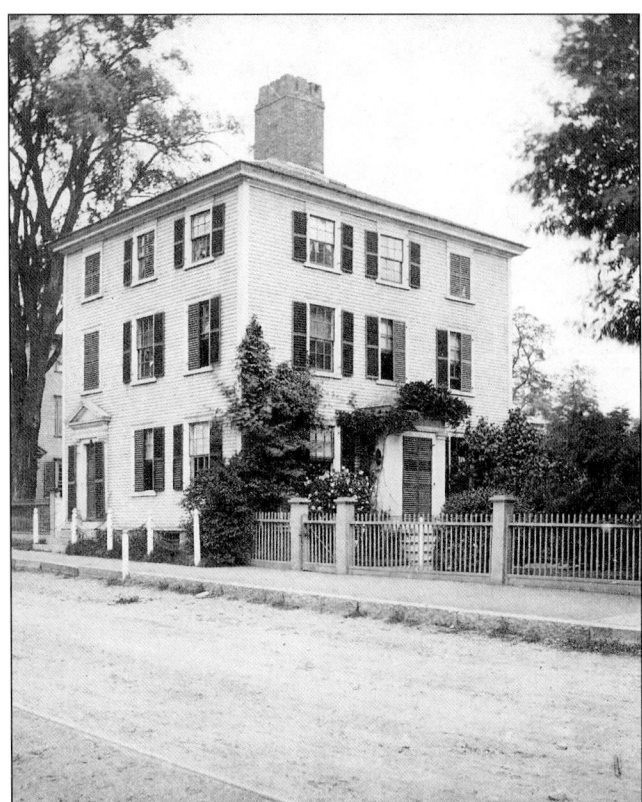

The Francis Boardman House, built 1782–1784 at 82 Washington Square East. George Washington, while visiting Salem in 1789, commented on the beauty and the architectural proportions of this newly built dwelling. This photographic view was taken in September 1873. (Courtesy D. Michel Michaud.)

Bridge Street, c. 1902. This large, two-family Greek Revival dwelling still stands at 126 and 128 Bridge Street, although the matched board facade and the classical cornice pediment have since been altered. Some of the etched panes of glass flanking the doors are still in place. (Courtesy John Hardy Wright.)

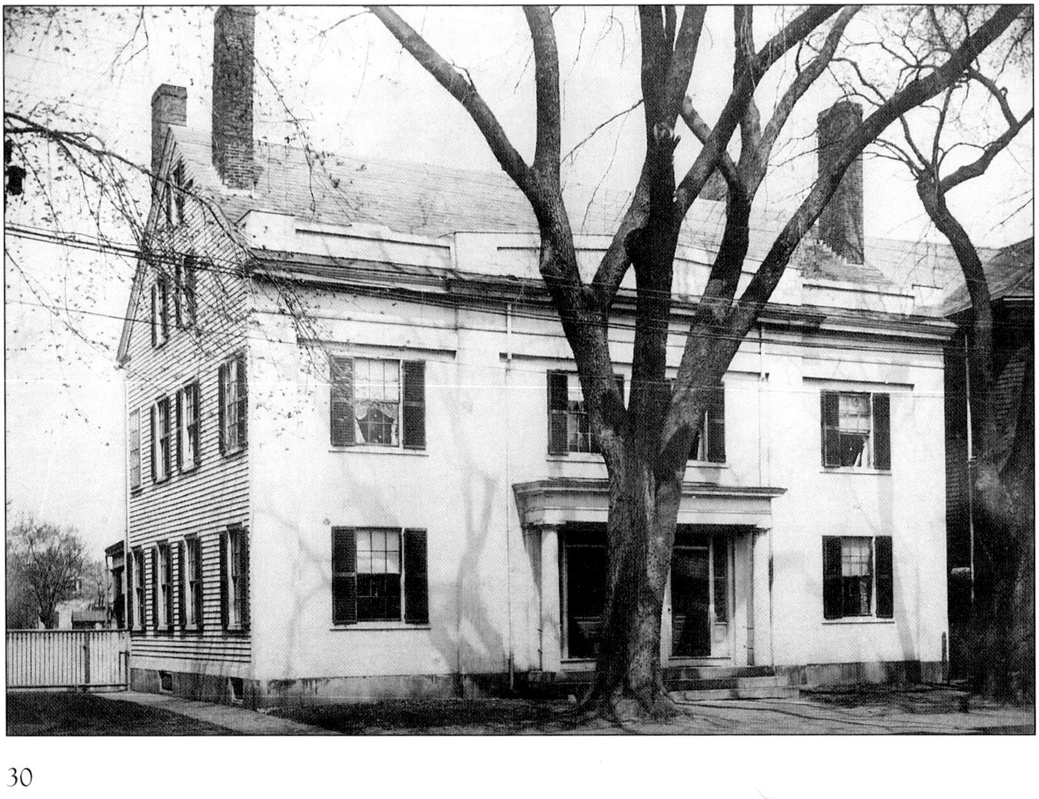

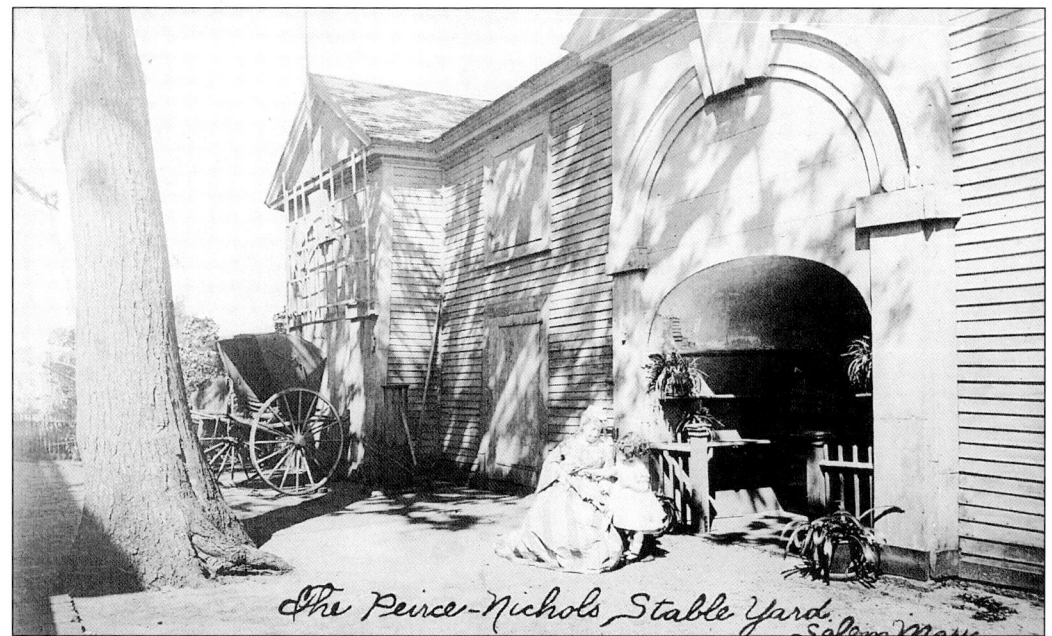

The carriage house of the Peirce-Nichols House, 80 Federal Street, restored in 1924–25 by architect William G. Rantoul (1867–1947). Charlotte Sanders Nichols, shown here, died in 1935. She was the last of three maiden sisters to live in the house. Her death ended the Nichols family occupancy. (Courtesy D. Michel Michaud.)

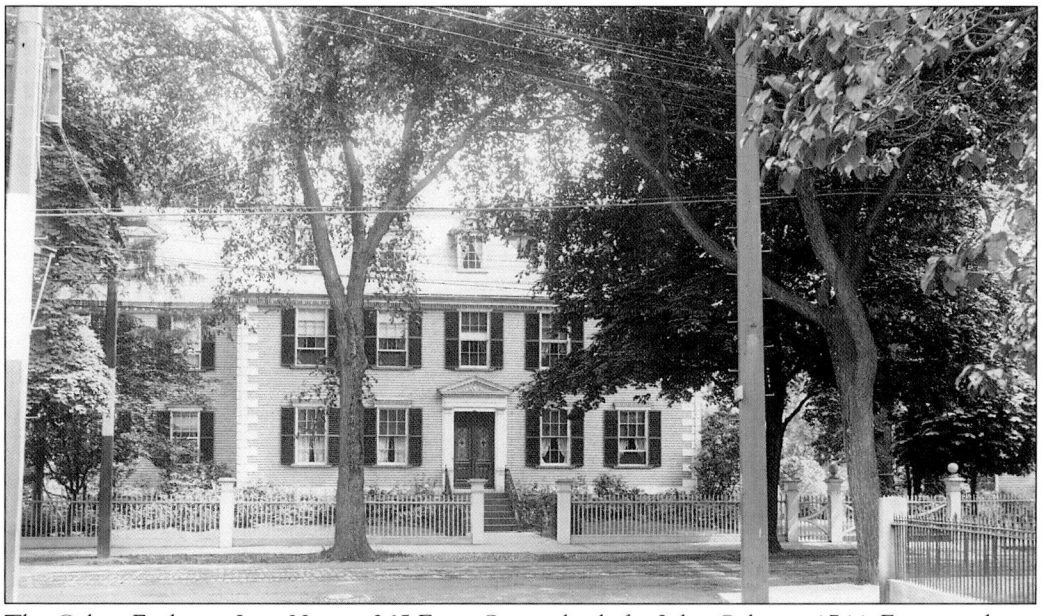

The Cabot-Endicott-Low House, 365 Essex Street, built for John Cabot c. 1744. For over thirty years it was the home of the Hon. William Crowninshield Endicott, justice of the Supreme Judicial Court and secretary of war under President Grover Cleveland. In 1890 the famous Civil War general William T. Sherman was entertained by the Endicotts. In 1894 Daniel Low, the enterprising merchant, bought the house and resided there until 1919. (Courtesy D. Michel Michaud.)

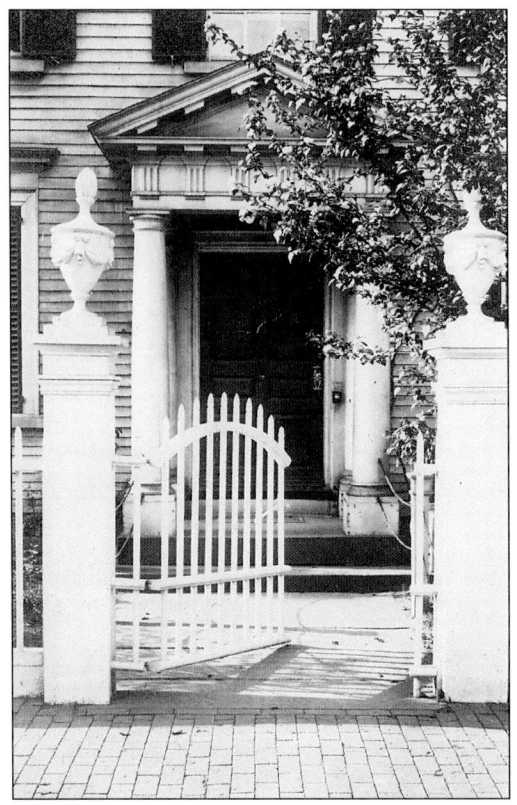

The doorway of the Peirce-Nichols House, 80 Federal Street, c. 1782. One of Salem's finest Georgian-style homes, the Peirce-Nichols House was designed by architect Samuel McIntire and was purchased by the Essex Institute in 1917. It is now a house museum. (Courtesy Pickering Foundation.)

The doorway of the Dodge-Shreve House, 29 Chestnut Street, built 1822–25. One of the unique features of the late Federal-style house was the marble bathtub installed in the basement, said to be the first in Salem. (Courtesy Pickering Foundation.)

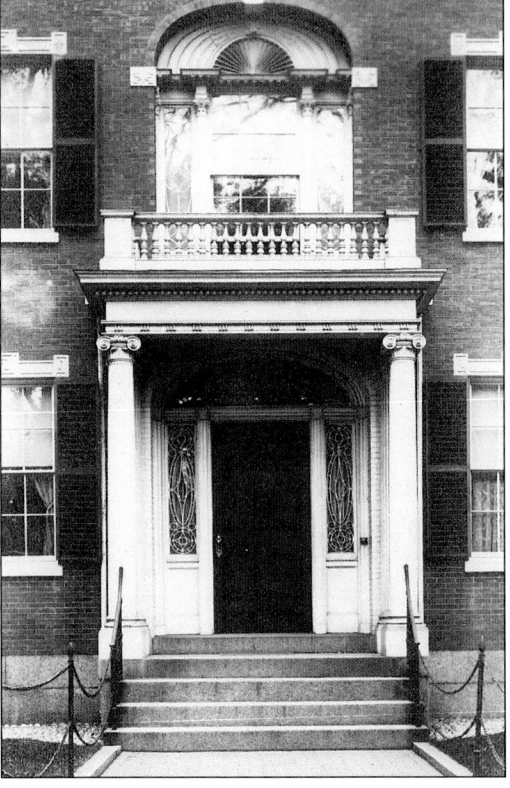

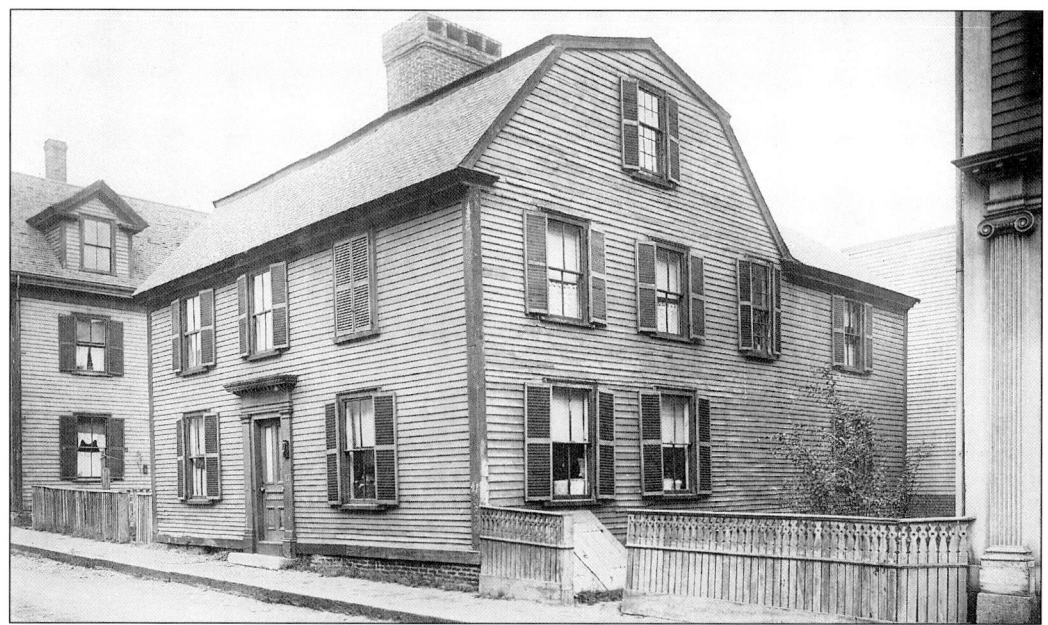

The birthplace of Nathaniel Hawthorne, 27 Union Street, built c. 1750. Hawthorne was born in the second-story northwest chamber of this gambrel-roofed house on July 4, 1804. In 1958 the house was purchased from the Catholic Archdiocese of Boston by The House of Seven Gables Settlement Association. It was moved in two parts to the association's complex at 54 Turner Street. The house has been meticulously restored and is open to the public. (Courtesy D. Michel Michaud.)

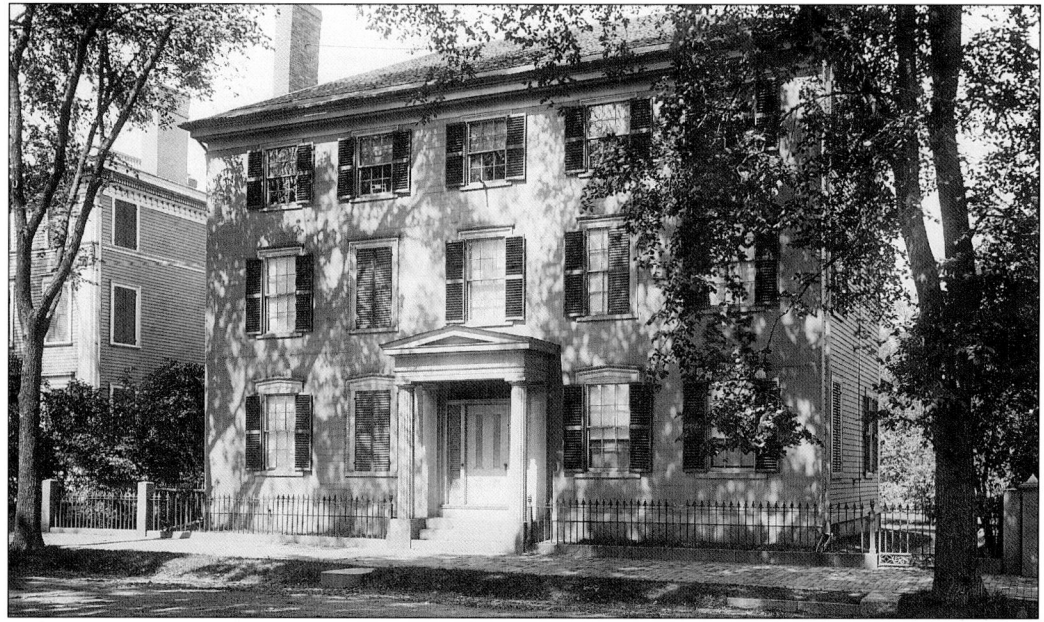

The Ichabod Tucker House, 28 Chestnut Street, built in 1800, remodeled and enlarged in 1846. Occupied by members of the Tucker, Cole, and Wilson families, the Ichabod Tucker House was probably the second dwelling on Chestnut Street, the first being the Bott-Fabens House at 18 Chestnut Street. It is shown here c. 1910.

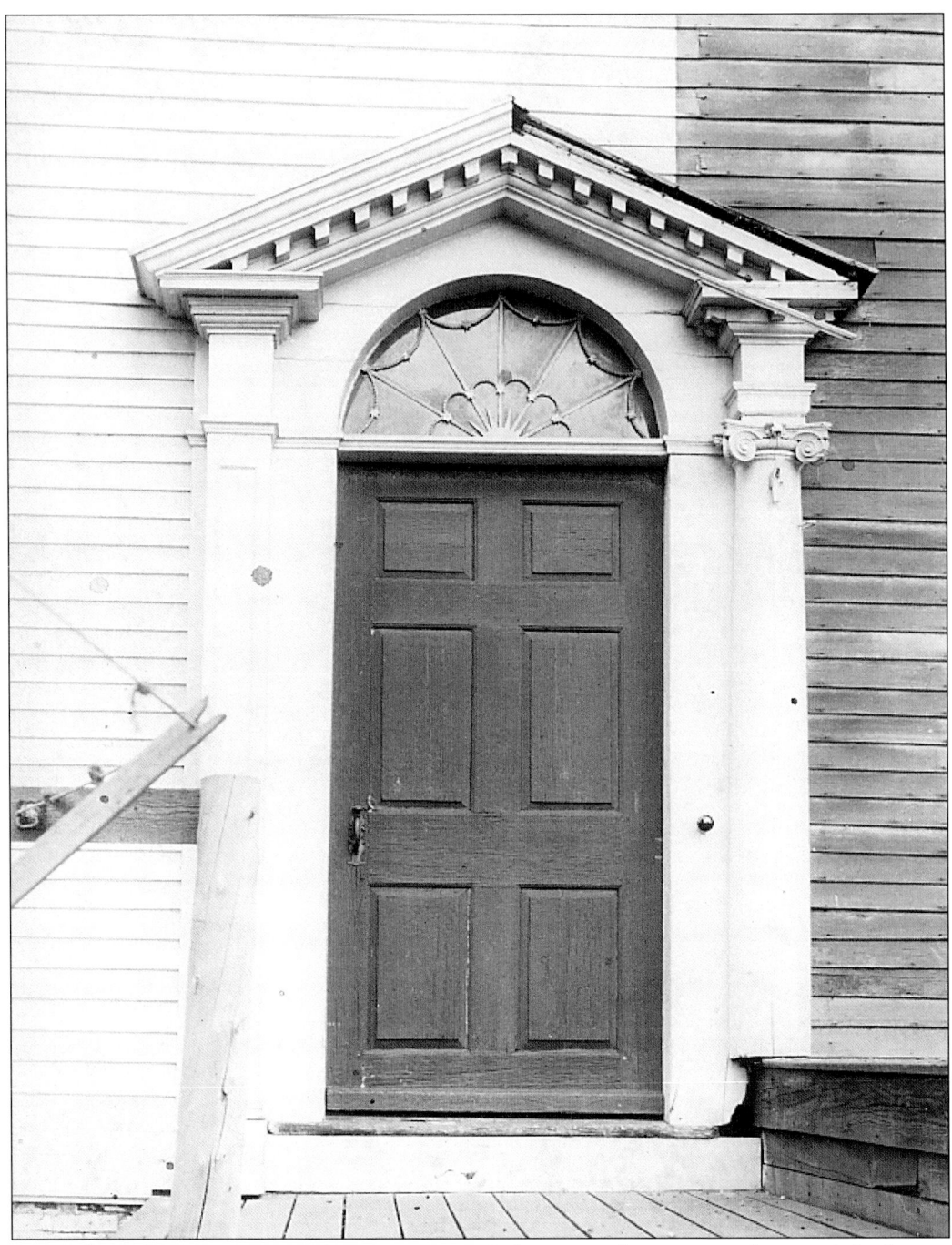

The Federal doorway at 118 Derby Street, c. 1890. It appears that two people owned this house. One owner let his side deteriorate, while the other maintained his property.

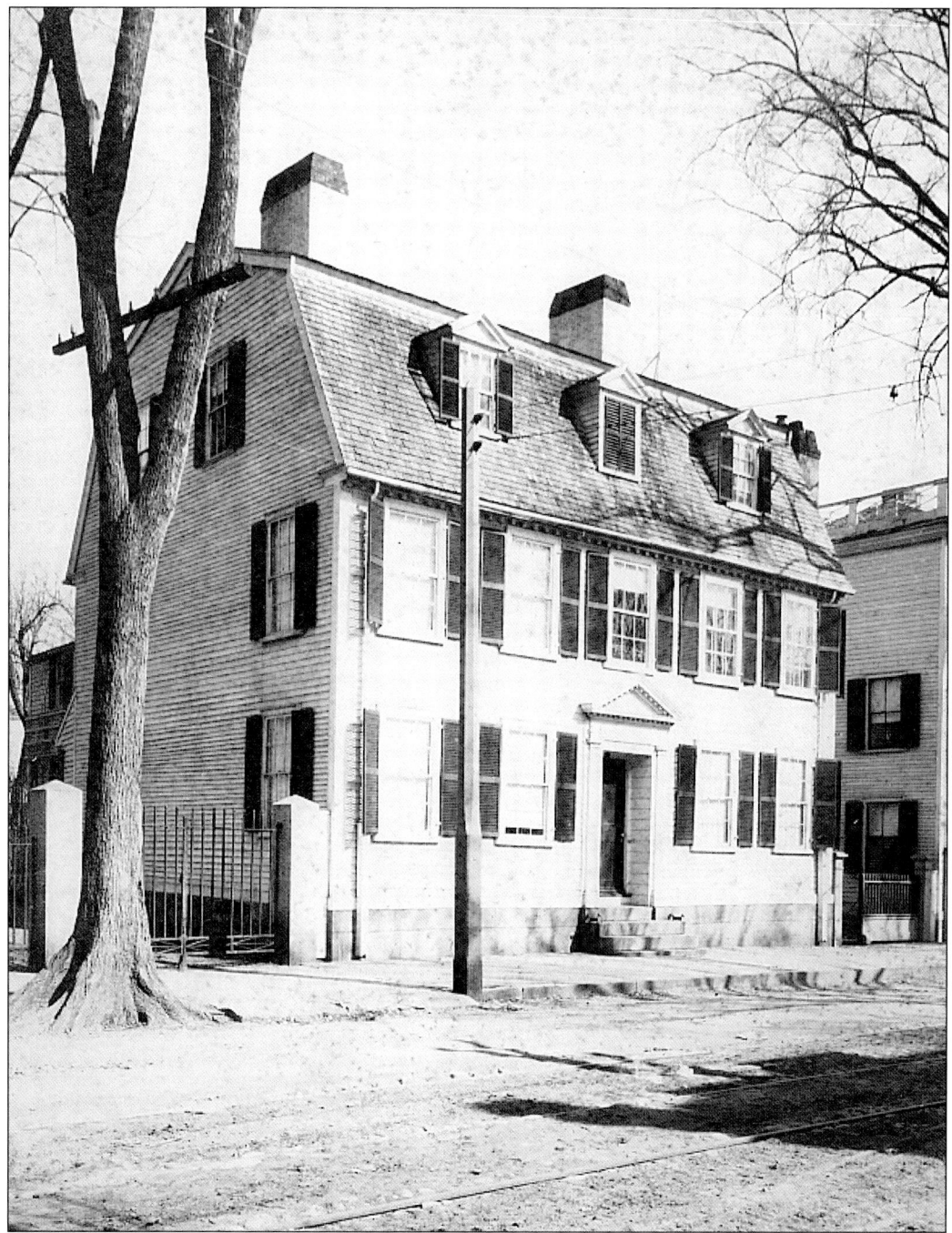

The Lindall-Gibbs-Osgood House, 314 Essex Street, built in 1755 for Mary Lindall. The house was later owned by the Appleton, Nichols, and Osgood families. In 1947 it was purchased by the Salem Chapter of the American Red Cross; today it serves as law offices. Note the Nathaniel Bowditch House on the right, which was moved around the corner in 1944 to North Street.

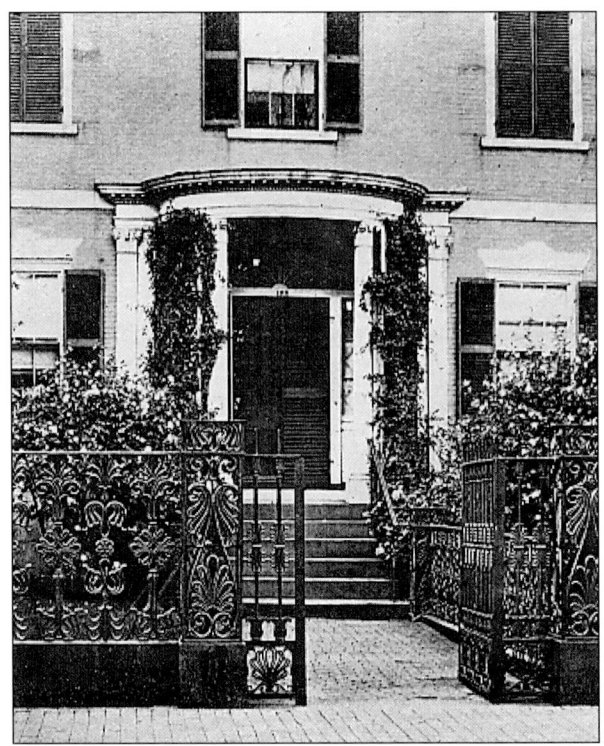

The doorway of the Gardner-White-Pingree House, 128 Essex Street, built 1804–05 by Samuel McIntire, architect. On April 6, 1830, Captain Joseph White was brutally murdered while sleeping in the upstairs chamber of his home. He received thirteen stab wounds to the heart and his skull was crushed. The perpetrators were Joseph and Frank Knapp, along with Richard Crowninshield Jr.

The Clifford Crowninshield House, 74 Washington Square East at Forrester Street, built 1804–06 by Samuel McIntire, architect. Captain James Devereux, an early owner of the house, was the first Salem ship captain to trade with Japan during the first decade of the nineteenth century. The building is shown here c. 1920.(Courtesy D. Michel Michaud.)

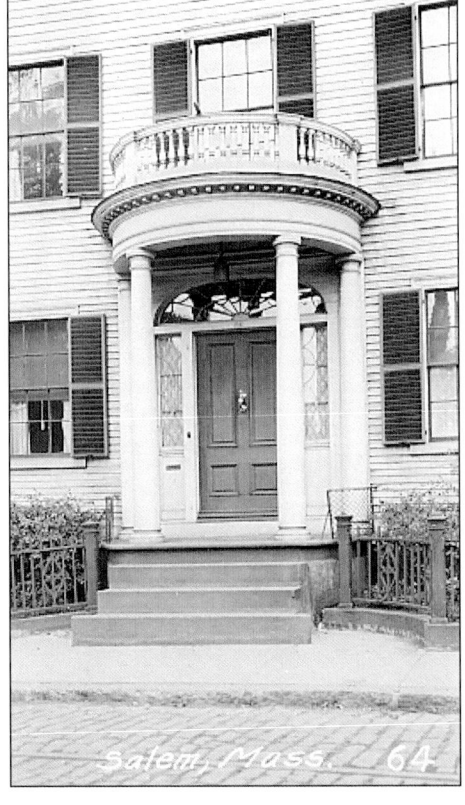

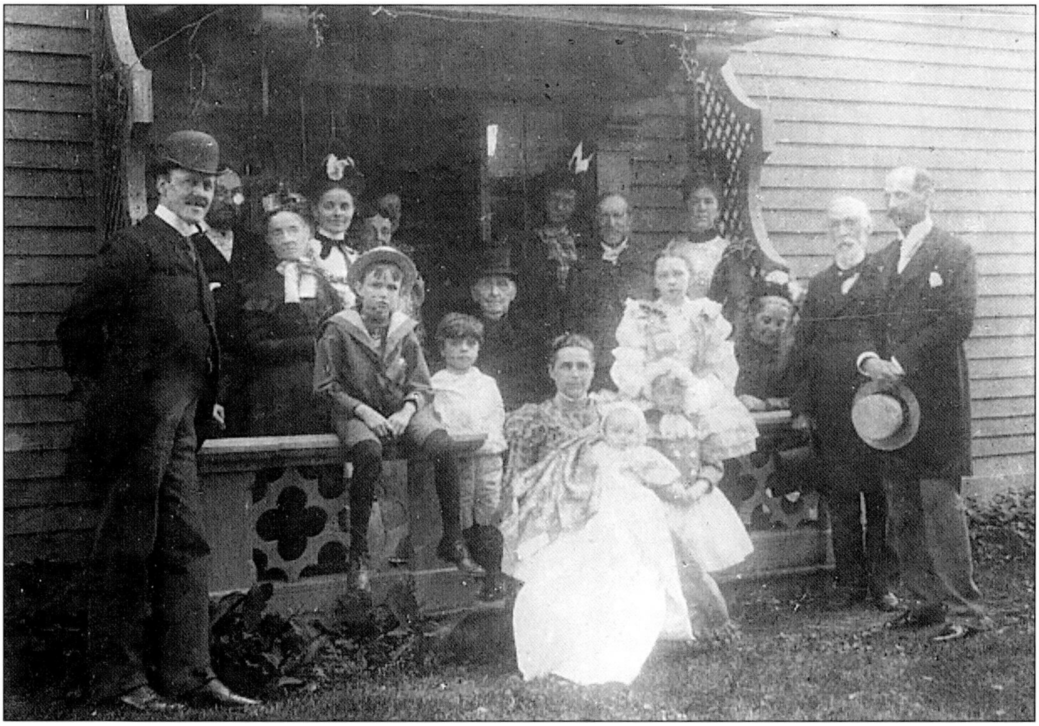

A group photograph of Pickering family members taken c. 1890 at 18 Broad Street. The quatrefoil motif railing and side latticework have since disappeared from the house. (Courtesy Pickering Foundation.)

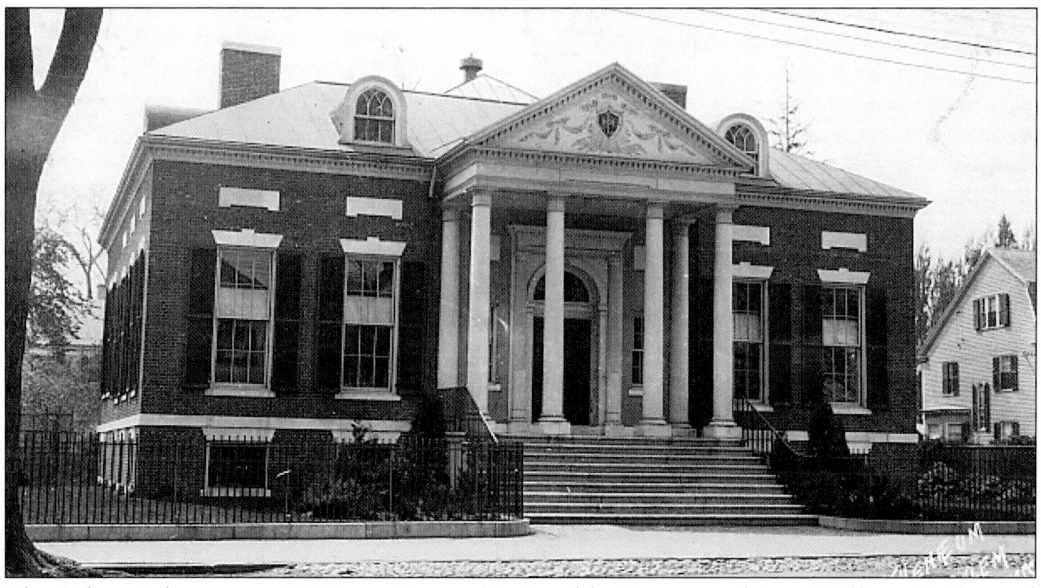

The Salem Athenaeum, 337 Essex Street. Designed by Boston architect William G. Rantoul (1867–1949) in 1906–07, this private library was incorporated in 1810. The Social Library of 1760 and the Philosophical Library of 1781 were its predecessors. The exterior, constructed in the Colonial Revival style, resembles "Homewood," a Baltimore mansion built in 1804. (Courtesy D. Michel Michaud.)

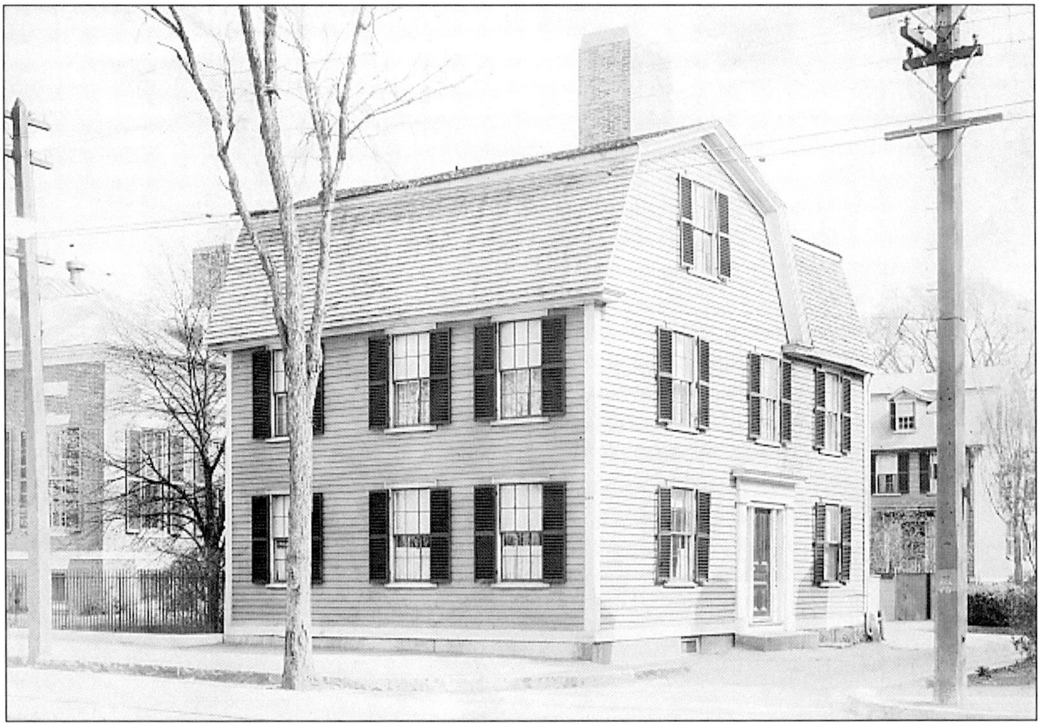

Front and rear views of the William T. Pickering House, 343 Essex Street at the corner of Botts Court. The house was built before 1736, and these photographs were taken around 1910. (Courtesy Pickering Foundation.)

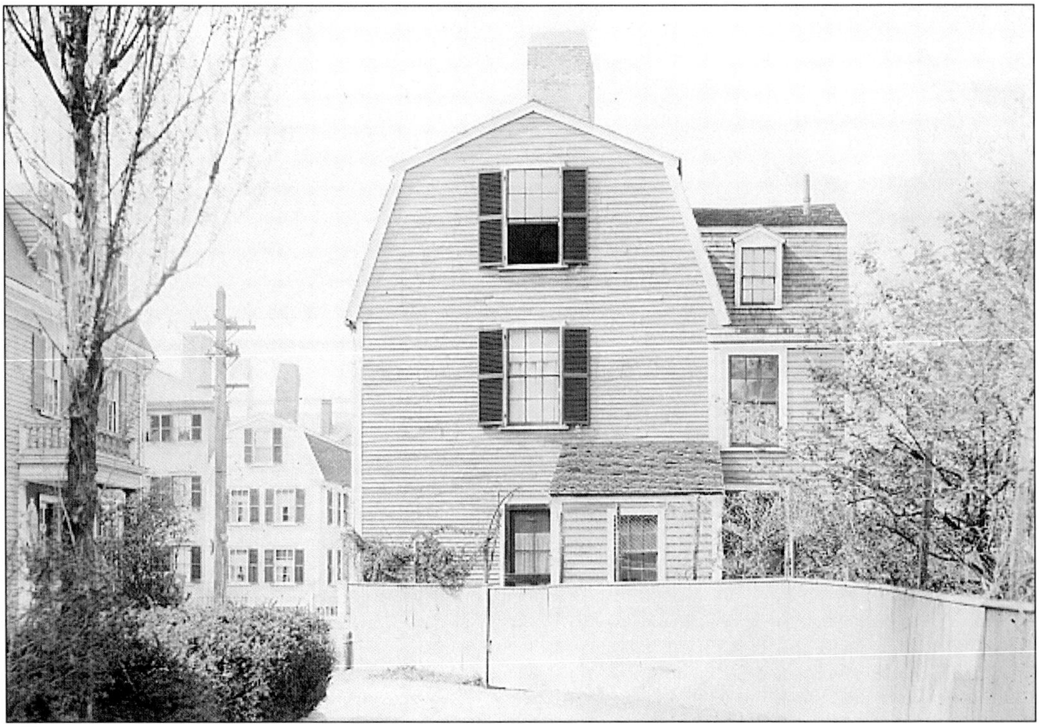

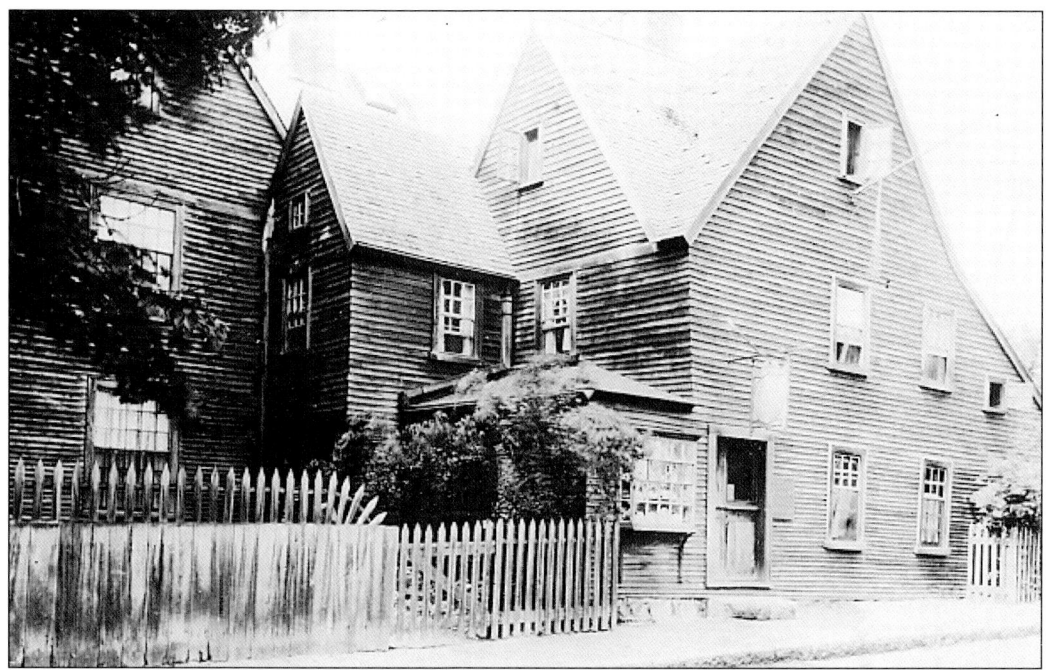
A Turner Street view of The House of Seven Gables. The house was made famous by renowned Salem author Nathaniel Hawthorne, whose book of the same name, published in 1851, won him acclaim as an writer. (Courtesy D. Michel Michaud.)

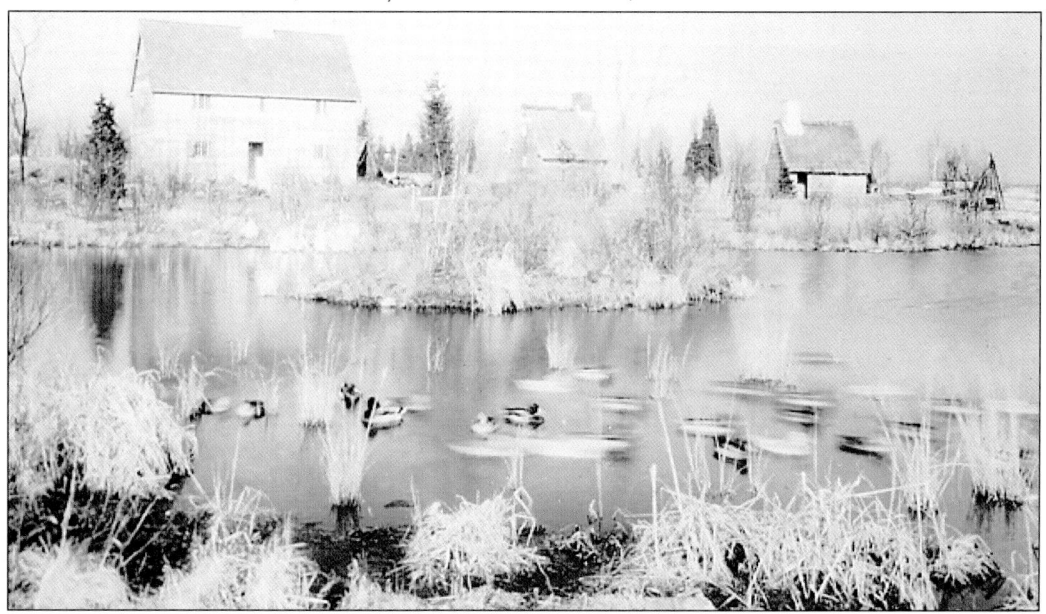
Pioneer Village, Forest River Park, 1930. The village is a reconstruction of an early seventeenth-century settlement. It was built for the Massachusetts Bay Tercentenary in 1930 under the supervision of George Francis Dow, a noted historian and curator at the former Essex Institute. Pictured here in this idyllic setting are the Governor Winthrop House and two thatched-roof cottages. The site is managed by The House of Seven Gables Settlement Association.

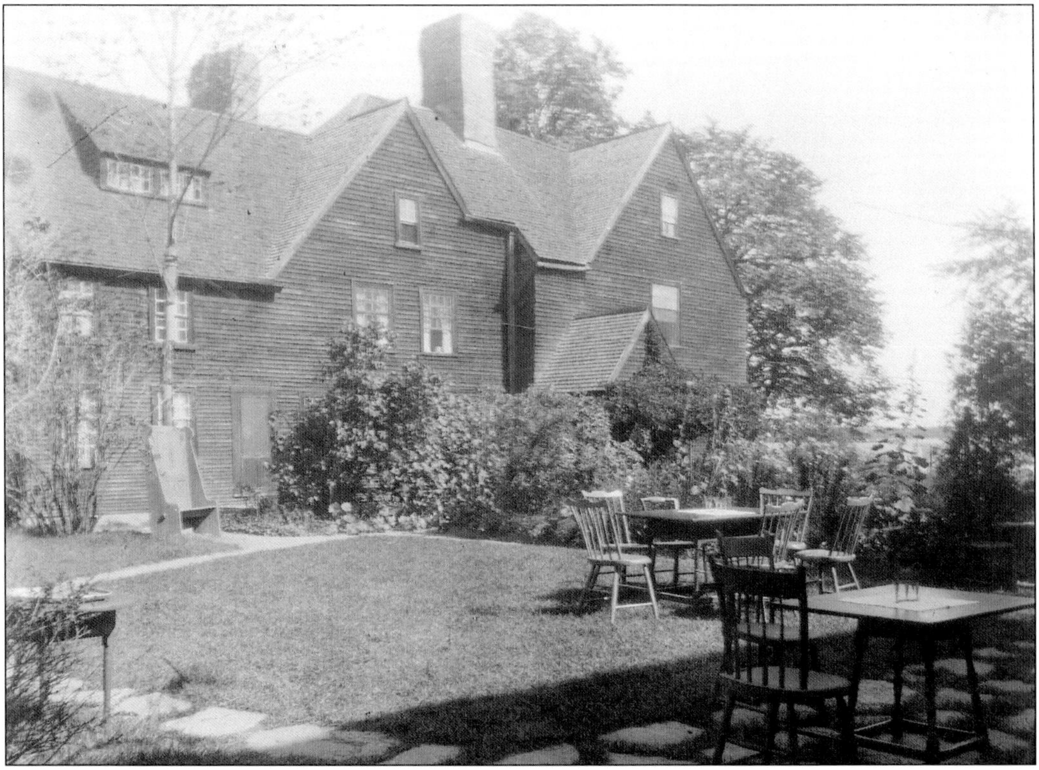

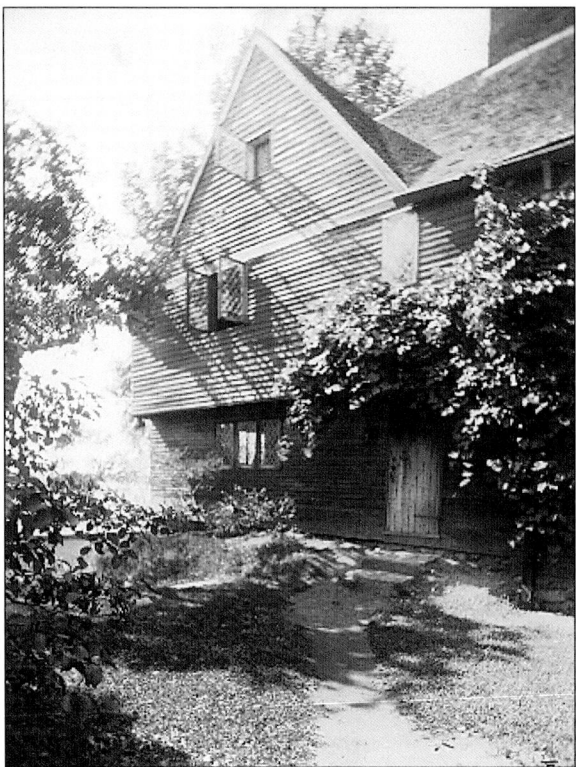

A garden view of The House of Seven Gables. Built in 1668, 54 Turner Street is owned by The House of Seven Gables Settlement Association. It was occupied by three generations of Turners and Ingersolls and a variety of other owners during the late nineteenth century. In 1908, Miss Caroline O. Emmerton purchased the house and restored it under the direction of the architect Joseph E. Chandler (1864–1945). In 1910 it was opened to the public for tours.

The Hooper-Hathaway House, built c. 1682, House of Seven Gables Settlement Association, 54 Turner Street. Originally located at 23 Washington Street, the Hooper-Hathaway House was moved to its present site in 1911 by Miss Emmerton. Known as the Old Bakery during the last half of the nineteenth century, it was moved in three parts and restored under the direction of Joseph E. Chandler.

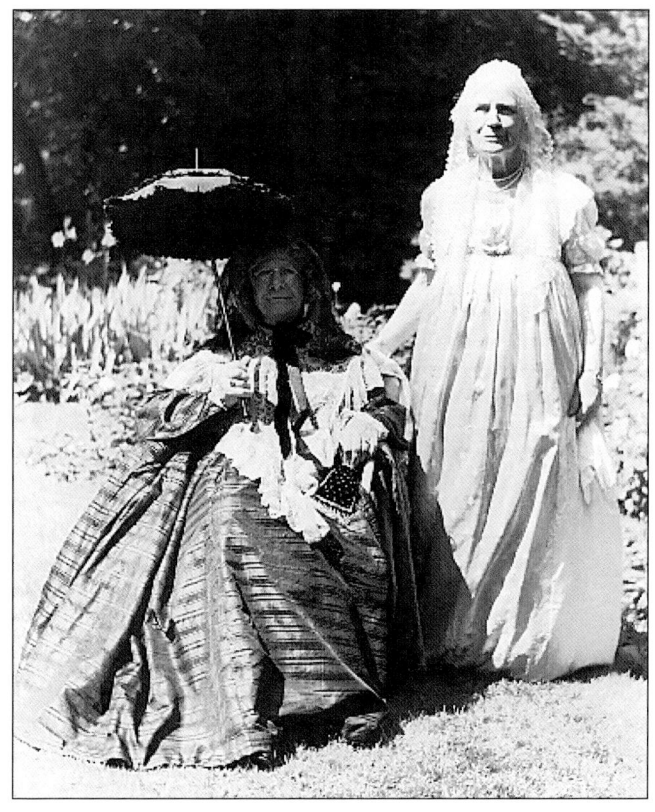

A portrait of Mrs. William H. Jelly (seated) and Mrs. John Pickering VIII (nee Anna Dane Varney). The ladies, dressed in old family garments, are celebrating Old Chestnut Street Days, c. 1926. (Courtesy Pickering Foundation.)

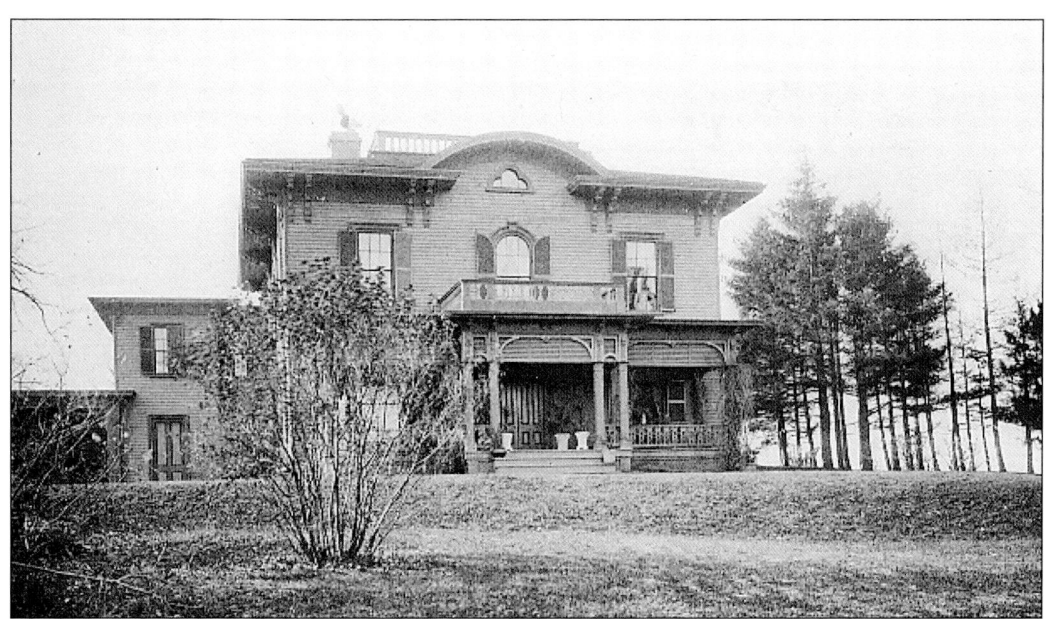

The residence of Mrs. George B. Loring, known as the Loring Farm, off Loring Avenue. It was purchased in 1915 for use as Saint Chretienne's Convent. In the 1970s, Salem State College acquired the compound as part of its expansion. (Courtesy D. Michel Michaud.)

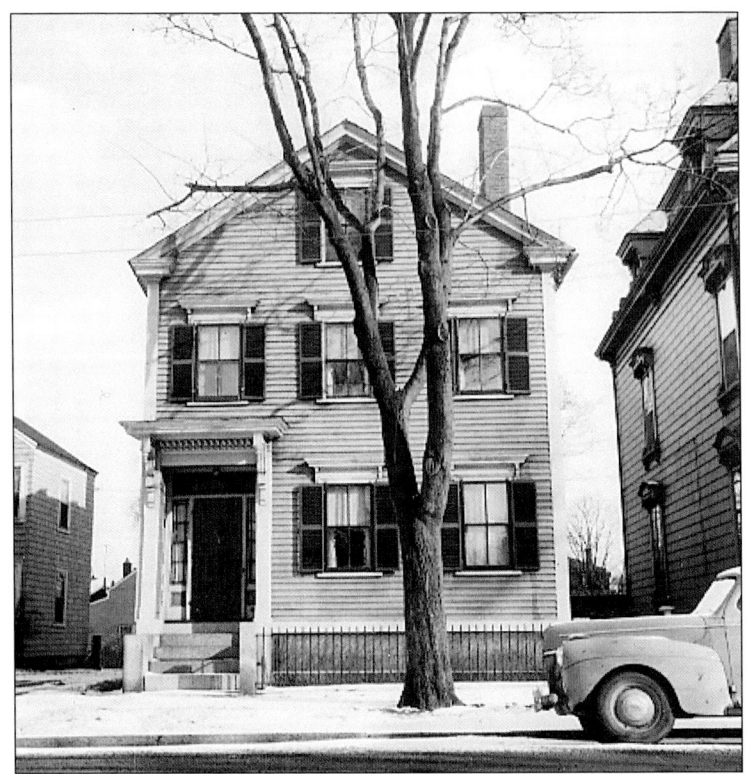

The house at 5 Winter Street. A then-fashionable Italianate bracketed door hood was added to this modest dwelling not too many years after it was built in 1839–40 for painter Samuel C. Clarke. John Kinsman, the superintendent of the Salem and Danvers Aqueduct Company, lived here during the late nineteenth century. Light opera singer Clara Emilio resided here when she starred in Gilbert and Sullivan operettas in the early twentieth century. (Courtesy John Hardy Wright.)

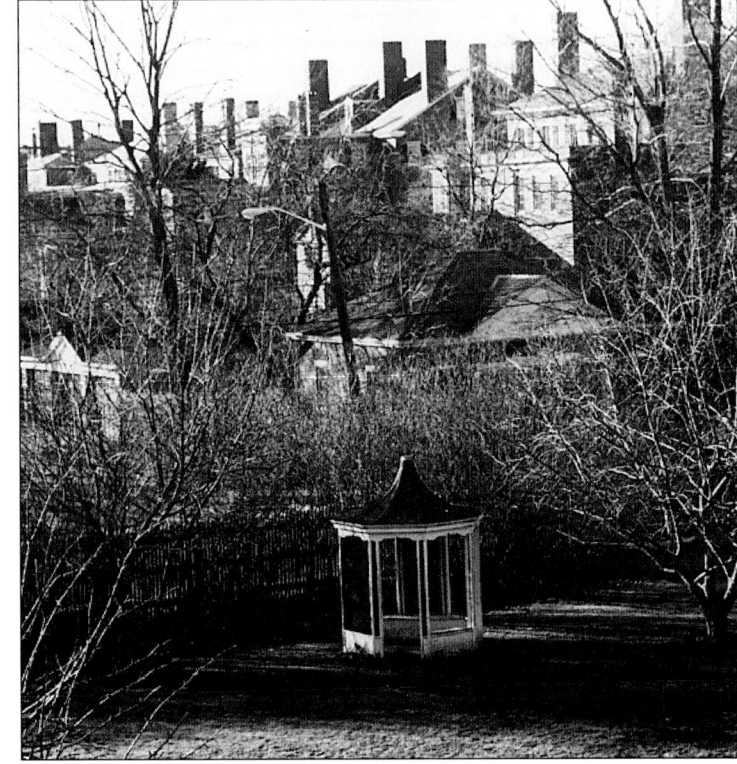

The gazebo on the grounds of the Pickering Foundation, 18 Broad Street. This photograph, taken from the skylight of the Pickering House, shows the roof lines of Warren and Chestnut Street houses. (Courtesy Pickering Foundation.)

# Three

# SALEM INTERIORS

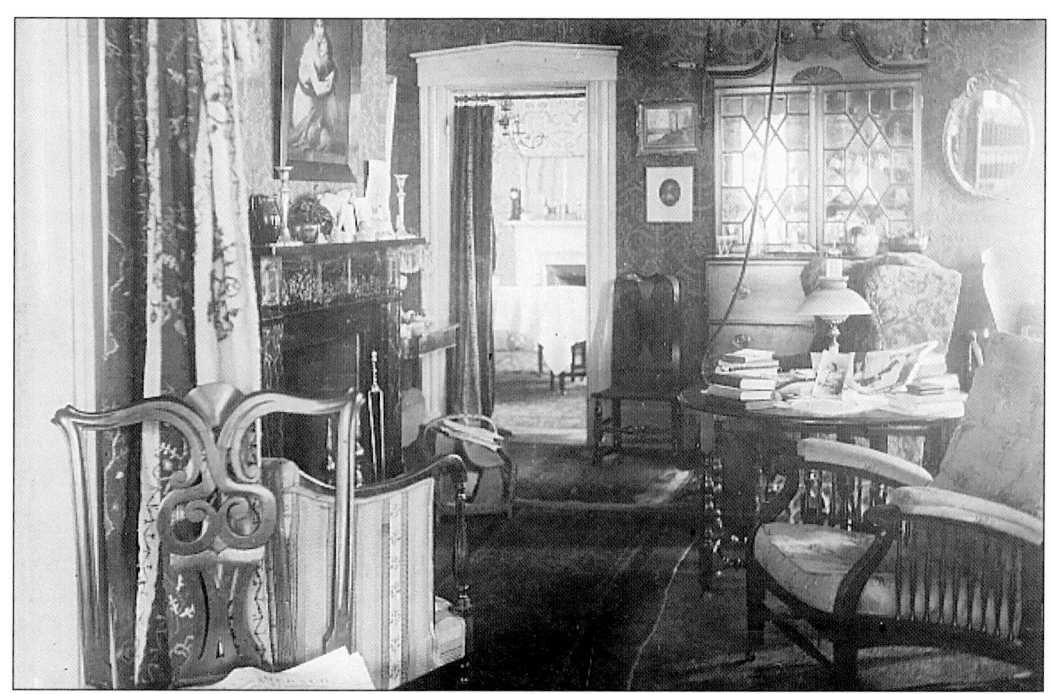

The interior of the Benson home, probably 46 Washington Square, c. 1895. Note the gas hose coming down from the ceiling fixture to illuminate the lamp on the gateleg table. (Courtesy Pickering Foundation.)

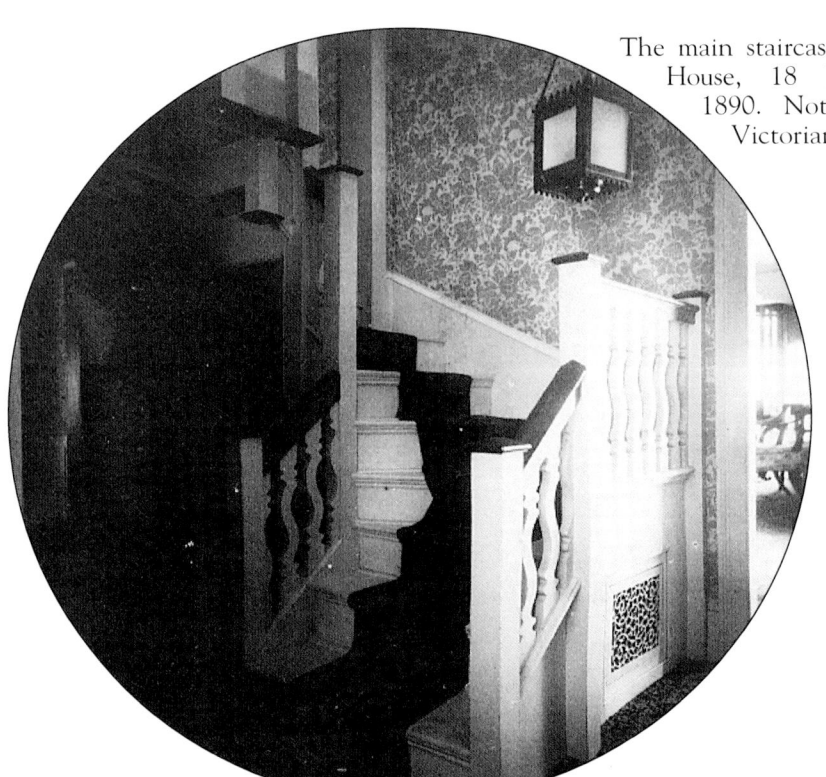

The main staircase of the Pickering House, 18 Broad Street, c. 1890. Note the undulating Victorian balusters.

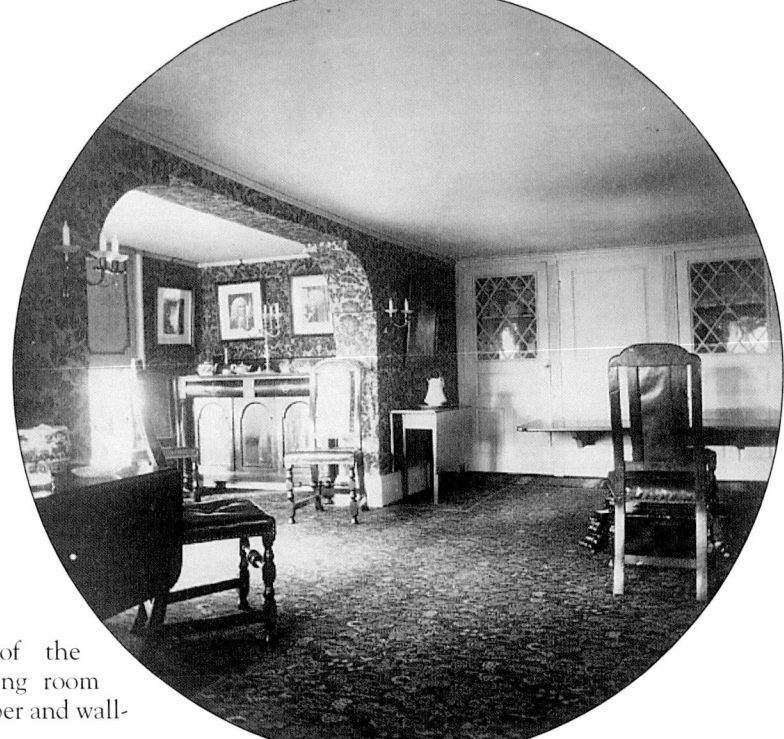

A c. 1890 view of the Pickering House dining room with Victorian wallpaper and wall-to-wall carpeting.

The parlor of the Pickering House. A heavy Victorian influence prevails in this eclectic decor. The portrait on the right is of John Pickering VI (died 1846) by Boston artist Chester Harding (1792–1866).

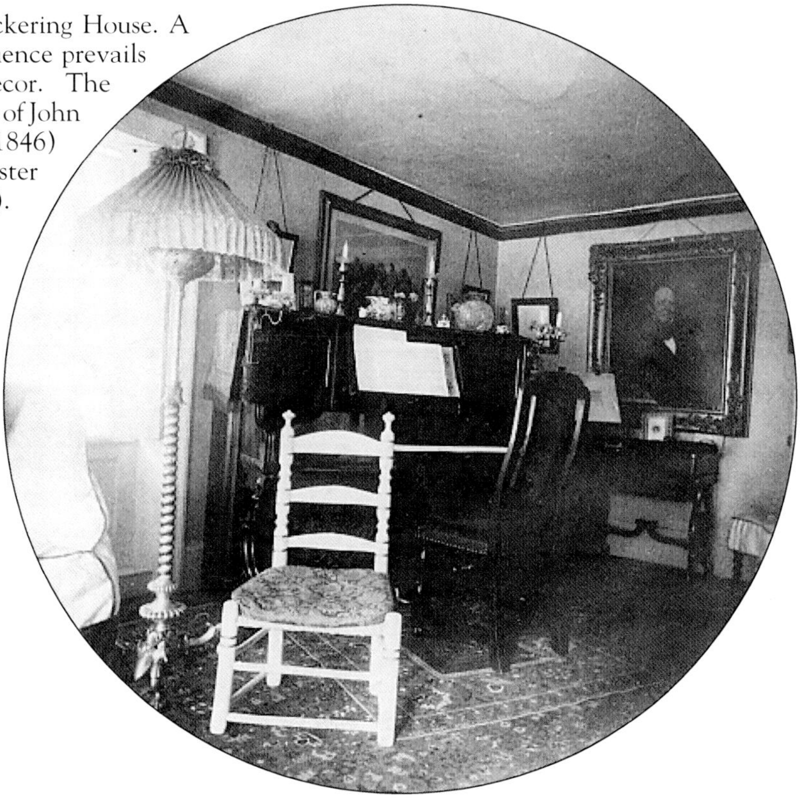

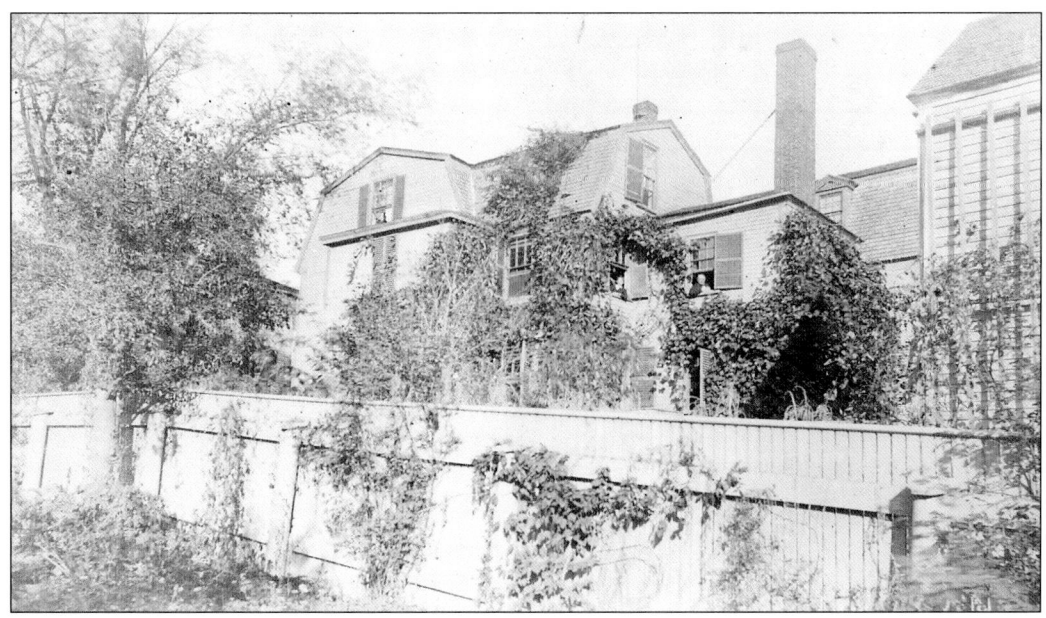

The rear garden view of the Benjamin Cox House on Norman Street at the height of the growing season. (Courtesy Pickering Foundation.)

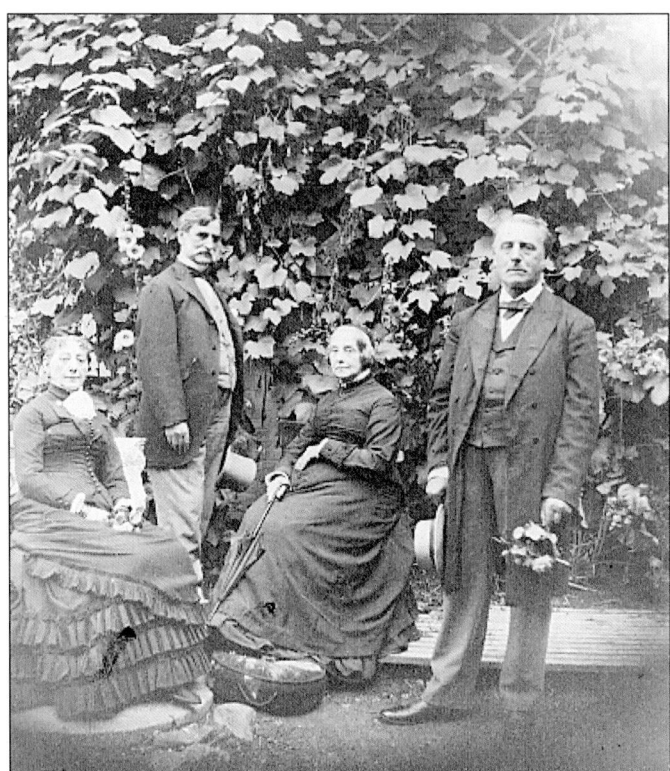

The garden at 21 Norman Street. From left to right are: Marianne Cox, Francis Cox, Sarah Cox Browne, and Edward Cox.

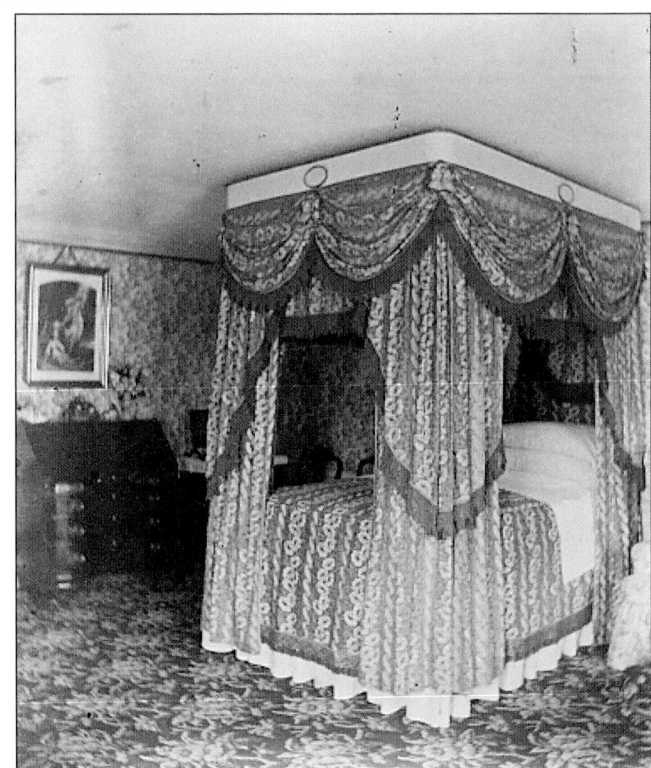

The master bedchamber of 21 Norman Street, c. 1890. The elaborately draped and festooned bedhangings in the master bedchamber add a touch of opulence to the surroundings. (Courtesy Pickering Foundation.)

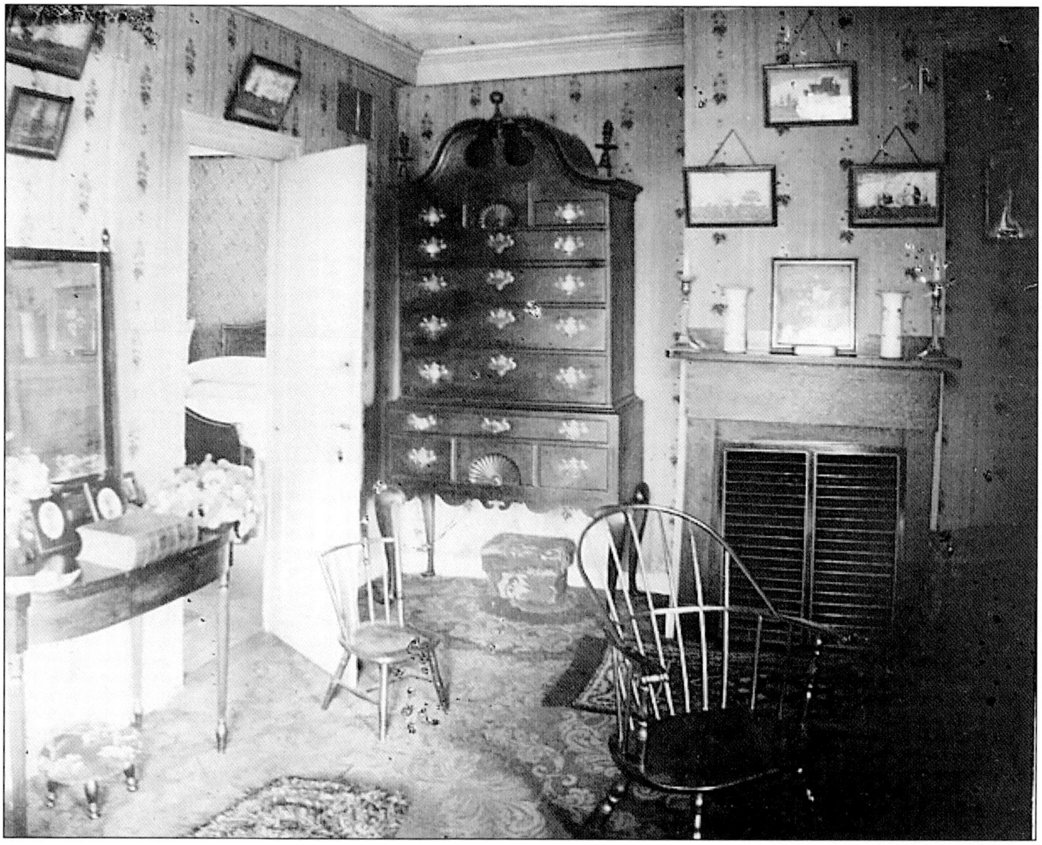

The upstairs bedchamber in the home of Benjamin and Sarah Smith Cox, 21 Norman Street. Family heirlooms such as a Salem Queen Anne bonnet-top highboy, a New England Sheraton card table, a sack-back Windsor armchair, and a child's rod-back side chair are displayed here. (Courtesy Pickering Foundation.)

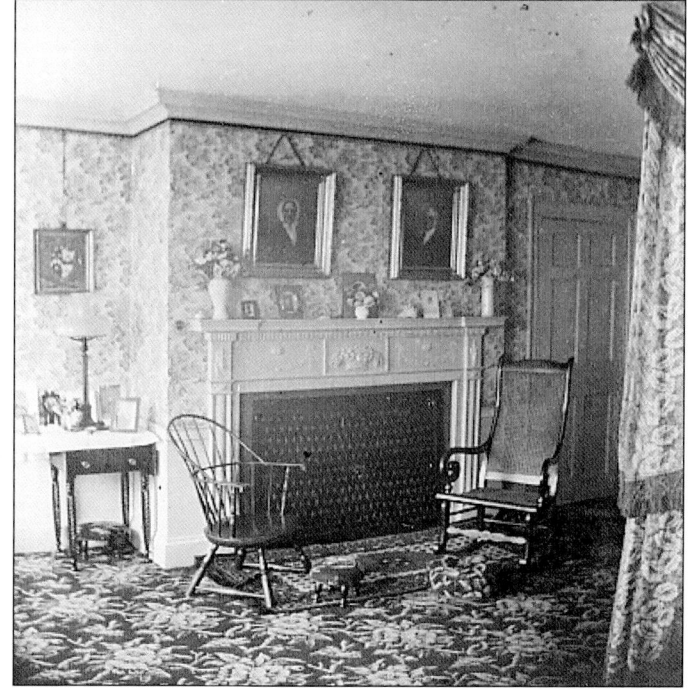

The bedroom fireplace in the Cox's Norman Street home. Portraits of Sarah Smith Cox and her husband Benjamin hang over the McIntire-designed mantel. (Courtesy Pickering Foundation.)

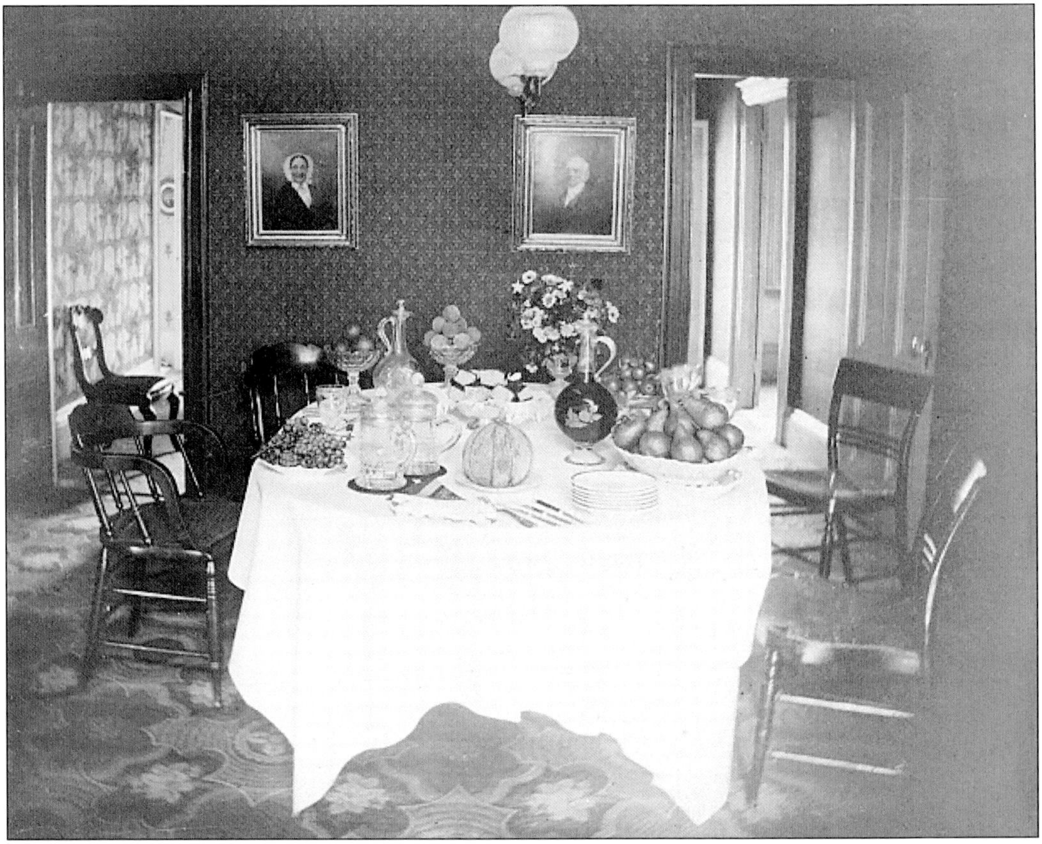

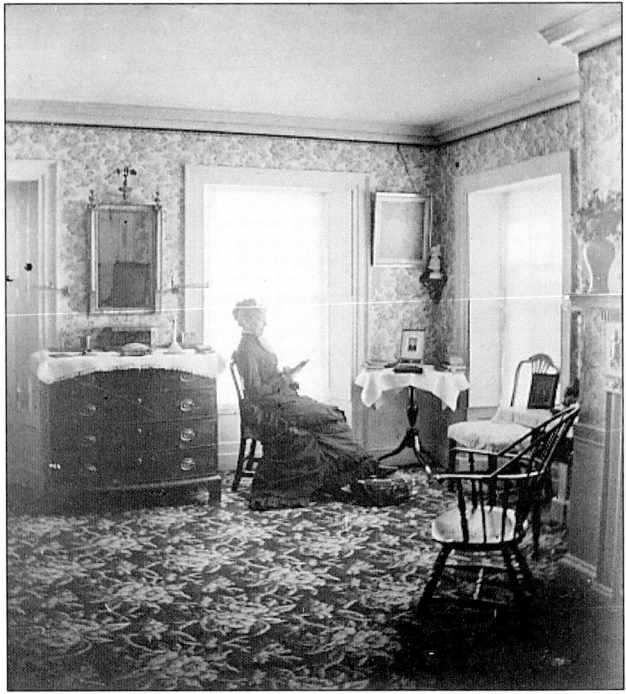

The dining room in the Cox home on Norman Street. The table is laden with fruits that were probably grown in the family garden. (Courtesy Pickering Foundation.)

The pleasures of a good book. Miss Marianne Cox finds a tranquil, sunny corner to read in her Norman Street home. Note the bow-front Hepplewhite chest of drawers and the Bilboa mirror. (Courtesy Pickering Foundation.)

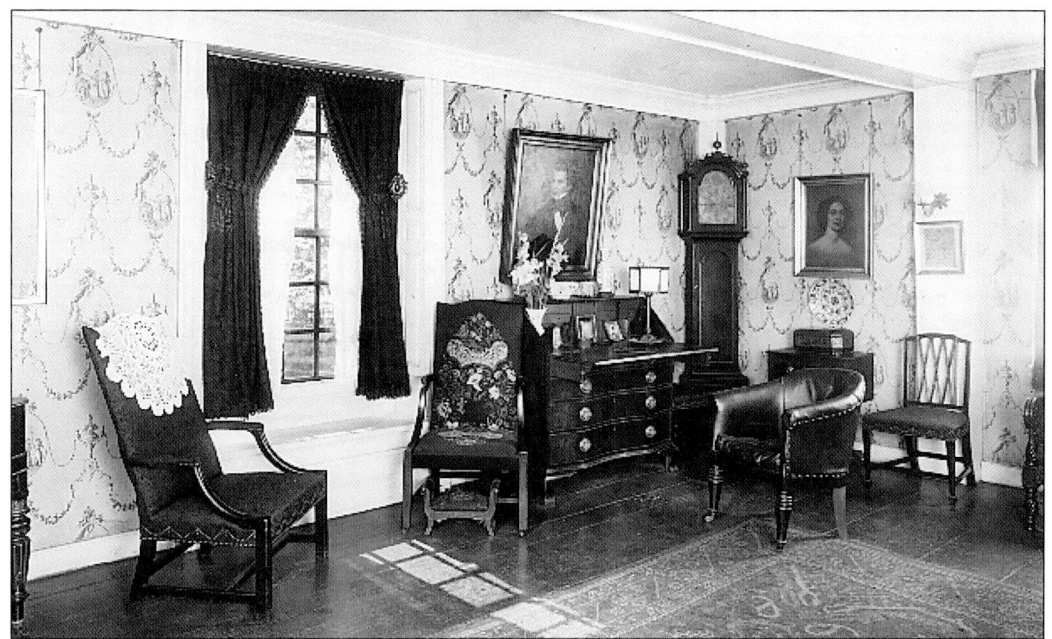

The parlor in The House of Seven Gables, 54 Turner Street, c. 1910. The Massachusetts reverse serpentine-front Chippendale desk was owned by the Hawthorne family. The leather-covered Sheraton bergére chair was said to be Nathaniel Hawthorne's favorite easy chair when he came to visit his cousin Susan Ingersoll.

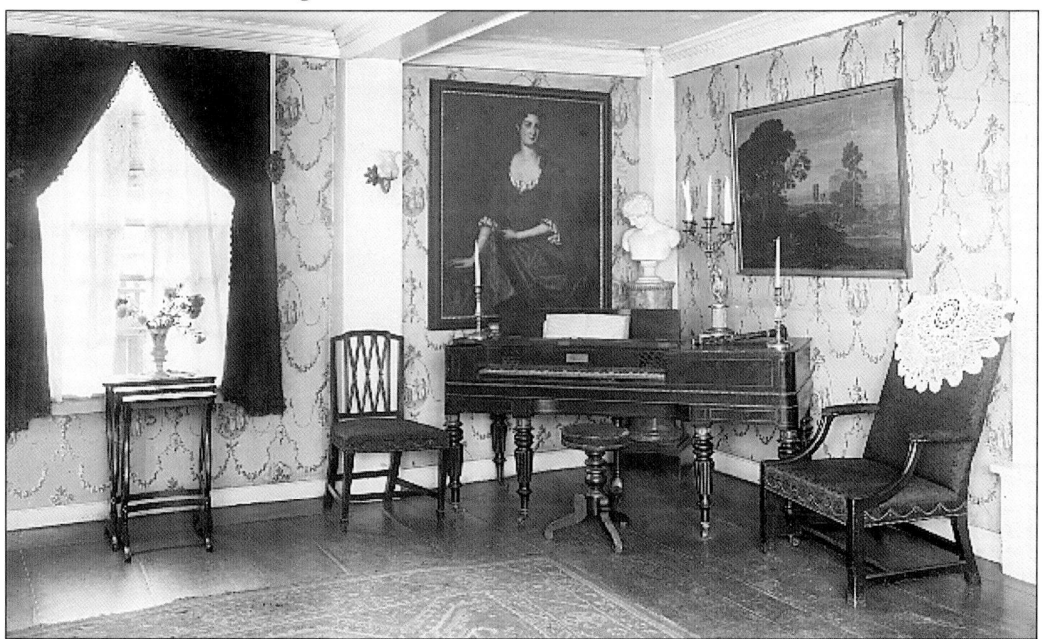

A different view of the parlor in The House of Seven Gables, 54 Turner Street, c. 1910. The pianoforte was made in Boston about 1820 by A. Babock for G.D. Mackay. The marble bust is of Antinous, the companion of the Emperor Hadrian. The neoclassical wallpaper in the "House of Seven Gables pattern" is a reproduction of an original paper found in the house and reproduced by Miss Caroline O. Emmerton.

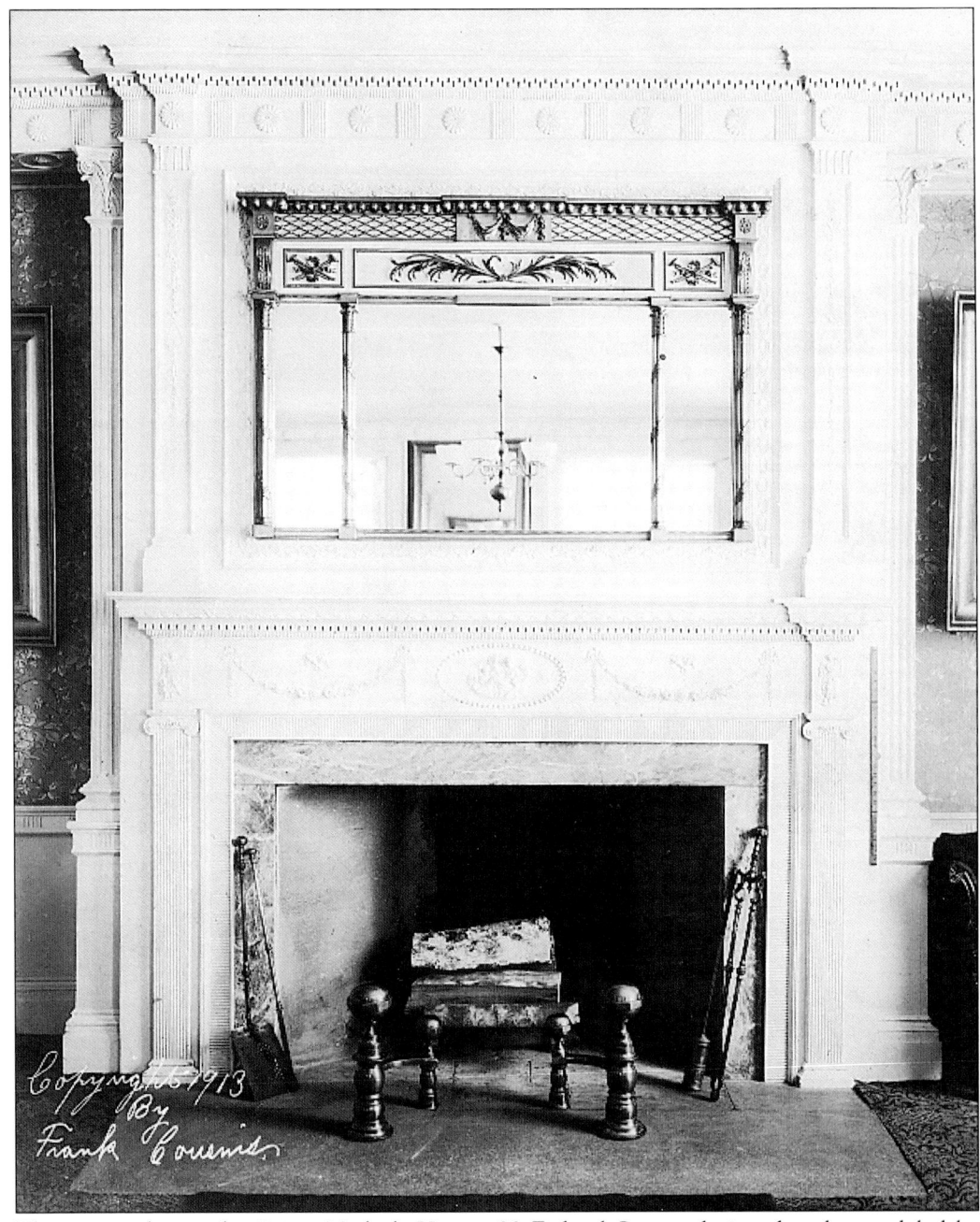

The east parlor in the Peirce-Nichols House, 80 Federal Street, designed and remodeled by Samuel McIntire in 1801 for the marriage of Sally Peirce to George Nichols.

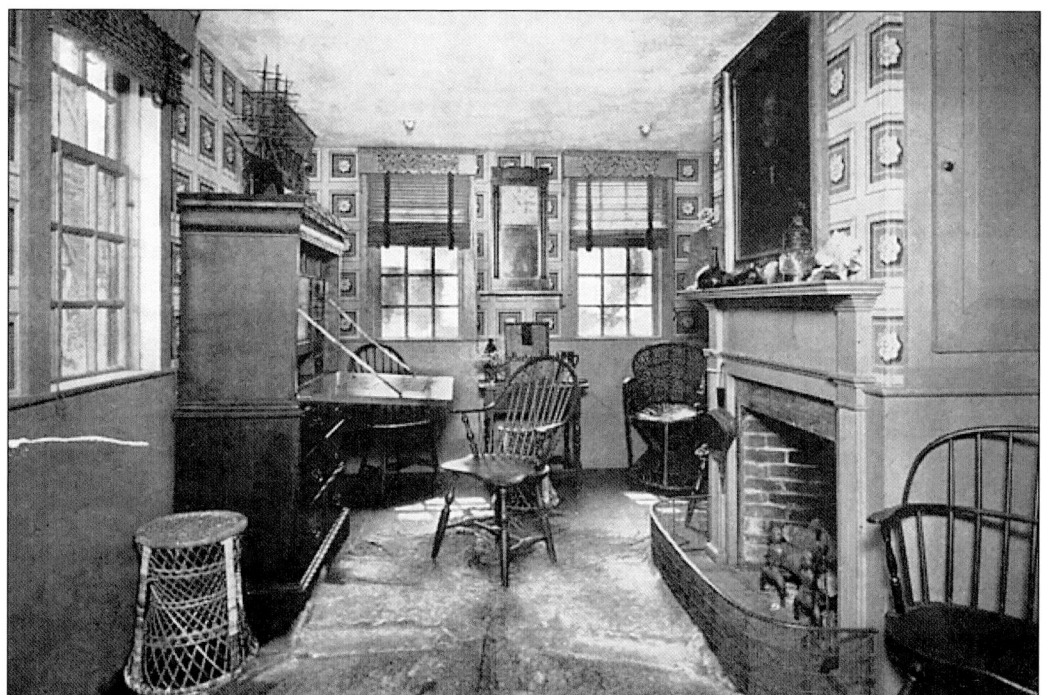

An interior view of the counting house on the grounds of The House of Seven Gables, 54 Turner Street. During the nineteenth century, it was common for merchants and sea captains to have an office, known as a counting house, where they transacted business. Sometimes this was a separate room within their home, or a small building on their property.

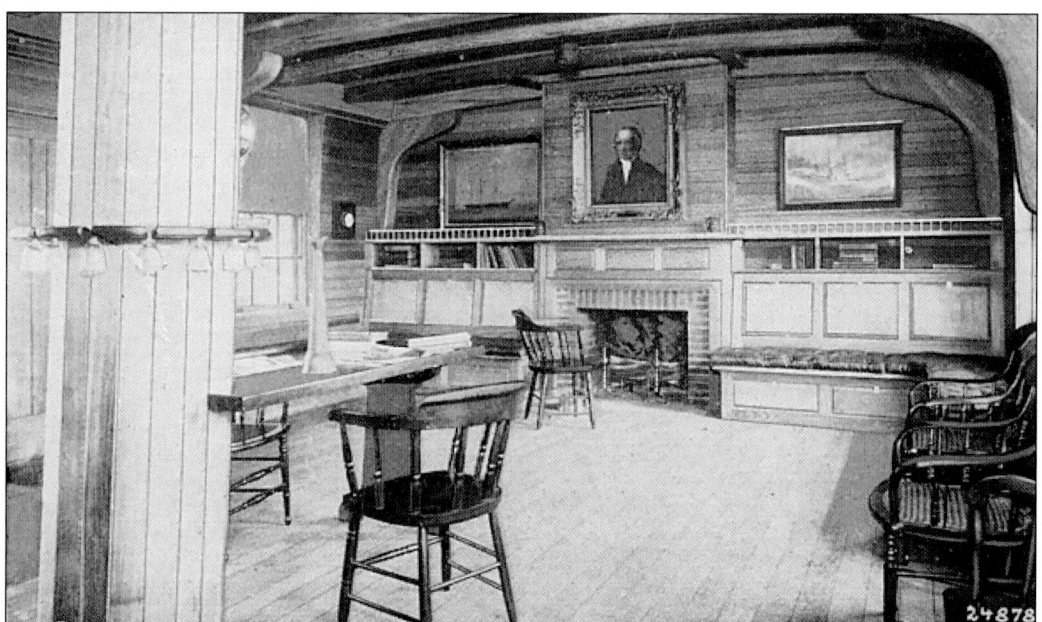

The Salem Marine Society headquarters on the roof of the Hawthorne Hotel, built in 1925. The society, formed in 1766, is the oldest charitable organization in the city. The interior of the headquarters was built to resemble a ship's cabin.

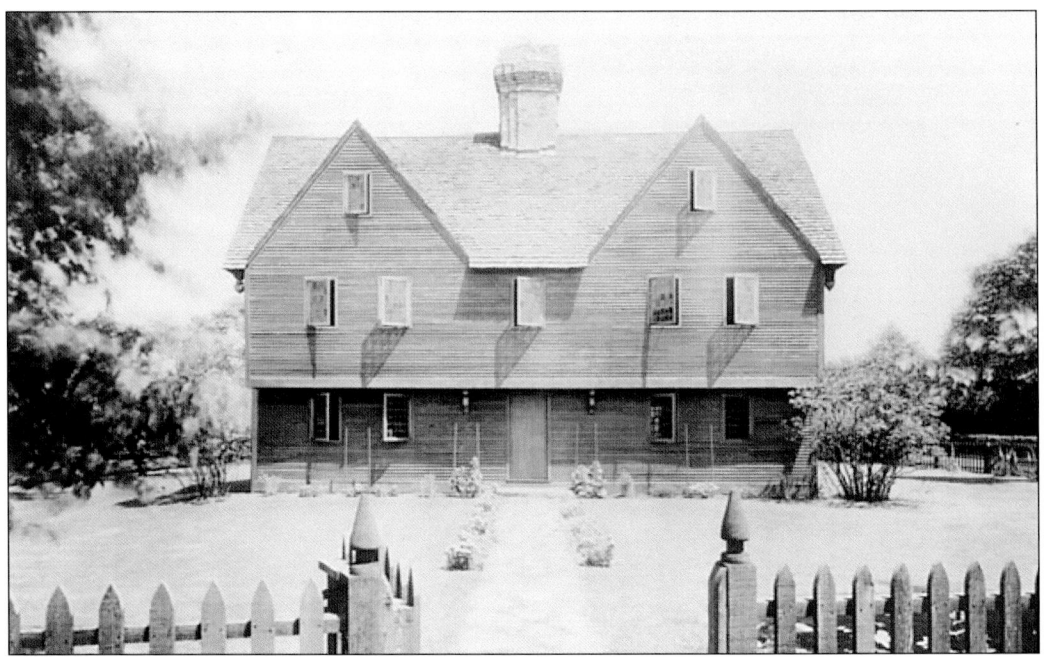

The Pequot House, 20 Congress Street, built in 1930 for the Massachusetts Bay Tercentenary celebration. The structure closely resembles the John Ward House, c. 1684, on the grounds of the Peabody Essex Museum.

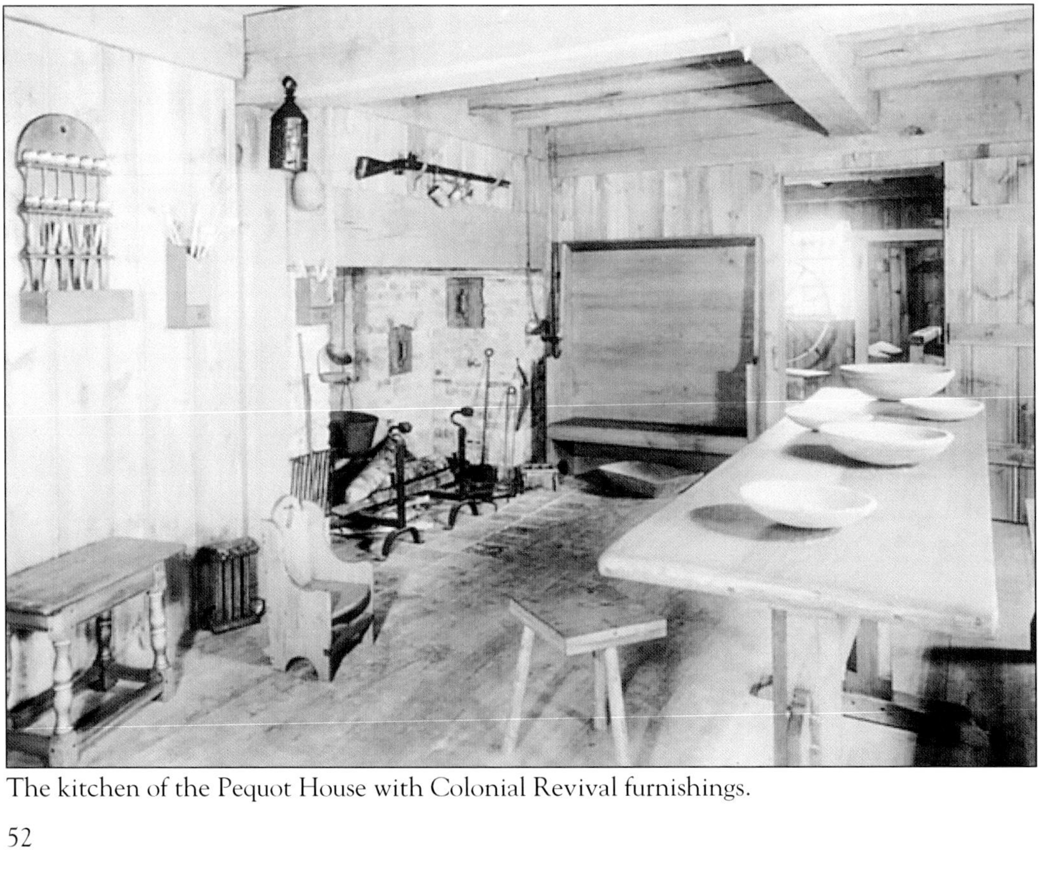

The kitchen of the Pequot House with Colonial Revival furnishings.

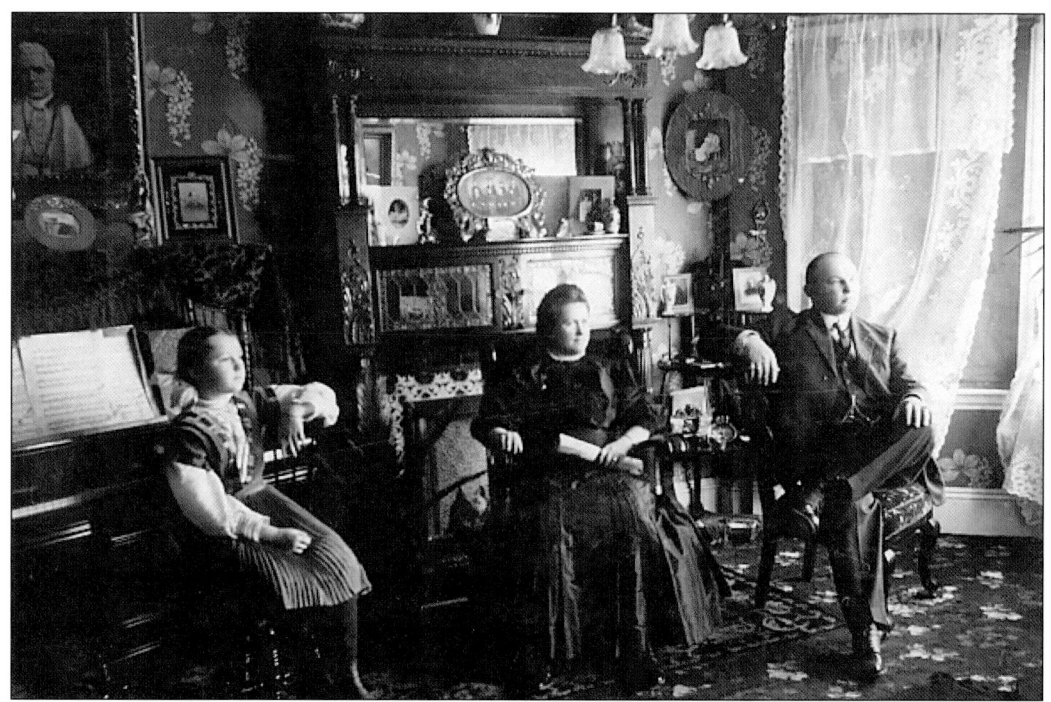

An interior parlor view of the home of Alfred Audet, his wife Eugenie, and daughter Marie Laure at 65 Palmer Street before the fire of 1914. (Courtesy D. Michel Michaud.)

A New Year's Eve dinner party in 1935 at the home of Martial Michaud and family, 48 Leavitt Street. The Michauds were members of Salem's large French-Canadian community. (Courtesy D. Michel Michaud.)

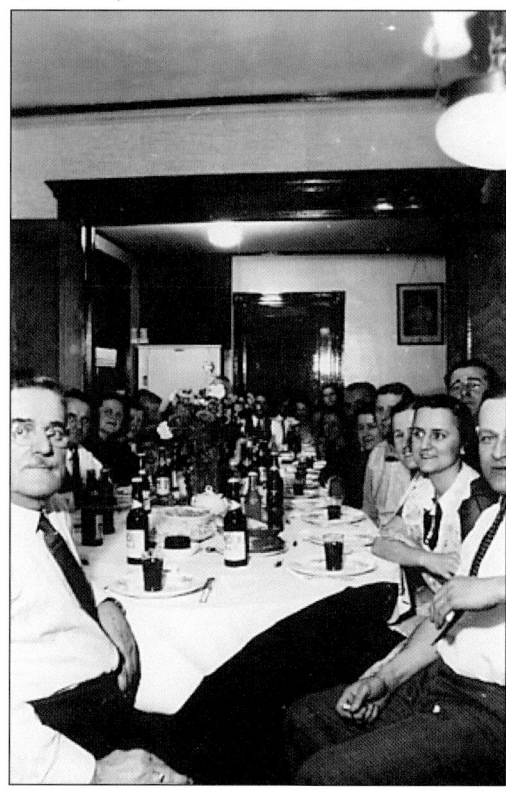

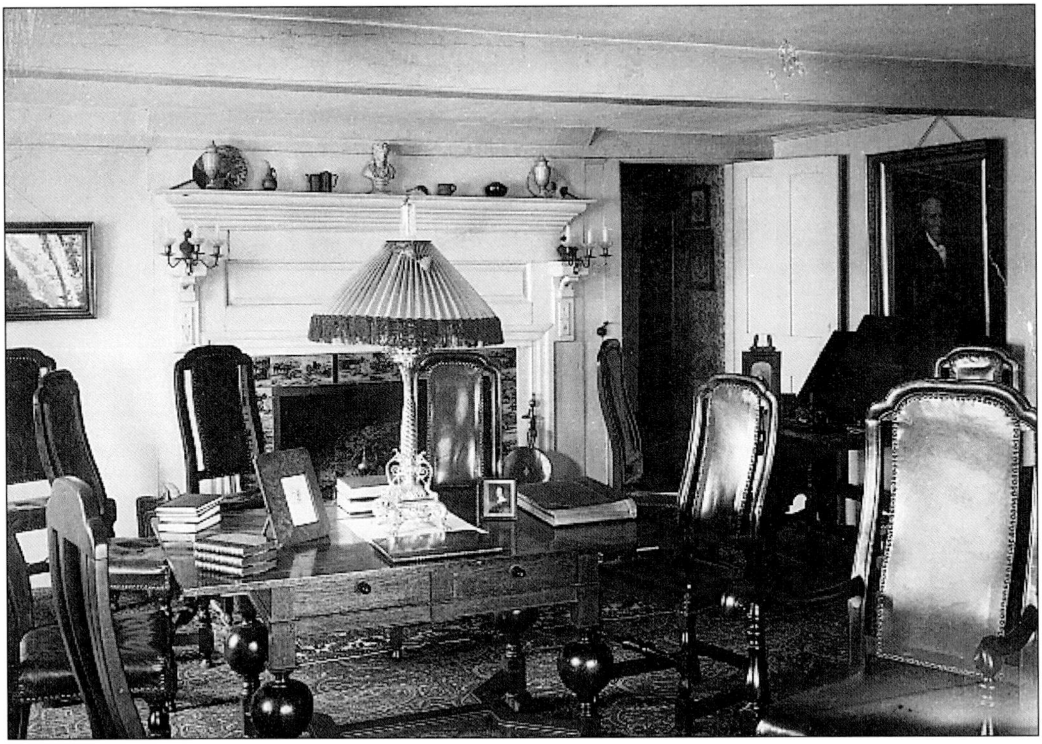

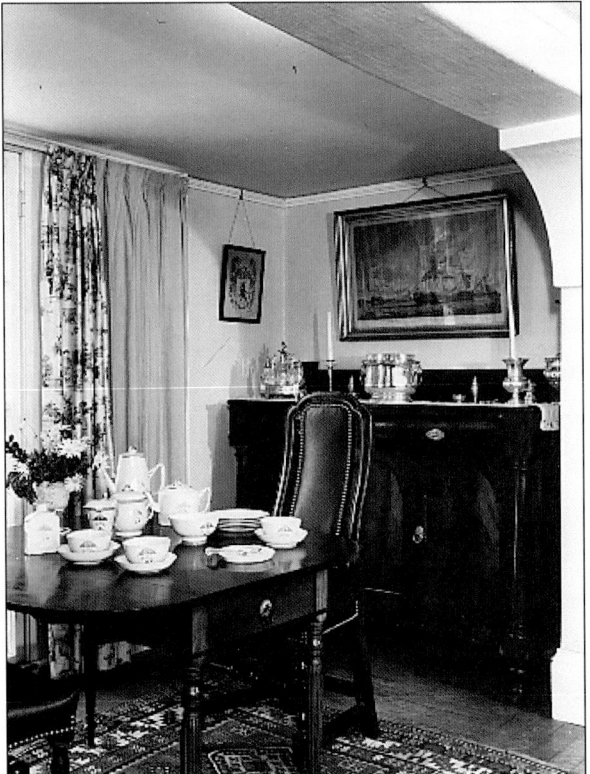

The library at the Pickering House, 18 Broad Street. The center oak table was brought to Salem from England by John Pickering in 1638; the Boston chairs date from about 1720 and were made by Theophilus Pickering. To the right hangs a portrait of Colonel Timothy Pickering (1745–1829) by artist Samuel Lovett Waldo (1783–1861).

The dining room alcove in the Pickering House, 18 Broad Street, c. 1950. On the center of the sideboard is a silver wine cooler presented to Colonel Timothy Pickering by President George Washington. On top of the Sheraton table is a Chinese export porcelain tea set that once belonged to the Cox family. (Courtesy Pickering Foundation.)

# Four
# Schools and Public Buildings

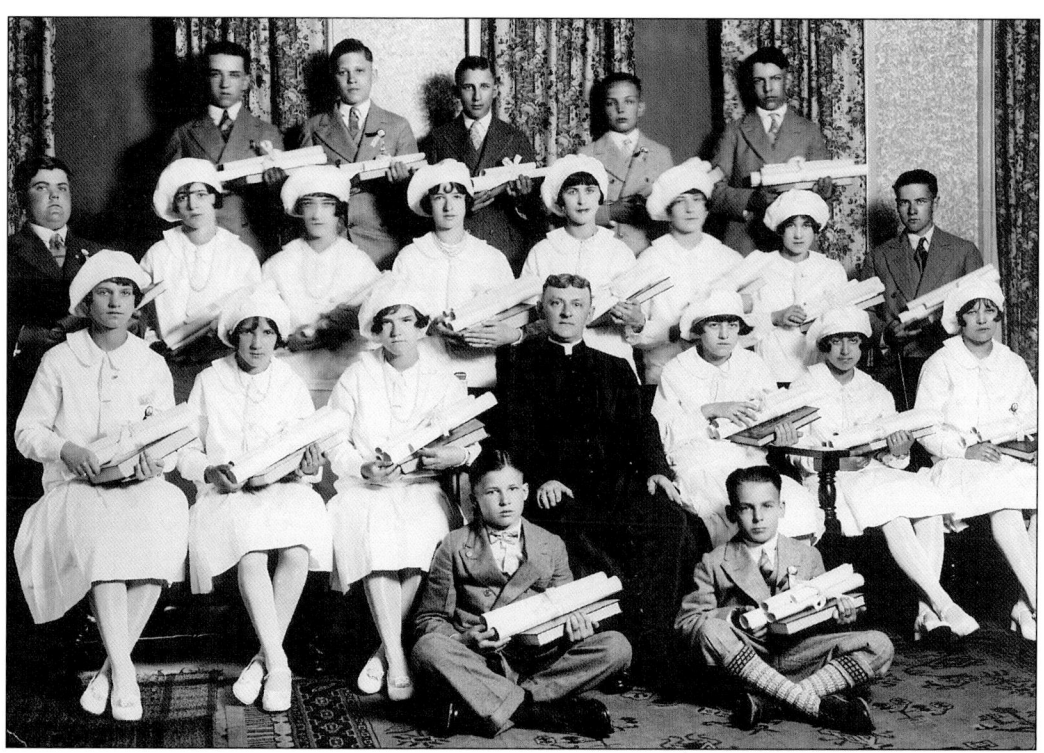

The graduating class of 1926 of Saint Anne's School in all their finery. Saint Anne's was formerly the Derby School on Jefferson Avenue. (Courtesy D. Michel Michaud.)

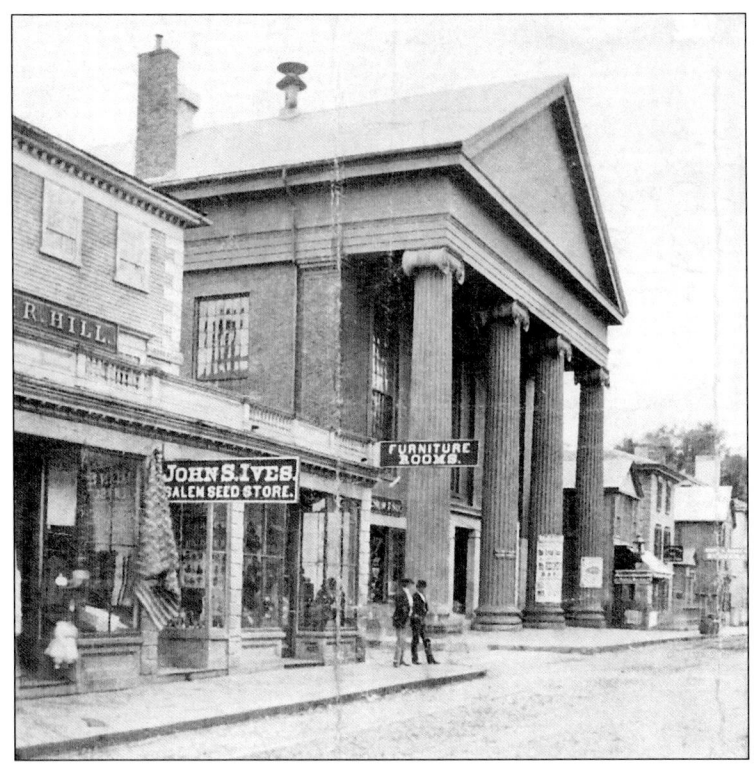

The Mechanic Hall Theatre. Located at the corner of Crombie and Essex Streets, the Mechanic Hall Theatre (on the right) was built in 1839 and destroyed by fire on February 4, 1905. The fire started from the moving picture projector and spread rapidly; there were over eleven hundred people in the theatre but all escaped safely. (Courtesy D. Michel Michaud.)

The Custom House, Salem Maritime National Historic Site, 178 Derby Street. The site was built in 1818–19, and remodeled in 1853–54. Nathaniel Hawthorne was appointed surveyor of the Port of Salem from 1846 through 1849. It is here that he found inspiration for his novel *The Scarlet Letter*, published in 1850. The balustrade is adorned with an enormous gilded American eagle carved by Joseph True of Salem.

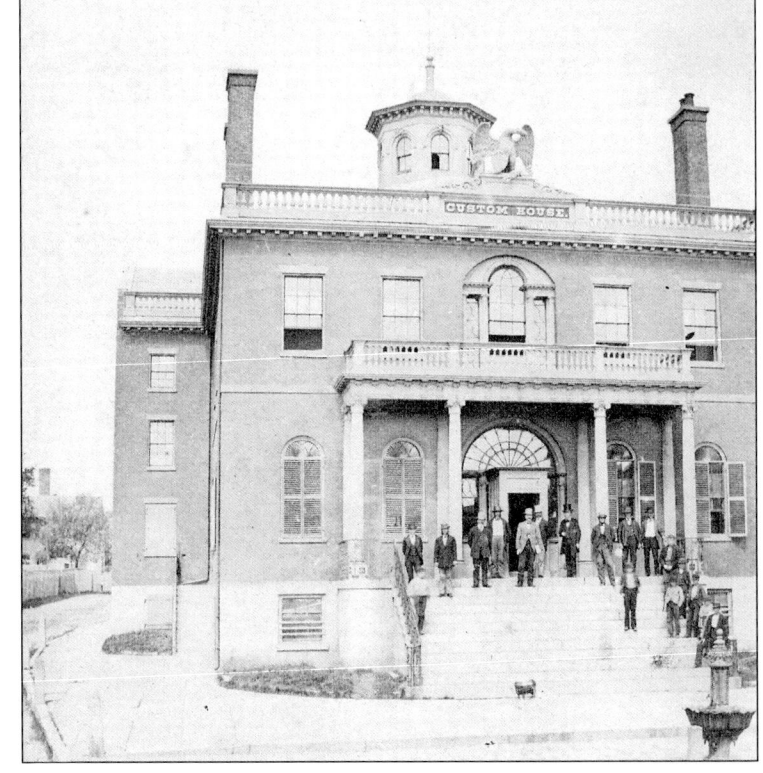

The Salem City Hall, 93 Washington Street, built in 1837 with funds from the surplus revenue of the United States Treasury. Notice the gilded eagle carved by Samuel McIntire on the crest of the Greek Revival building. It originally sat on top of the gateway at the western entrance of Washington Square (Salem Common). (Courtesy D. Michel Michaud.)

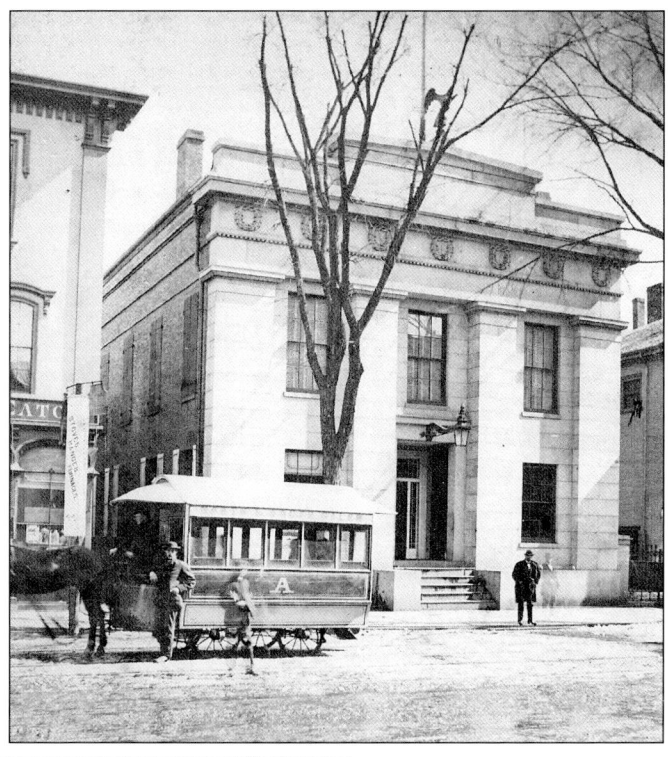

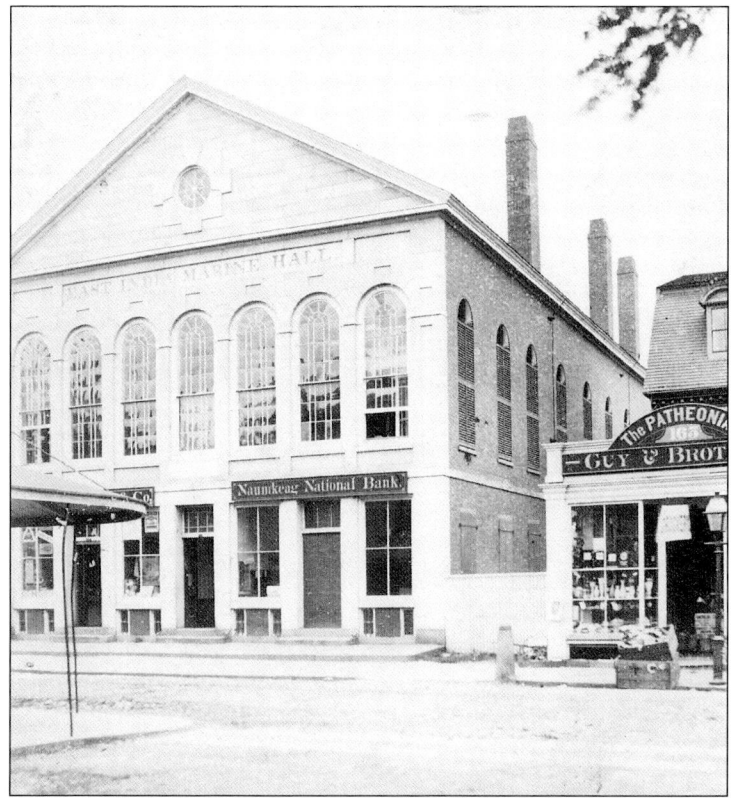

The East India Marine Hall, built in 1825–26 for the East India Marine Society, 161 Essex Street. Over the years, the building's name was changed successively to the Peabody Academy of Science, the Peabody Museum, and finally the Peabody Essex Museum. Founded by sea captains in 1799, this is the oldest continuously operated museum in the country. The partial view on the right is the Colonel Benjamin Pickman House at 165 Rear Essex Street. This photograph was taken *c.* 1870. (Courtesy D. Michel Michaud.)

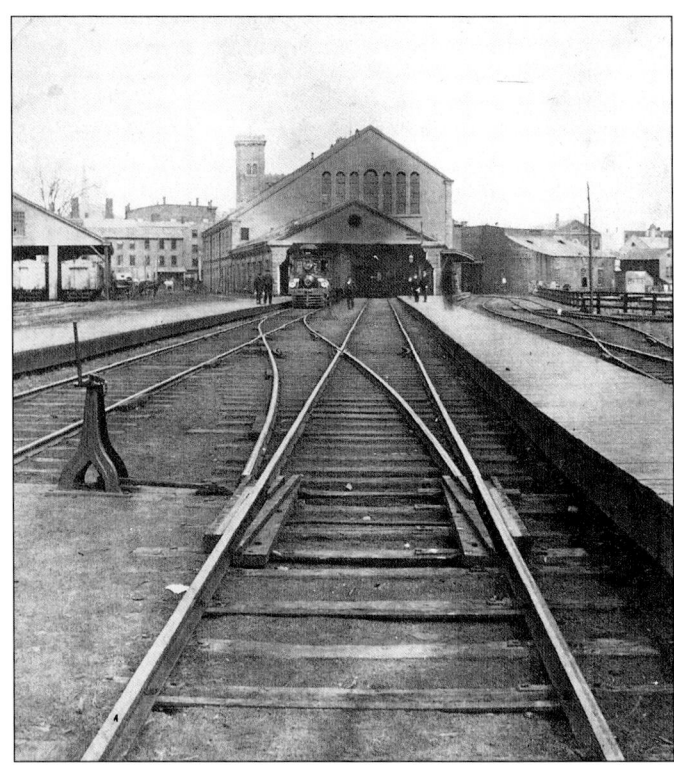

A rear view of the masonry Boston & Maine Railroad station, c. 1870. (Courtesy D. Michel Michaud.)

Bentley School, 50 Essex Street, built in 1861 as a grammar school. The tower housed a bell cast in 1801 by Revere and Son, Boston. The rooster weather vane that capped the cupola and bell were from the East Church on Essex Street. Today, both rooster and bell are preserved at the Peabody Essex Museum. In the twentieth century, the top two floors were removed and the first floor contained the Gardner Maynard Jones Memorial Library, a branch of the Salem Public Library. (Courtesy D. Michel Michaud.)

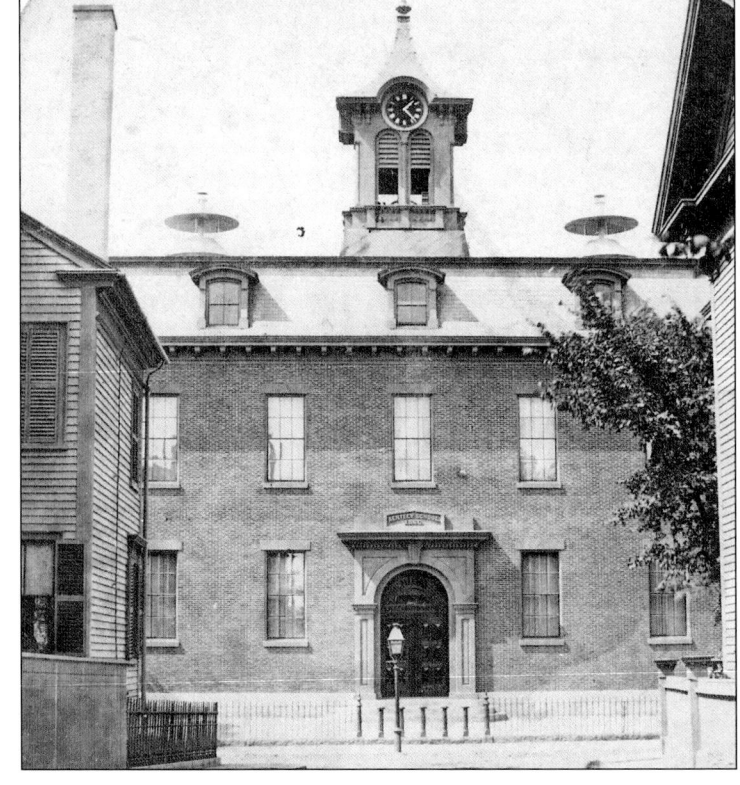

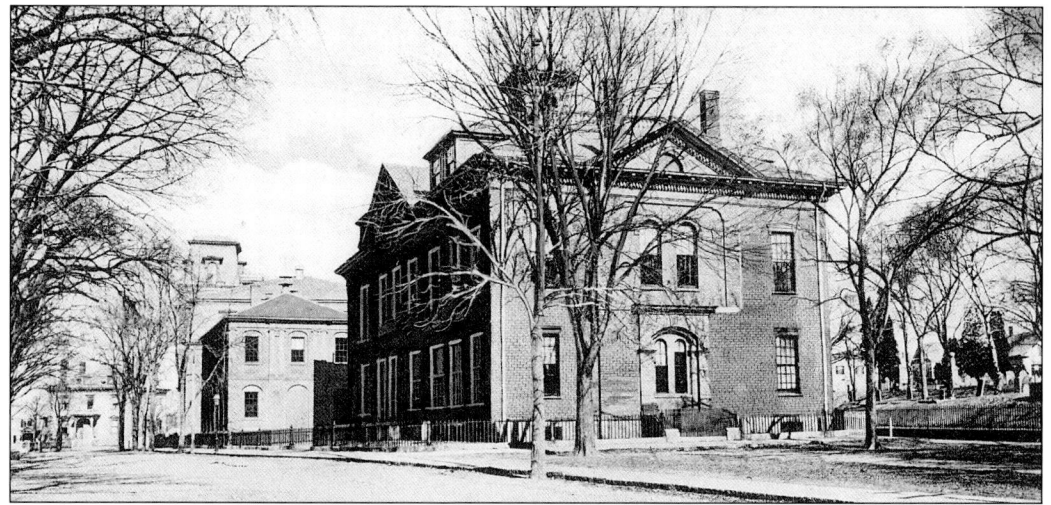

Salem High School, 5 Broad Street, built in 1855–56 according to a design by Enoch Fuller (1828–1861) of Salem. Next to this Italianate brick building is the former Oliver School, constructed in the Federal style in 1818–19. These buildings are bordered by the Broad Street Cemetery.

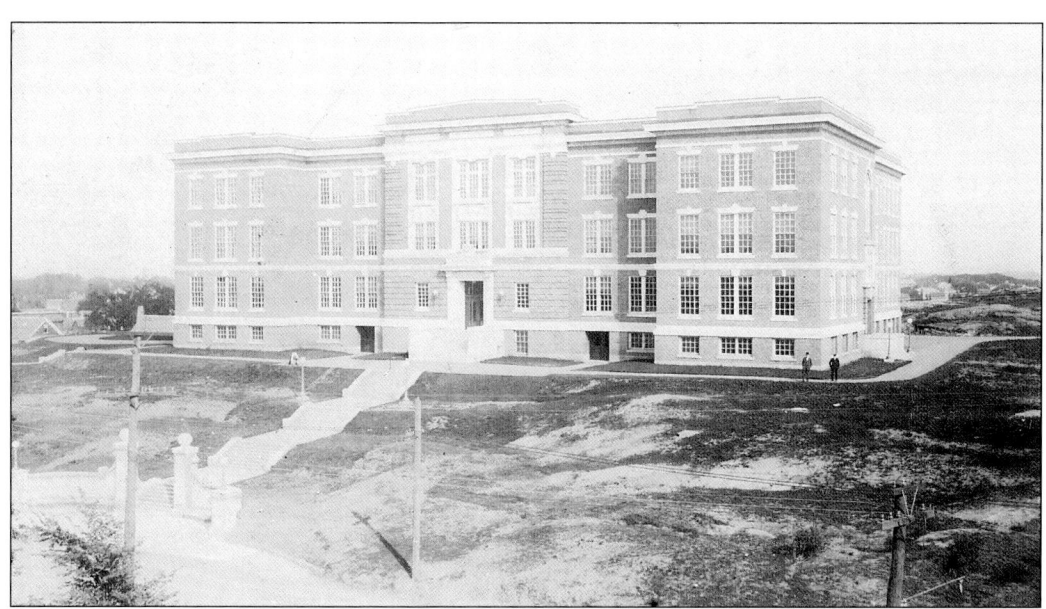

Salem High School, Highland Avenue. Salem High School moved from its Broad Street home to this location on Highland Avenue in 1909, when this building—designed by the architects Kilham and Hopkins of Boston—was built.

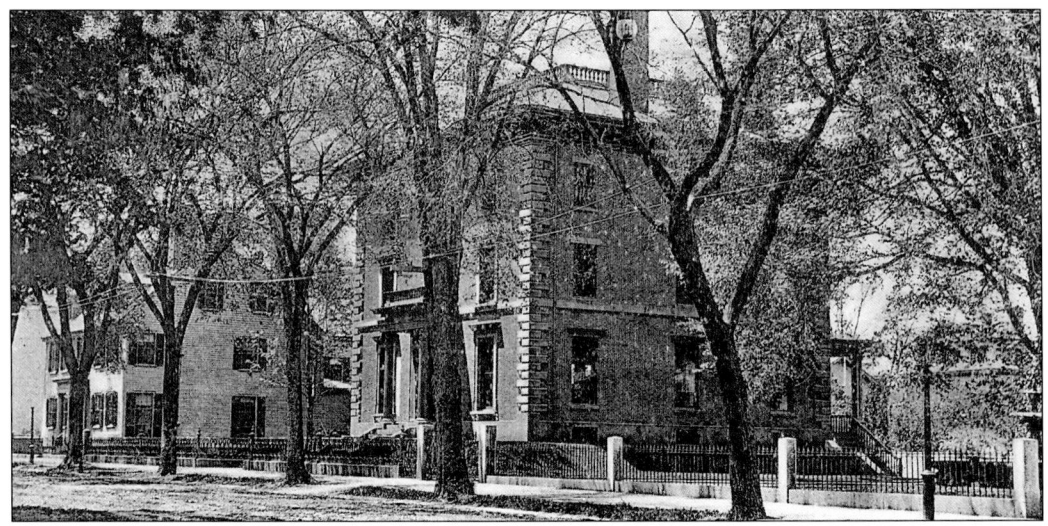

The Salem Public Library, 370 Essex Street. Formerly the home of Captain John Bertram (1796–1882), this building was built in 1855. After Captain Bertram's death his heirs donated the land and building to the city for use as a library. Opening day was July 8, 1889. This c. 1900 postcard shows the building before the 1911–12 addition.

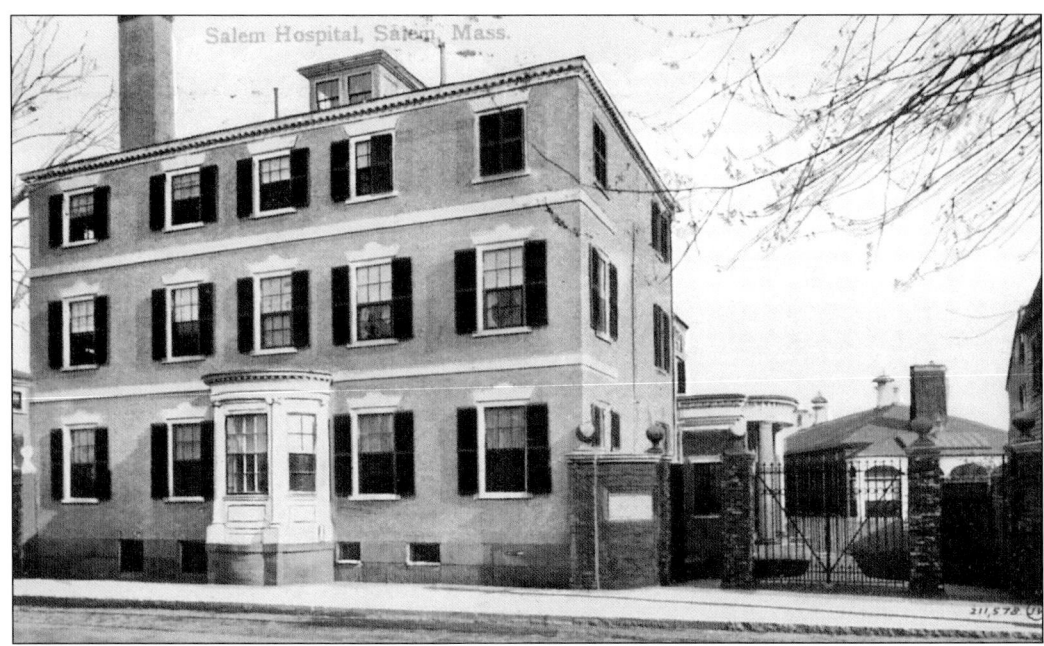

Salem Hospital, 31 Charter Street, first a private home and the birthplace of Stephen H. Phillips, attorney general of Massachusetts and Hawaii. The hospital was founded by Captain John Bertram in 1873. Damaged in the fire of 1914, the building was torn down during Salem's period of urban renewal in the 1970s. The health facility moved in 1916–17 to its present location at 81 Highland Avenue.

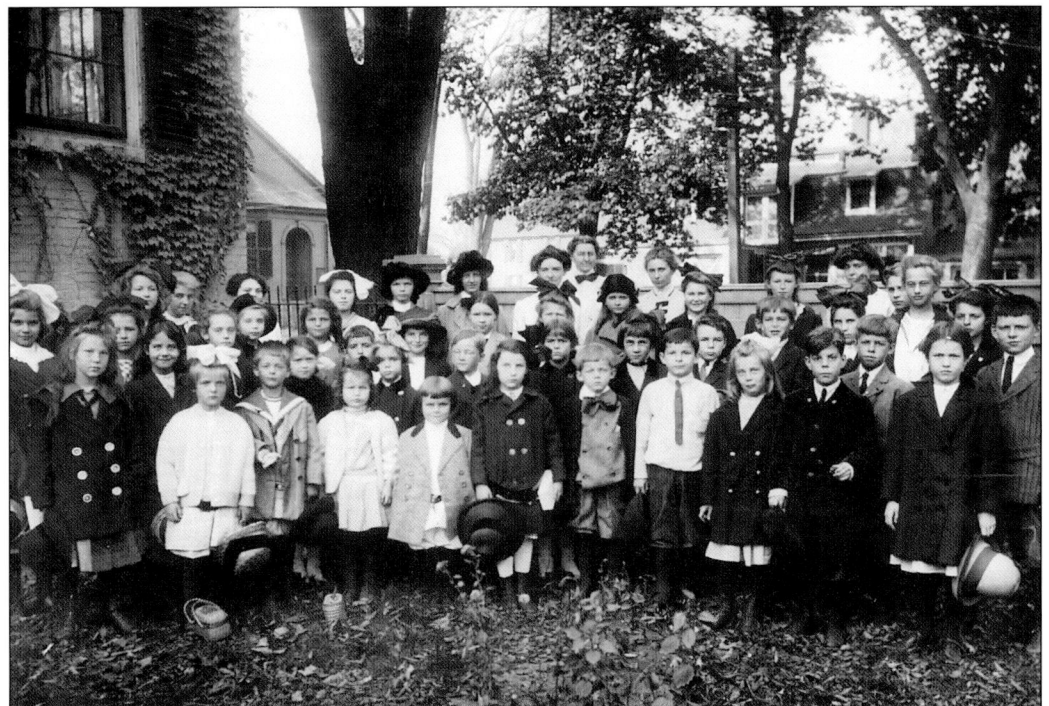
A group photograph of children in Miss Howe's school, c. 1906. The school was located at 2 Chestnut Street. (Courtesy Pickering Foundation.)

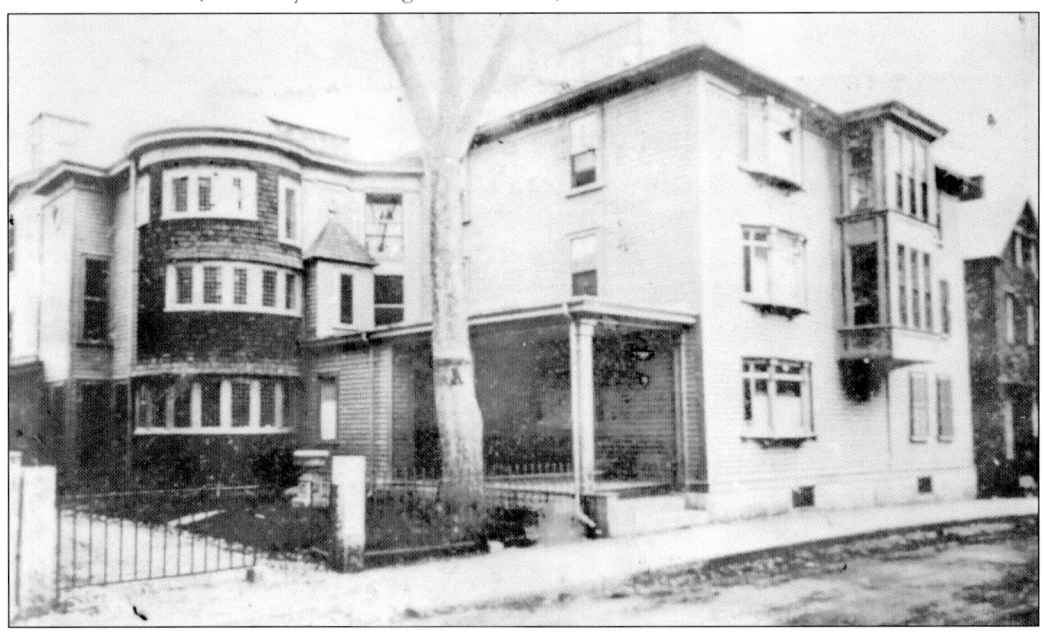
The site of the Witchcraft Jail, 4 Federal Street, at the corner of Saint Peter Street. In 1763 a new jail was built to replace the old jail of 1684, using some of the framing timbers of the original structure. In 1813, a new facility of Rockport granite was erected and the 1763 building was converted into a dwelling. These structures were torn down in the mid-1950s to make way for New England Telephone Company's expansion.

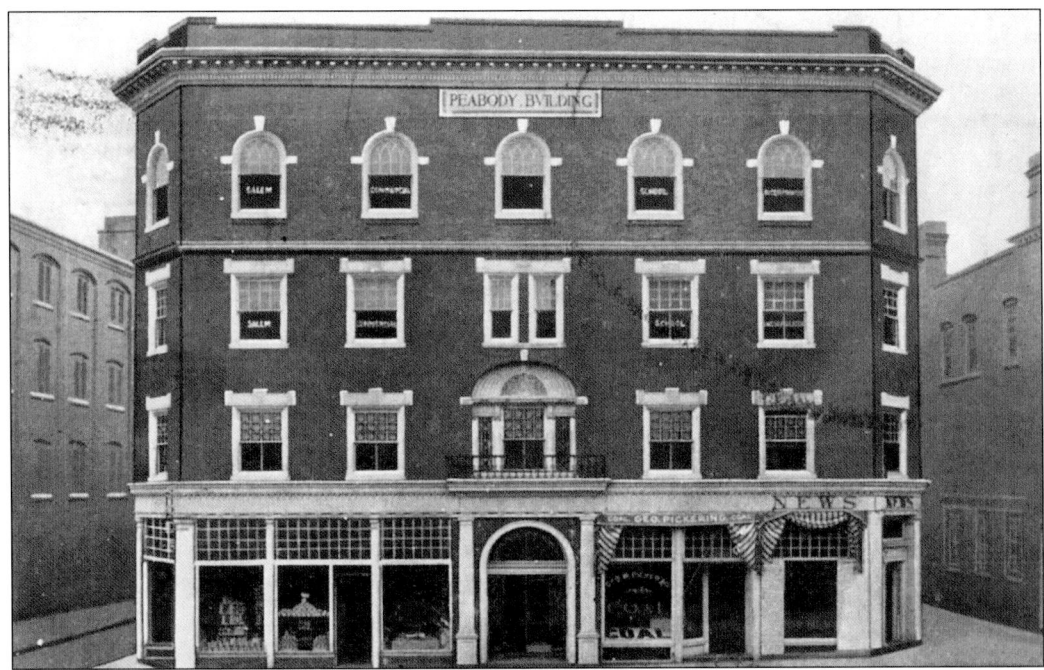

The Peabody building, 120–128 Washington Street, erected as the headquarters of the *Salem Evening News* in 1889. The two upper floors were used by the Salem Commercial School. The building, named after S. Endicott Peabody, is shown here *c.* 1910

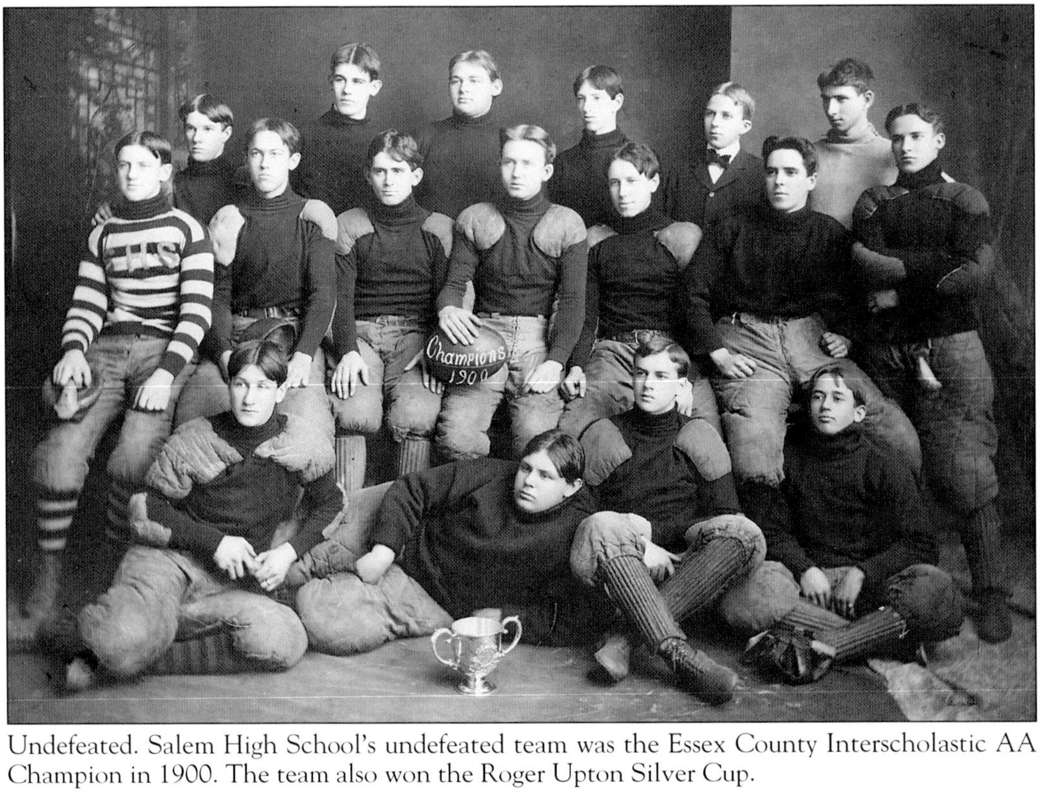

Undefeated. Salem High School's undefeated team was the Essex County Interscholastic AA Champion in 1900. The team also won the Roger Upton Silver Cup.

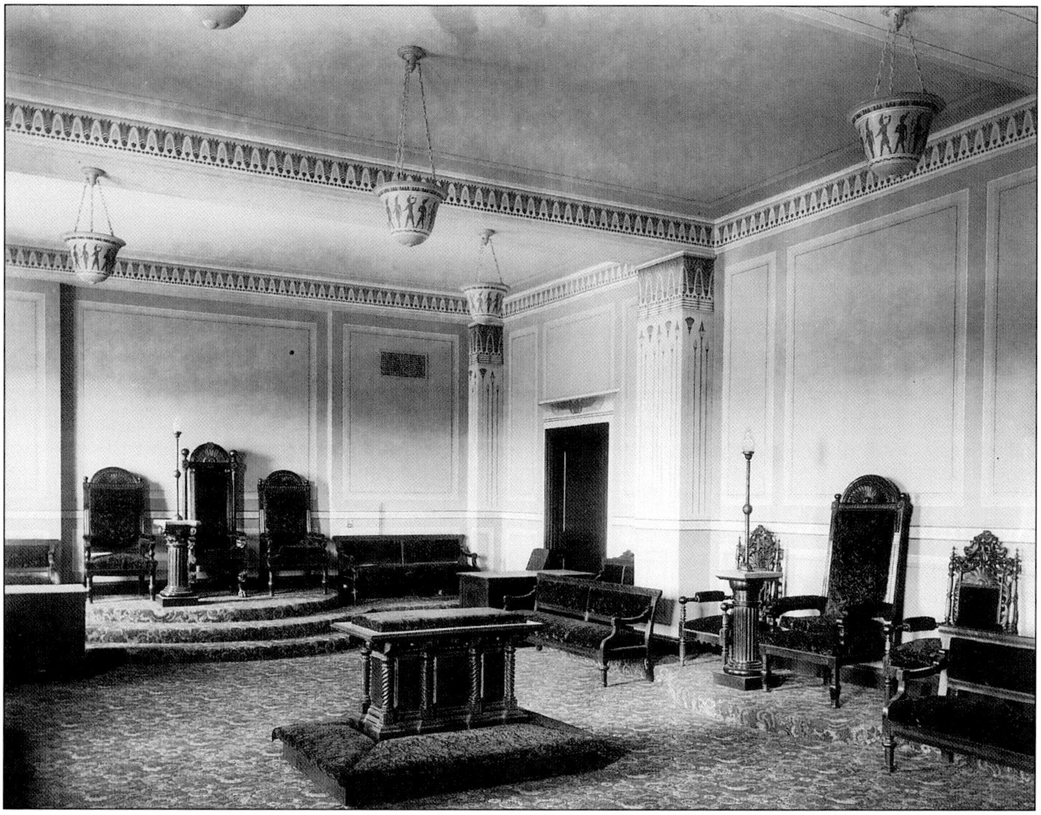

The interior of the Masonic Temple, corner of Washington and Lynde Streets. The temple was built in 1915–16 by Lester S. Couch of Little and Brown in the Colonial Revival style. Notice the Egyptian imagery stenciled on the frieze and the light fixtures. A fire destroyed the top two stories in 1982; they were subsequently rebuilt.

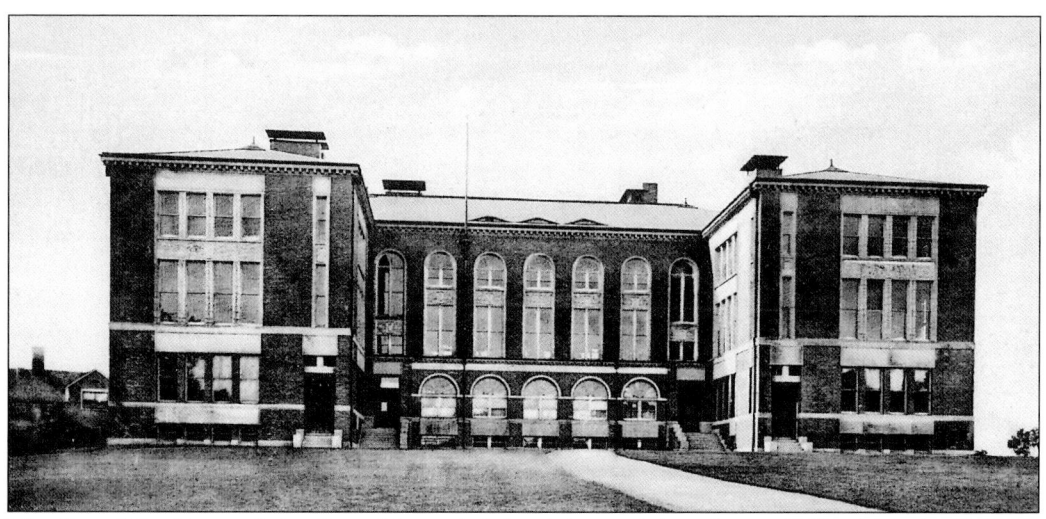

The "new" building of the State Normal School (now Salem State College), built 1893–96 by architect J. Philip Rinn. The building is located at the intersection of Lafayette Street and Loring Avenue. A State Normal school first came to the city in 1854.

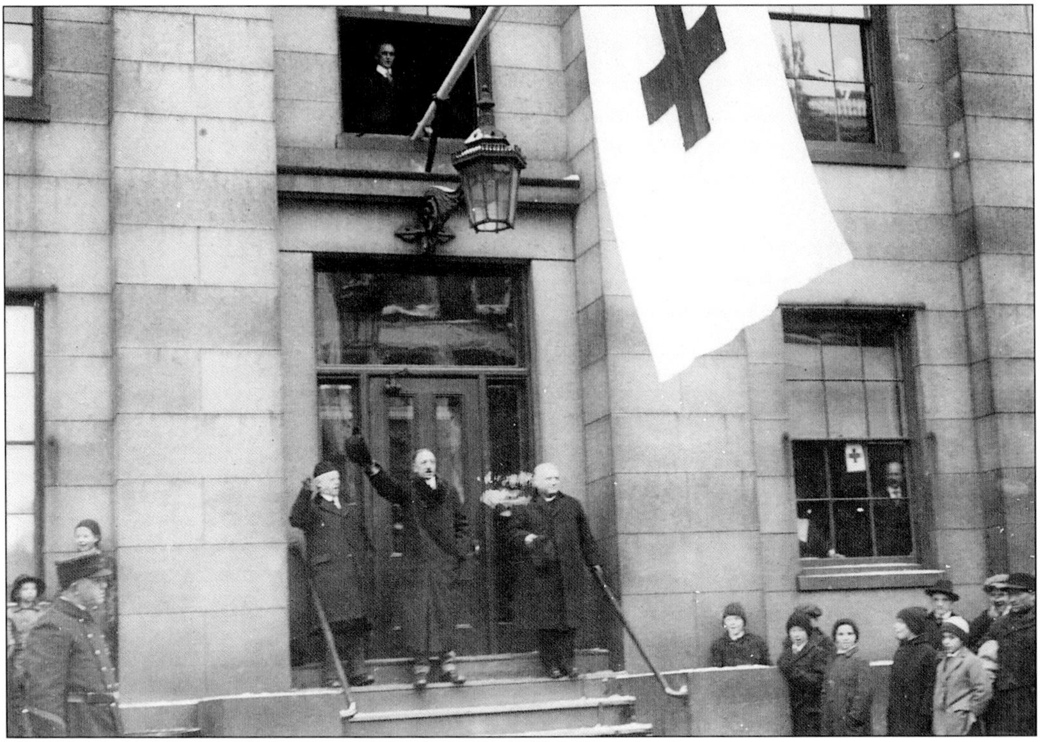

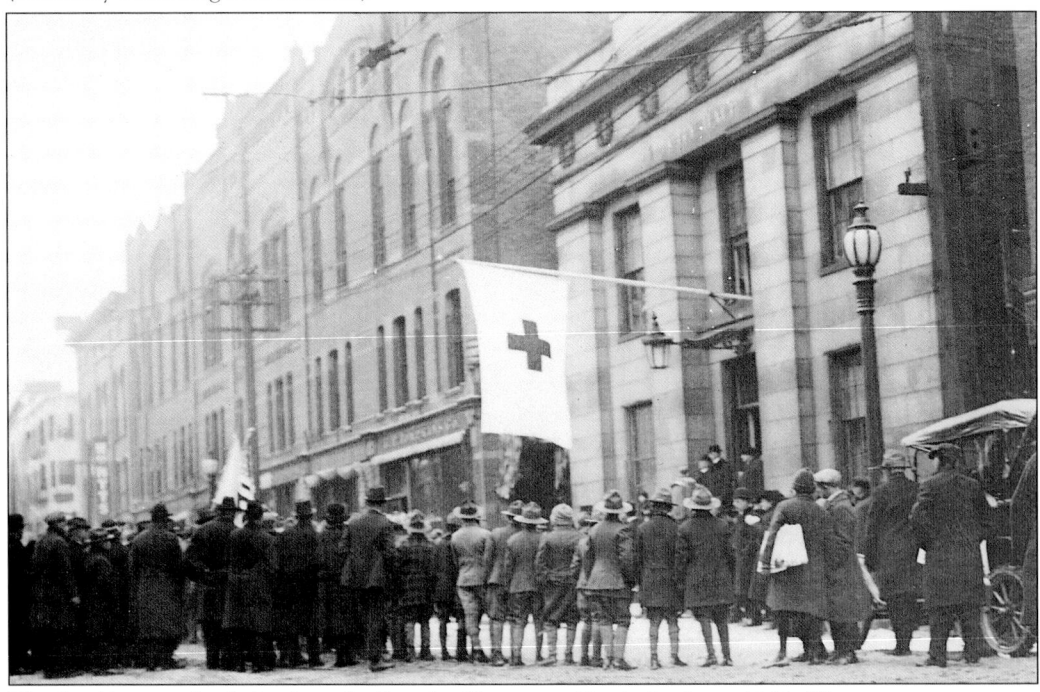

Mayor Henry P. Benson of Salem (center) during a World War I rally at city hall in 1917. (Courtesy Pickering Foundation.)

The building to the left of city hall is the Kinsman Block, built in 1882. The upper stories are used as the Odd Fellows Hall and various offices; the lower level serves the retail trade.

The Second Corps Cadet Armory, 136 Essex Street, built in 1908 after the demolition of the Colonel Francis Peabody House. In 1982 a fire destroyed this building. The drill shed in the rear has been restored. The facade is still standing as a burnt-out ruin and is threatened with demolition.

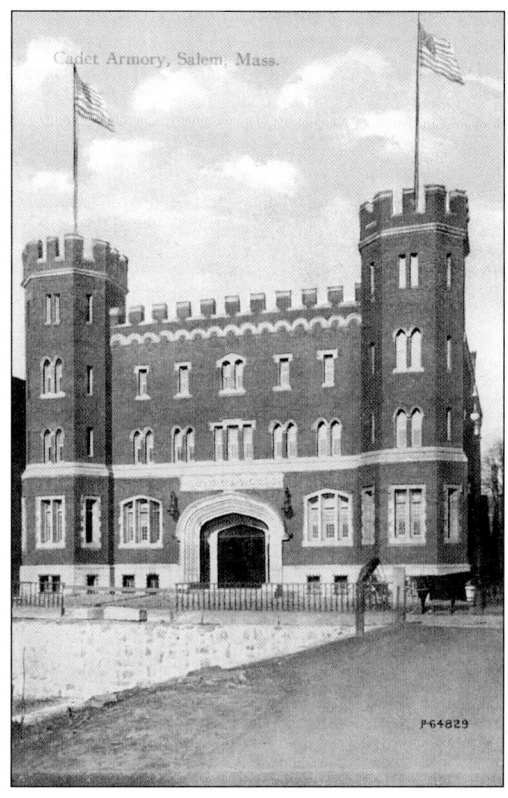

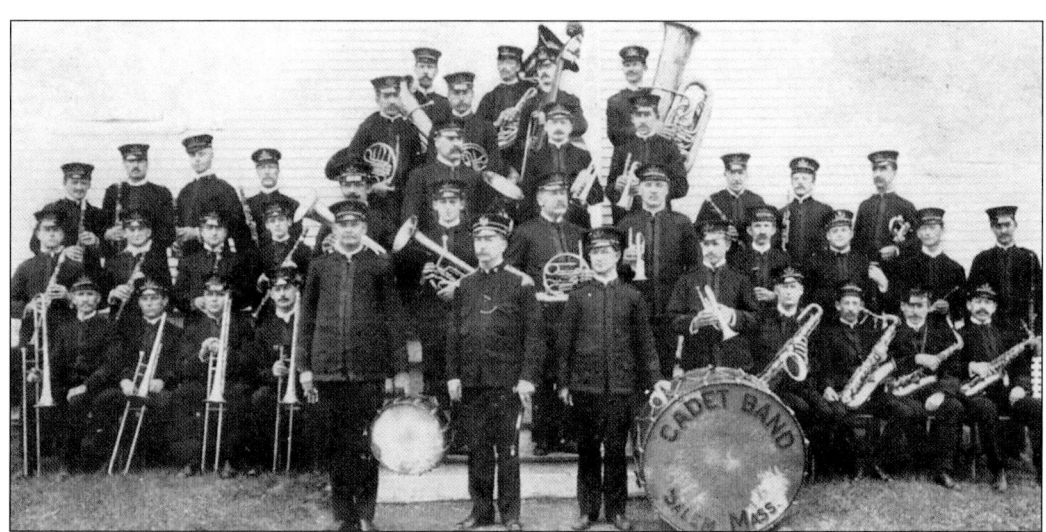

The Salem Cadet Band, 1897. Organized in 1878 for the Second Corps of Cadets, it was the authorized band of the Ancient and Honorable Artillery Company of Boston. (Courtesy D. Michel Michaud.)

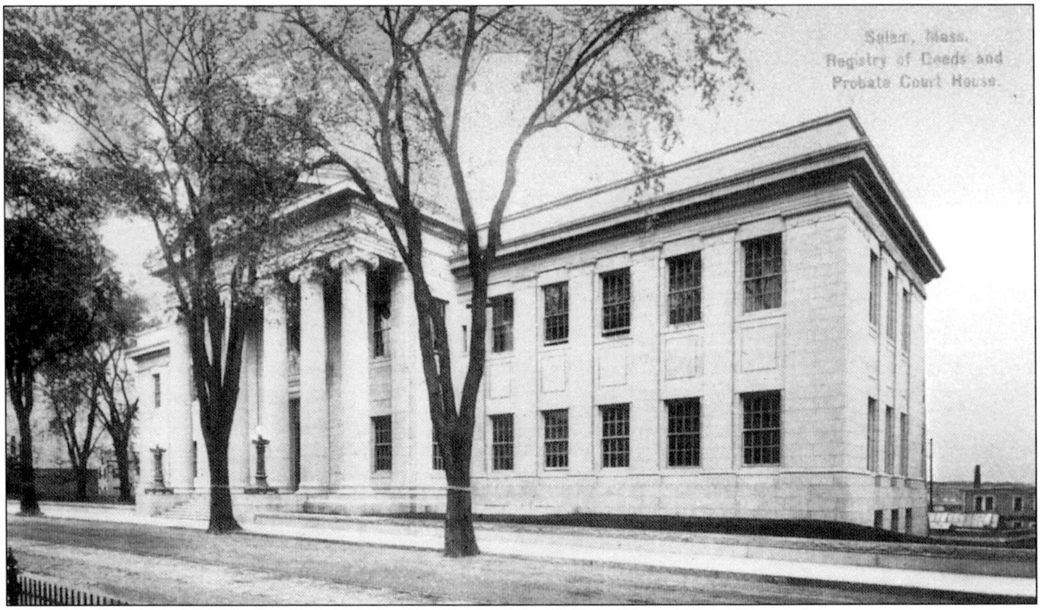

The Registry of Deeds and Probate Court House, 42 Federal Street. An imposing granite facade with its six Ionic columns was opened for use on July 31, 1909; the architect was Clarence H. Blackall (1857–1942) of Boston.

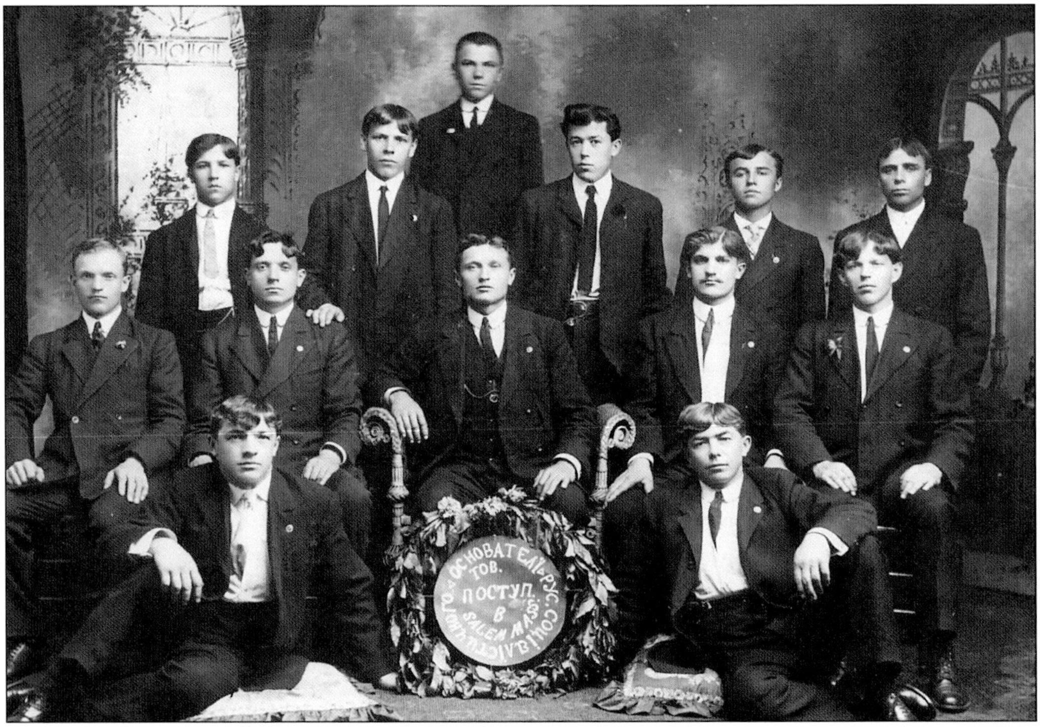

Founders of Socialism, c. 1900. A substantial number of Ukrainian immigrants settled in Salem at the turn of the century. Immigrant life was often centered around a church, in this case Saint Nicholas Russian Orthodox Church. The religious affiliation of this group is unknown. (Courtesy D. Michel Michaud.)

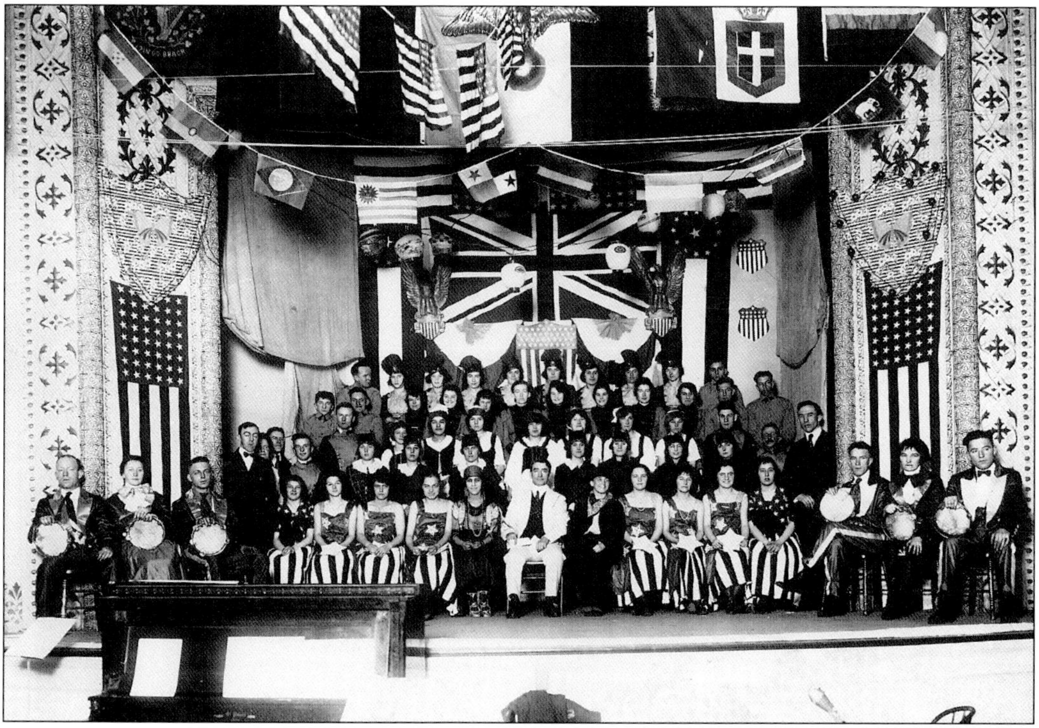

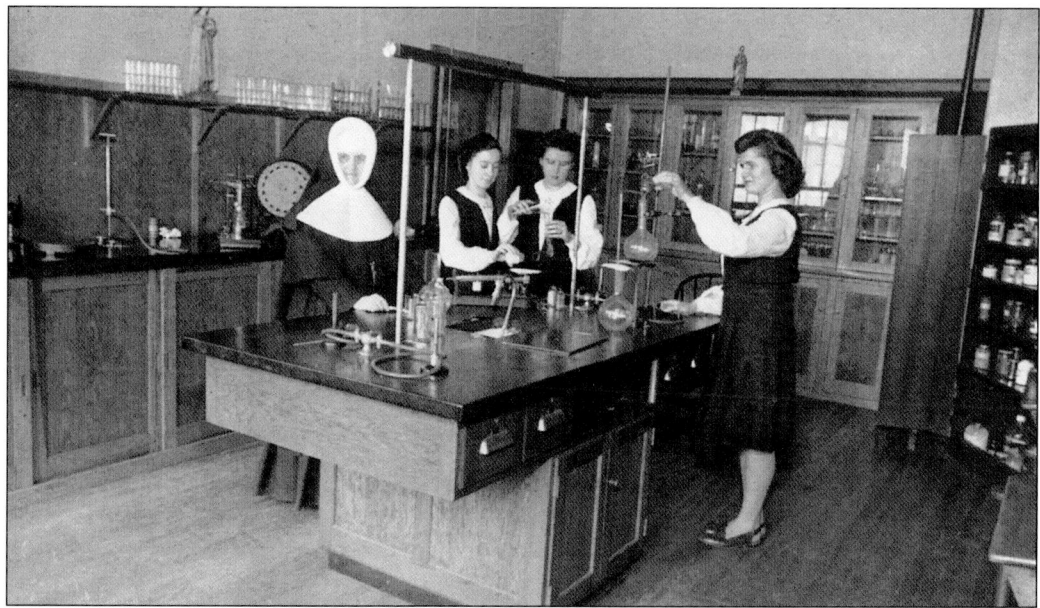

A minstrel show at the Now and Then Hall, 36 Washington Square South, January 29 and 30, 1920. The association was organized in 1886 with the provision that they would meet "Now and Then." The entrance was at 102 Essex Street and the hall could seat nine hundred people. (Courtesy D. Michel Michaud.)

Students from Saint Joseph's Academy on Harbor Street. Classes for the students (who were mainly of French-Canadian descent) were conducted in French. These students are in the chemistry laboratory with Sister Superior Georges-Francois in 1947.

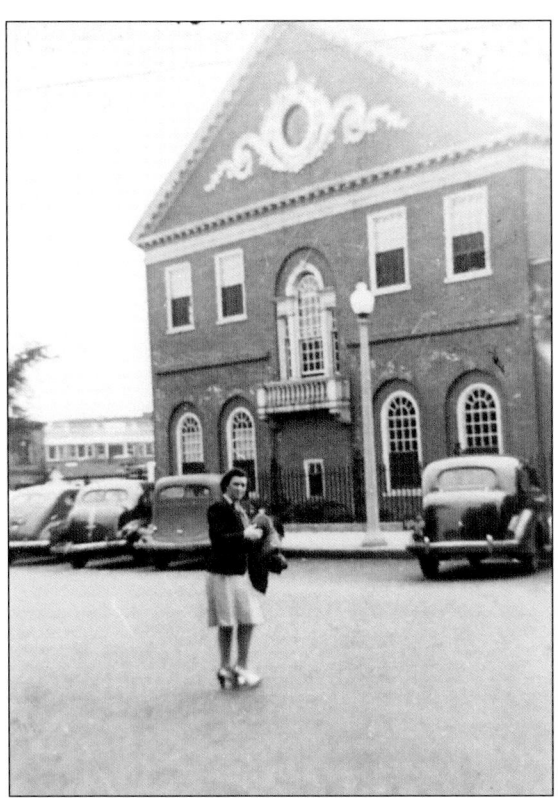

Rita Russell crossing Norman Street, July 1949. In the background is the Colonial Revival United States Post Office building, designed by Philip Horton Smith and built in 1932.

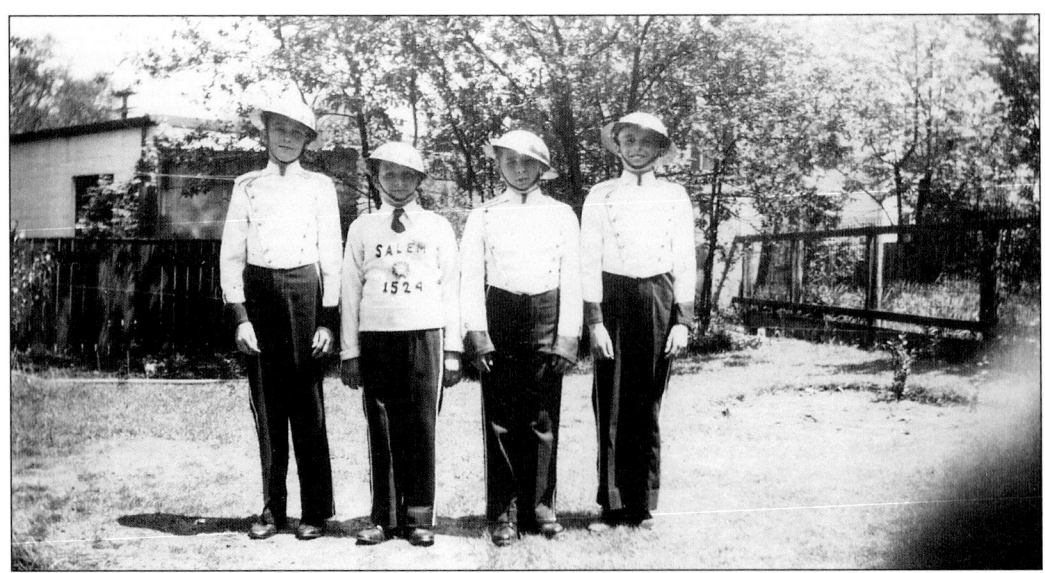

Four lucky lads getting ready for a parade, c. 1940. They represent Veterans of Foreign Wars Witch City Post #1524.

# *Five*
# CHURCHES

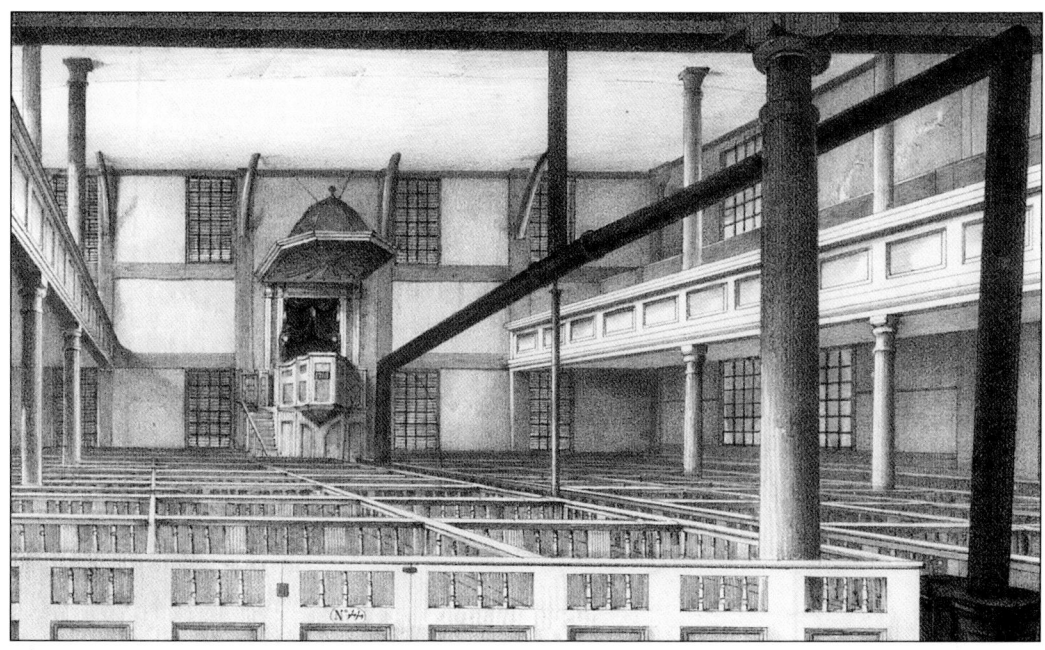

The interior of the East Church. Note the early heating device installed in the aisle. (Courtesy John Hardy Wright.)

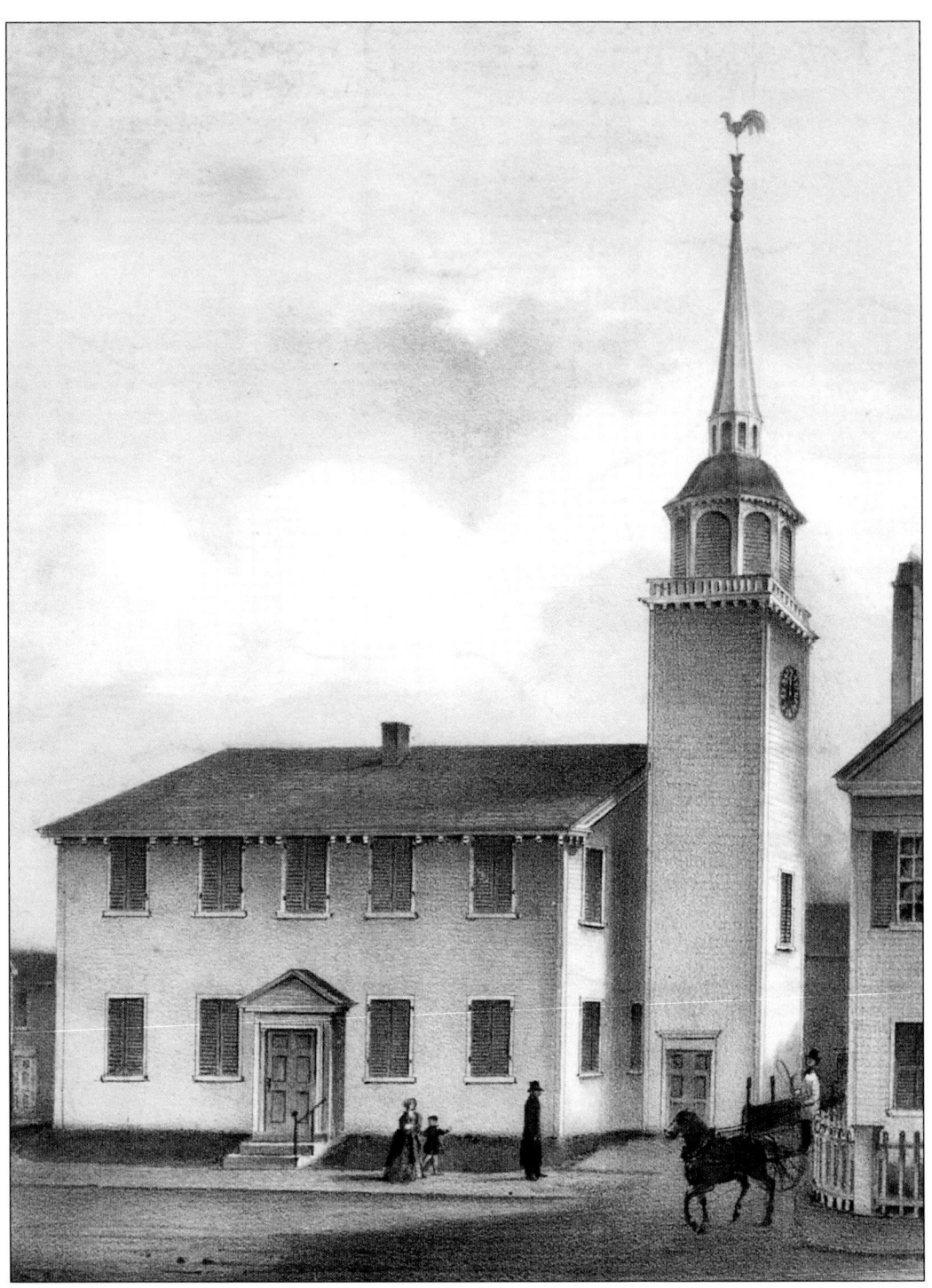

A John H. Bufford lithograph of the East Church in Salem, drawn by Daniel M. Shephard of Salem, c. 1840. Built in 1718, this structure stood on the corner between Bentley and Hardy Streets from 1783 to 1819. The famous diarist and historian Dr. William Bentley (1759–1819) preached here. (Courtesy John Hardy Wright.)

The original Grace Episcopal Church, 381 Essex Street. The church was built in 1858 and is shown here c. 1870. The current stone edifice was built on the site of this demolished building in 1926. (Courtesy D. Michel Michaud.)

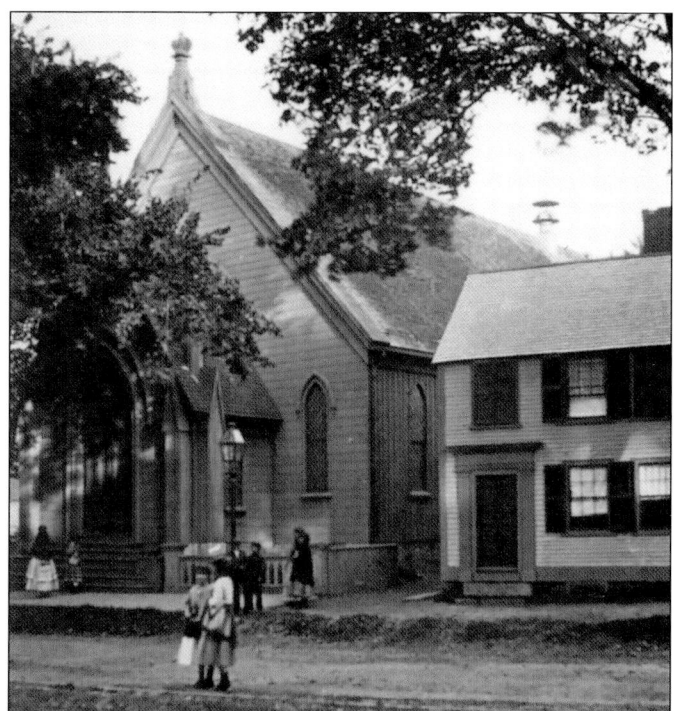

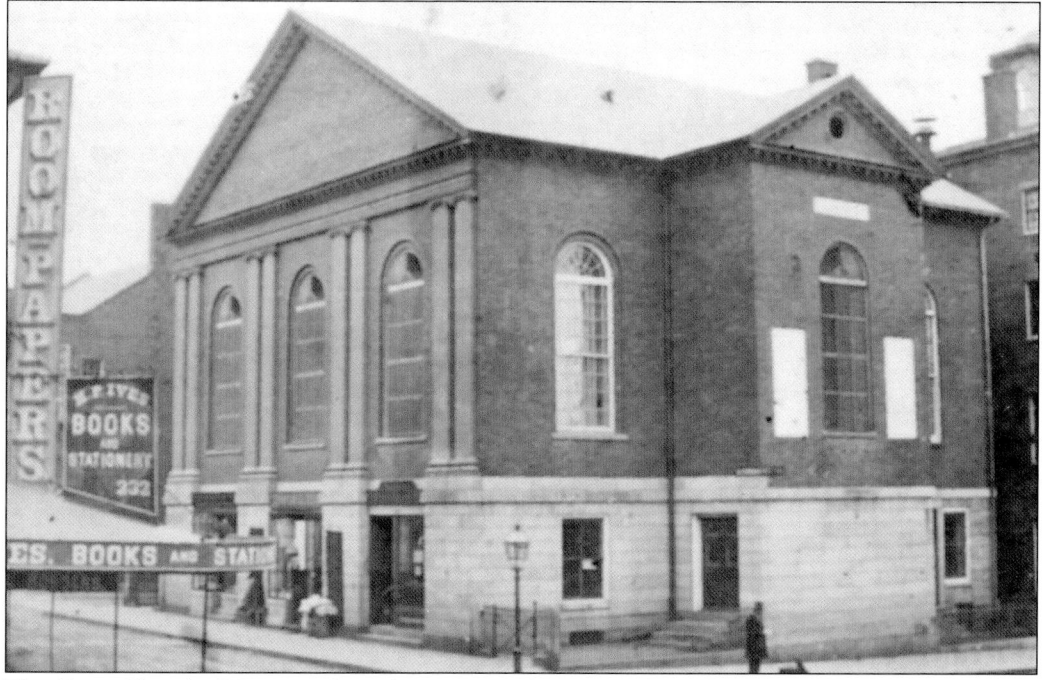

The First Church (Unitarian) at the corner of Essex and Washington Streets, c. 1875. The building was erected in 1826 and remodeled in 1875. The congregation merged with that of the North Church in 1923. The present location of the First Church is at 316 Essex Street. The building served for decades as the jewelry store of Daniel Low & Company. (Courtesy D. Michel Michaud.)

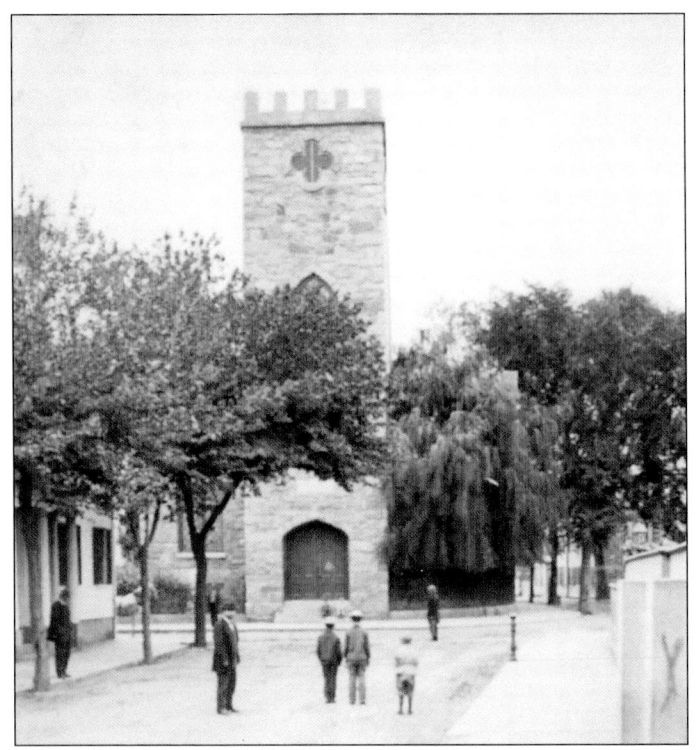

Saint Peter's Church, built in 1833 in the then popular Gothic Revival style at the corner of Saint Peter and Brown Streets. The church was one of the earliest organized in Salem and boasts the oldest church bell in the city. It is shown here c. 1870. (Courtesy D. Michel Michaud.)

The interior of the Universalist Church on Rust Street, c. 1872. The Federal-style brick building was originally built in 1808. The church is decked out in typical Victorian floral decorations, probably as a memorial to the man portrayed in the oval frame in the center of the photograph. (Courtesy D. Michel Michaud.)

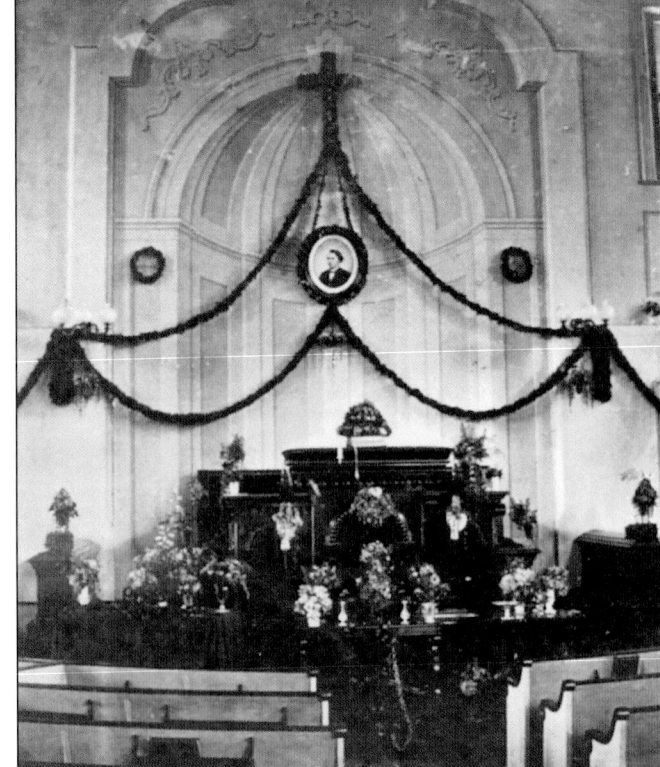

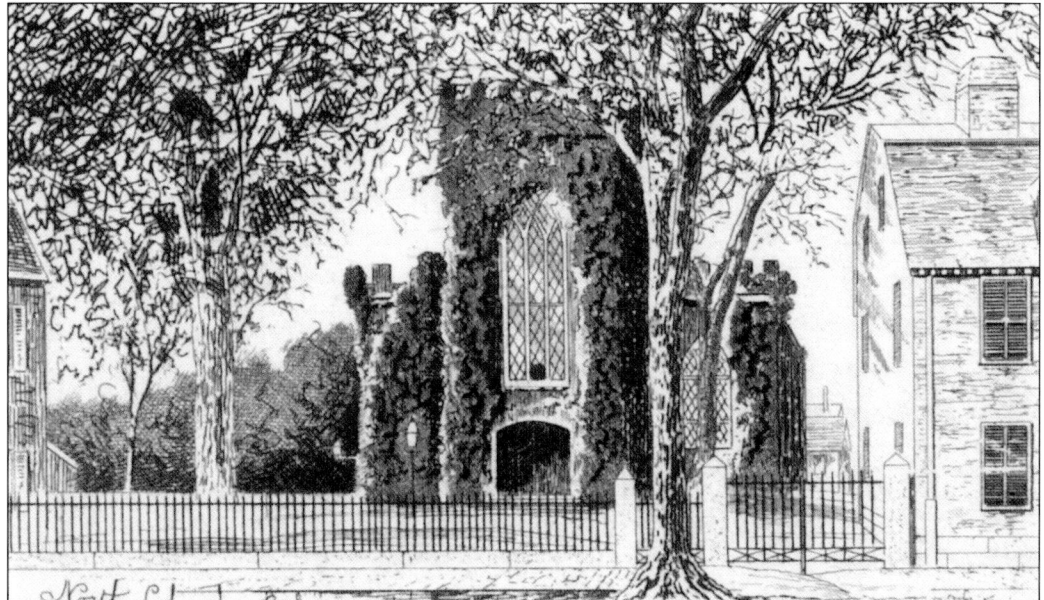

A copper plate engraving of the North Church, 316 Essex Street, by Salem artist George Merwanjee White (1849–1915). The North Church was built in 1835 under the direction of Boston architect Gridley J.F. Bryant. This Gothic Revival granite building contains the family pew of Nathaniel Hawthorne and stained-glass windows by L.C. Tiffany and John LaFarge. (Courtesy John Hardy Wright.)

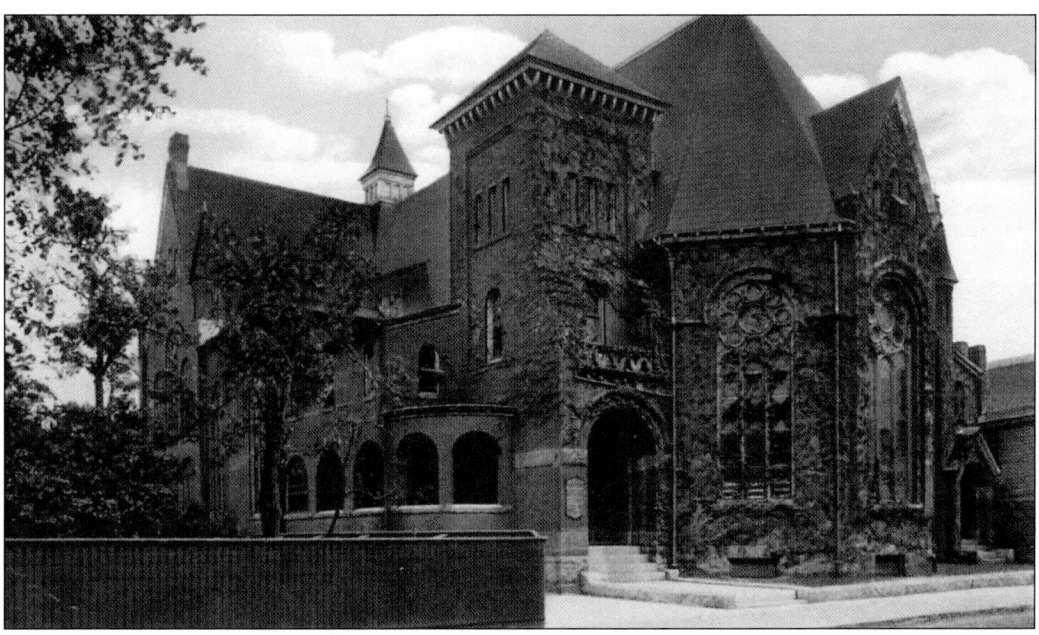

The handsome Wesley United Methodist Church, 10 North Street. This church was built in 1888–89 in the Romanesque Revival style.

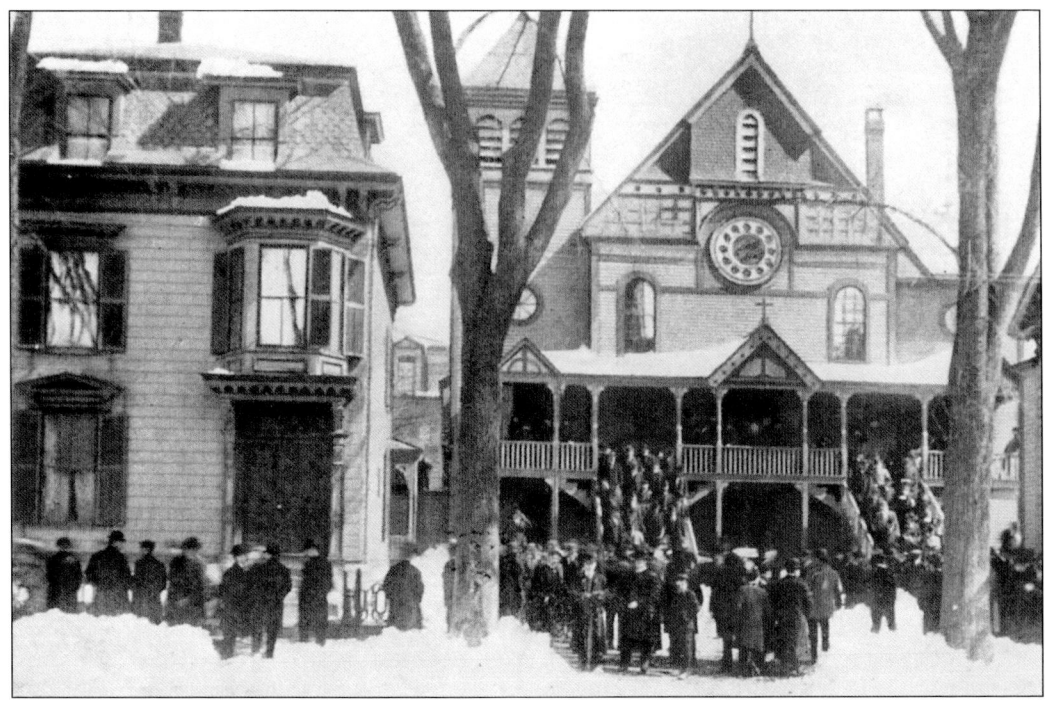

Saint Joseph's French Church, 135 Lafayette Street, built in 1885. Saint Joseph's parishioners were French-Canadian immigrants and their descendants who came to find work originally at the Pequot Mills. (Courtesy D. Michel Michaud.)

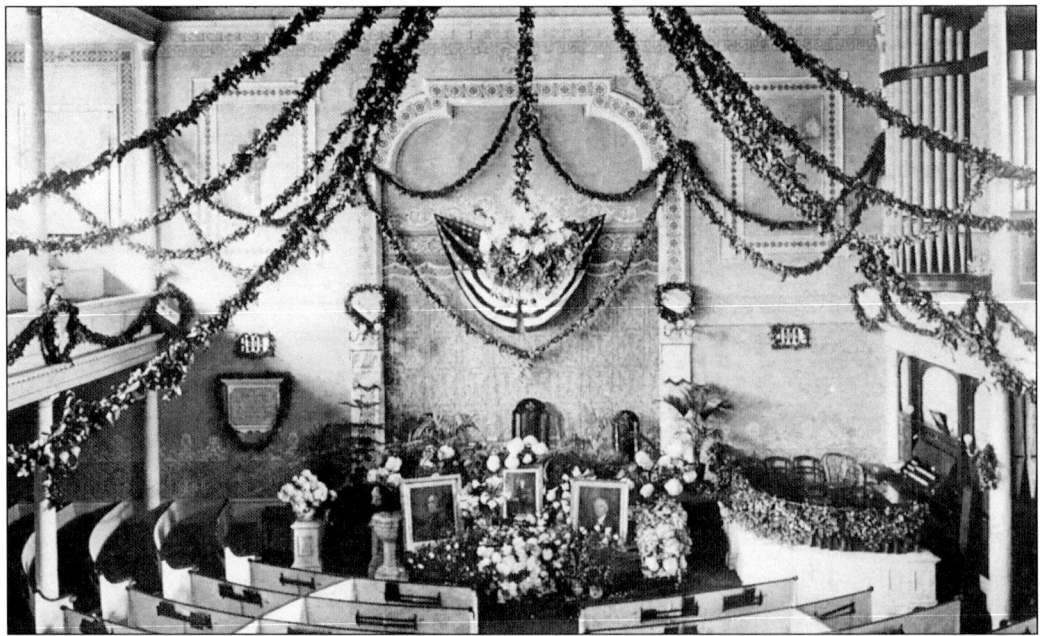

The Universalist Church on Rust Street, 1909. The church has been remodeled several times; compare this postcard with the earlier view. This image shows the interior ornately decorated for the church's centennial.

The Tabernacle Church (United Church of Christ), Washington at Federal Streets, built in 1924. The Tabernacle Church was the third church erected at this site. The Colonial Revival building with parish house in the rear is one of the finest in Salem. The cars date the photograph to shortly after the church opened.

The Charter Street Burial Ground, the oldest graveyard in the city. The tombstone of "Doraty, wife to Philip Cromwell," dated 1673, is said to be the oldest. This photograph was taken before the Salem Fire of 1914, which destroyed all the buildings in the background.

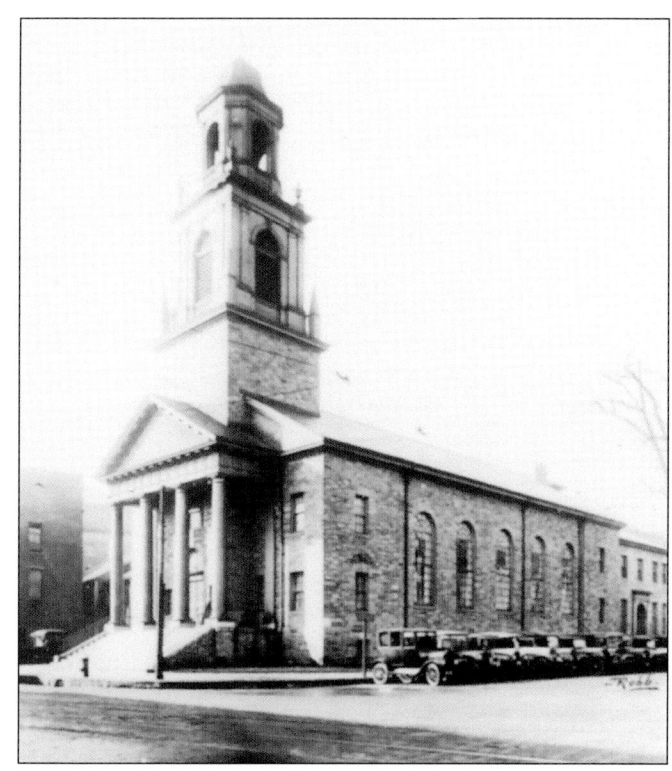

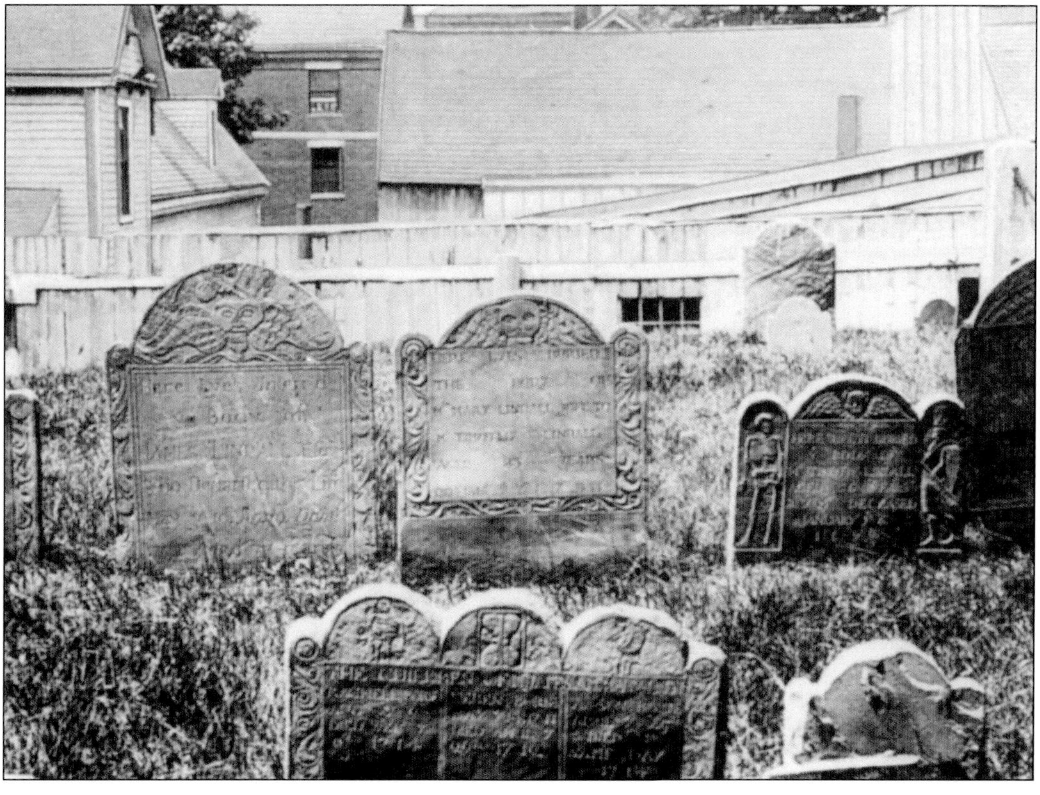

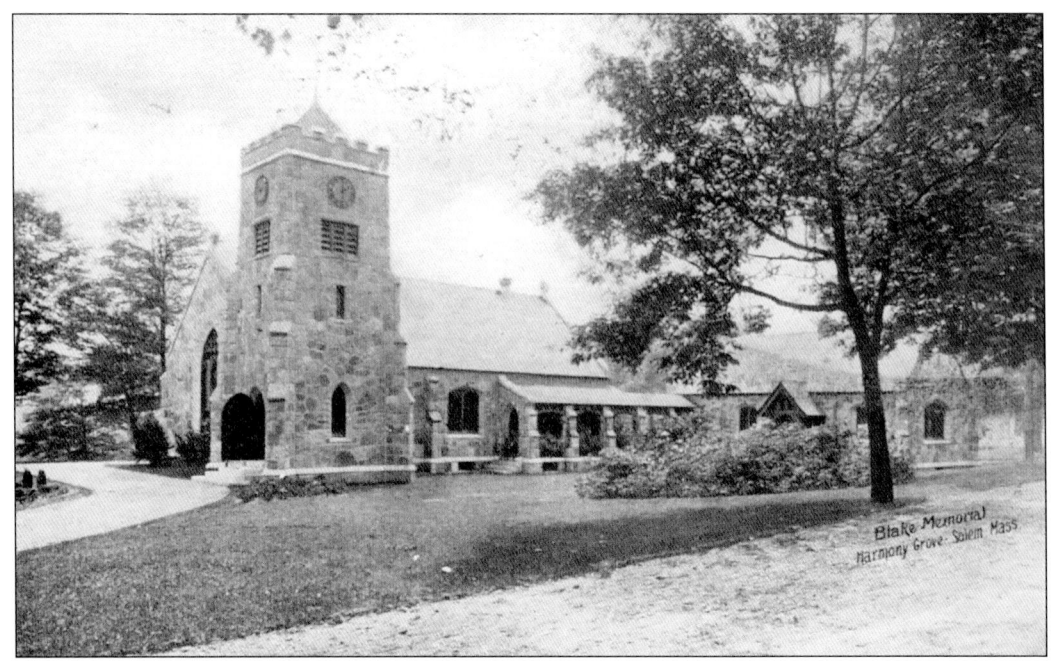

Harmony Grove Cemetery, one of the earliest rural cemeteries in Essex County. The burial ground dates to 1840. The Blake Memorial Chapel was built in 1905 in memory of Mrs. Nancy C. Blake's son, George Harrison Blake. The chapel boasts a series of outstanding stained-glass windows.

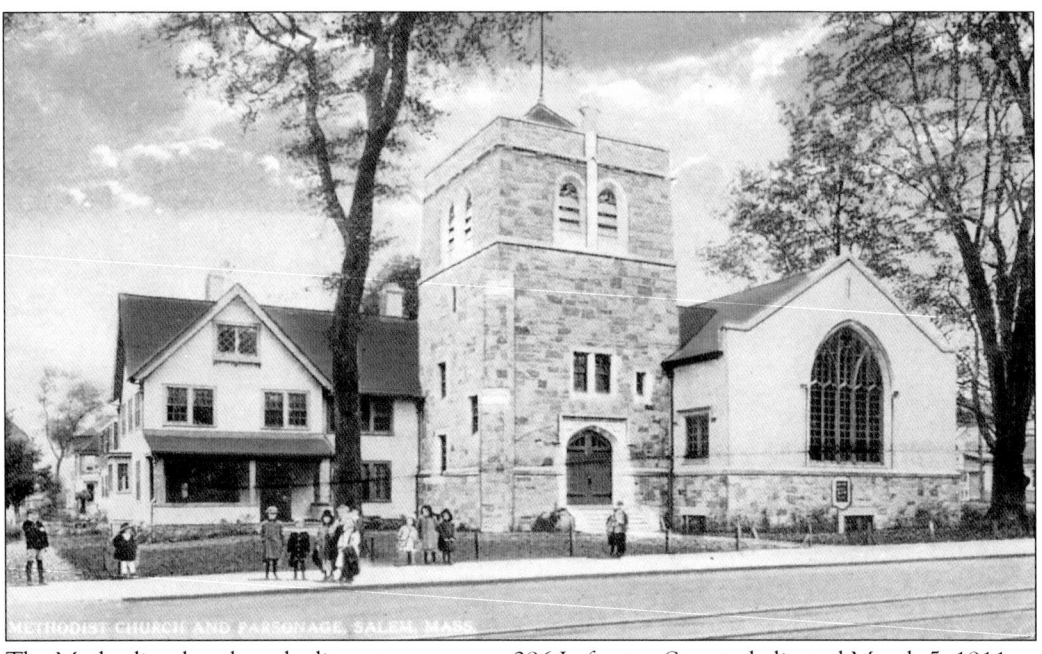

The Methodist church and adjacent parsonage, 296 Lafayette Street, dedicated March 5, 1911.

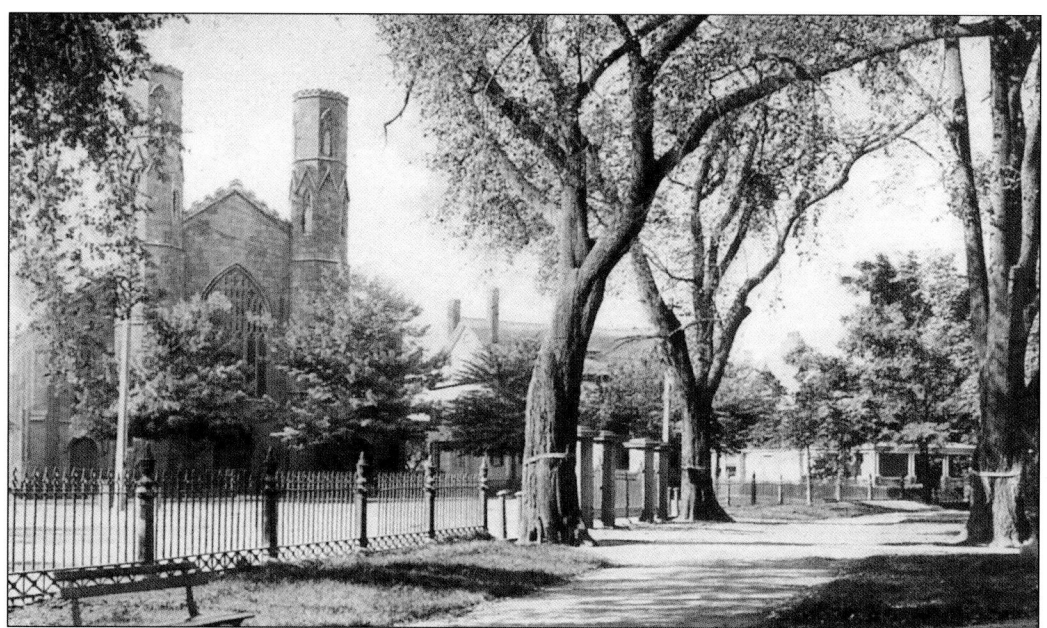

The Second Unitarian Church at 19 Washington Square, designed by New York architect Minard Lafever (1798–1854) in 1846. The upper stories of the octagonal towers were removed in the mid-1920s. The church was beset by fire in 1902 and again in 1969, when the flames consumed the Automobile Museum. In 1972, the interior was rebuilt and the building now houses one of Salem's most popular tourist attractions, the Salem Witch Museum.

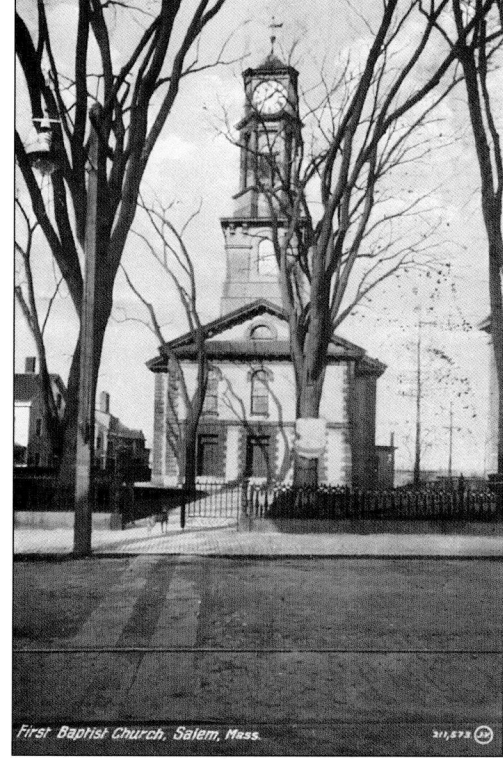

The First Baptist Church, 56 Federal Street. Construction started on this building in 1805. Almost twenty-five years later, in 1827, the church was remodeled and enlarged. The stately tower was added at that time. The edifice was again remodeled in 1868, 1877, and 1909. The steeple was removed in 1926 due to the high cost of maintenance.

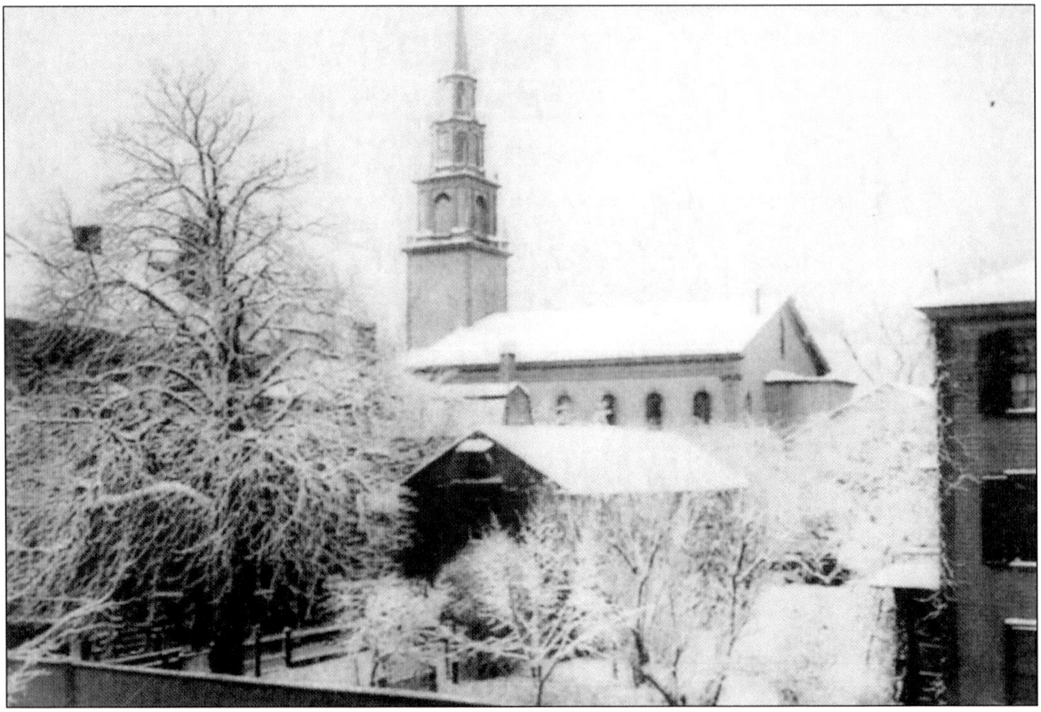

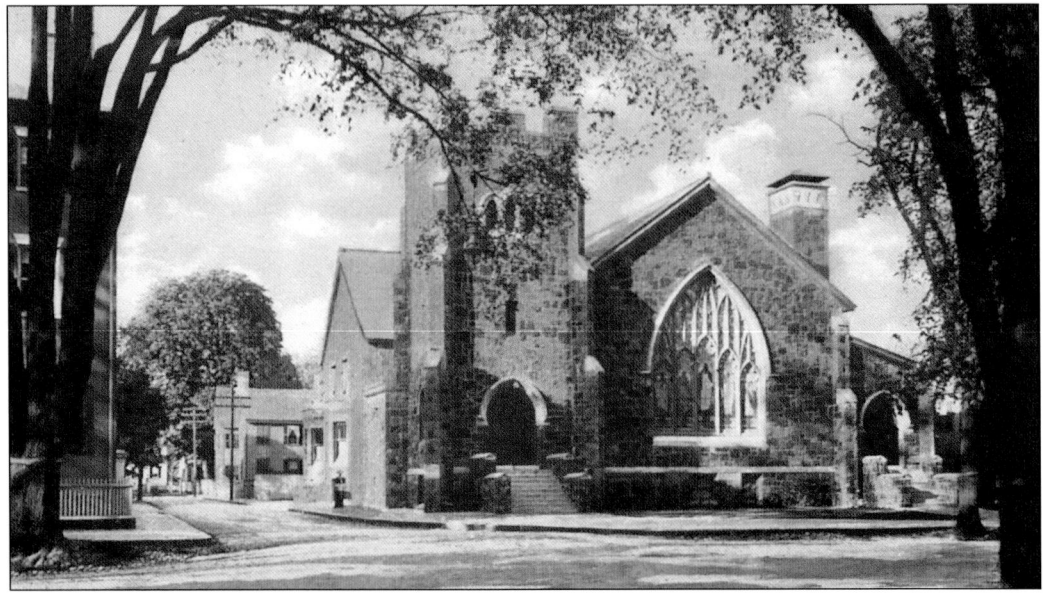

The South Church, built 1804, formerly situated at the corner of Chestnut and Cambridge Streets. Samuel McIntire (1757–1811) was the architect. The church was destroyed by fire in 1903.

The new South Congregational Church on the corner of Chestnut and Cambridge Streets. This Gothic Revival building was built in 1907 on the site of the former church, which was destroyed in 1903. In 1927 the church was sold to the Calvary Baptist Congregation. In 1950 the church closed and the building was razed shortly thereafter to make way for a park named in the honor of Salem's most famous architect.

Saint Anne's Catholic Church on Jefferson Avenue. This imposing wood-frame building was situated on a high vantage point at Castle Hill. Built in 1901, this French church suffered a devastating fire in 1982. (Courtesy D. Michel Michaud.)

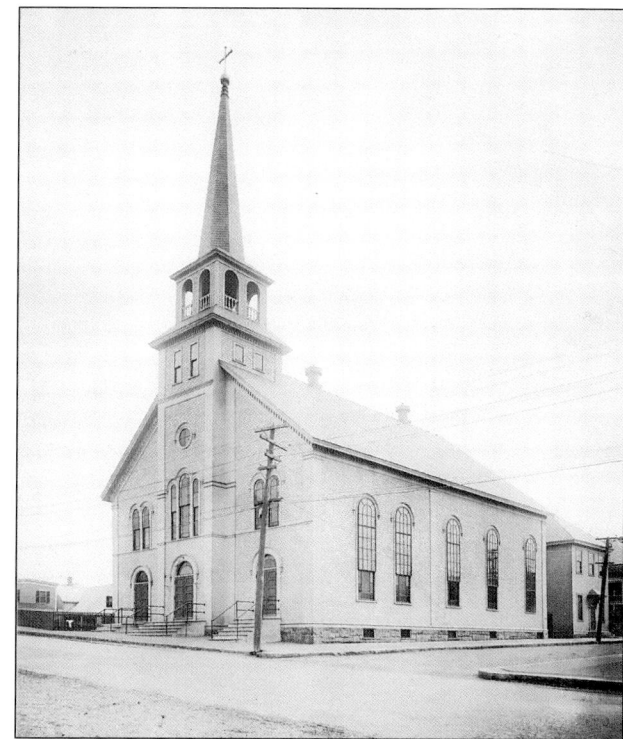

The elaborate interior of the former Saint Anne's Church on Jefferson Avenue in 1926. (Courtesy D. Michel Michaud.)

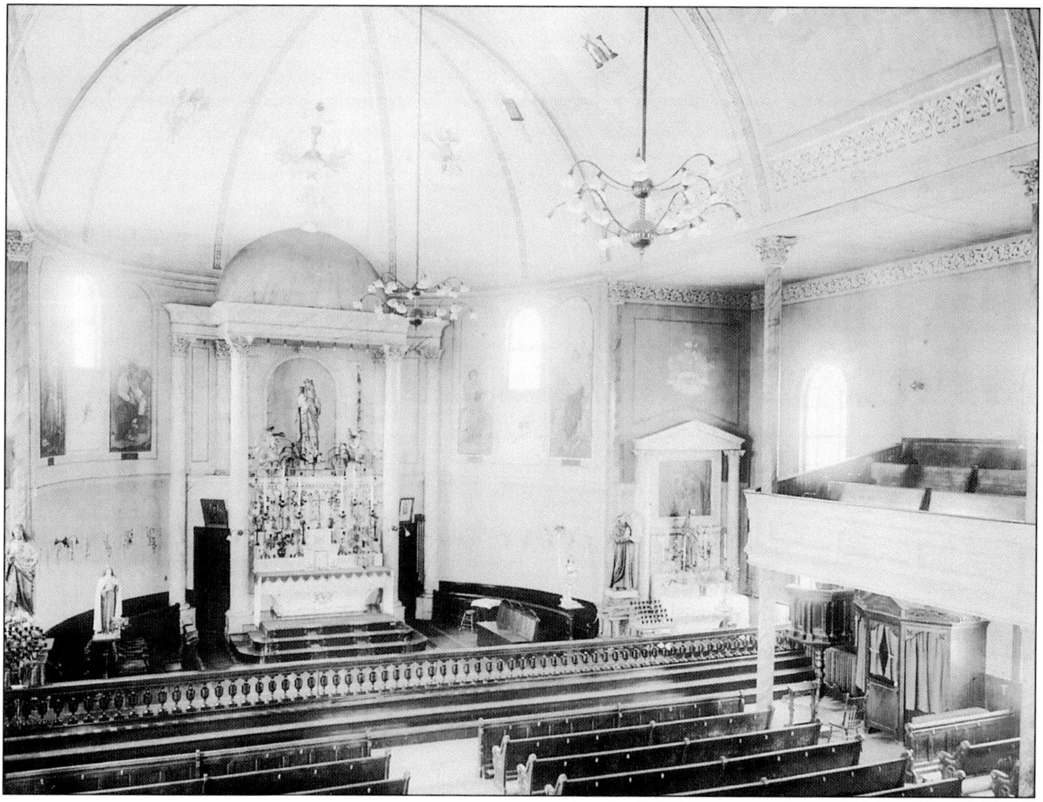

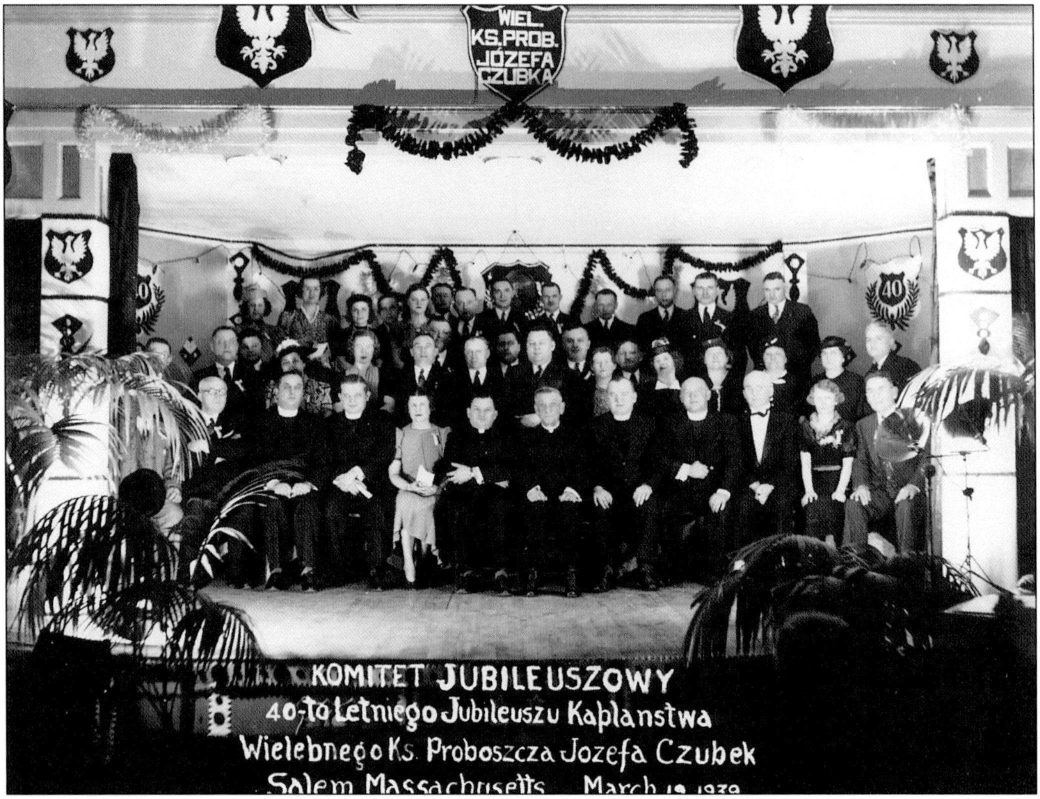

Salem's Polish community. Salem has a large Polish community that is centered around its church. Here the Jubilee Committee celebrates the 40th Anniversary of Father Jozefa Czubek in March 1939. (Courtesy John Kobuszewski.)

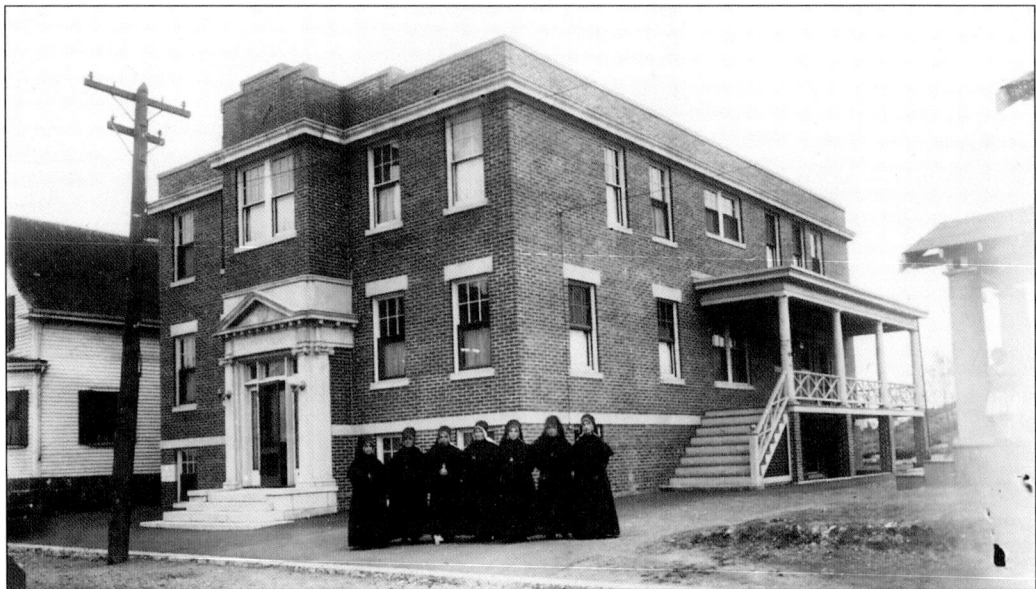

The convent of Saint Anne's parish on Cleveland Street, built in 1921. (Courtesy D. Michel Michaud.)

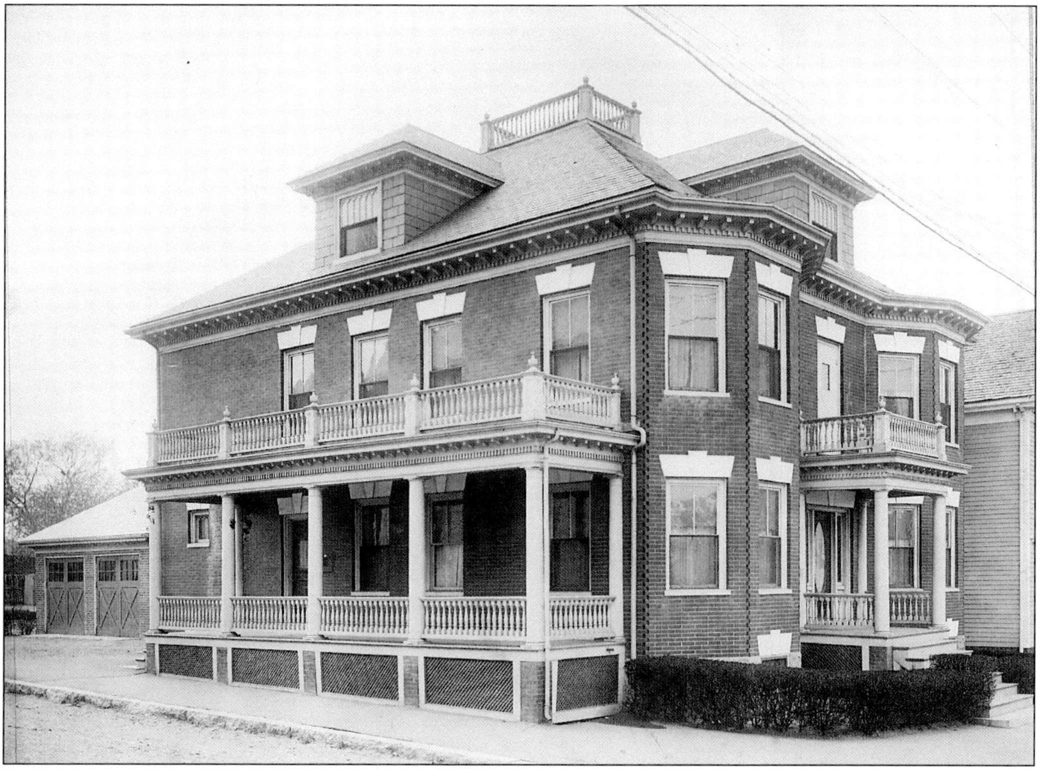

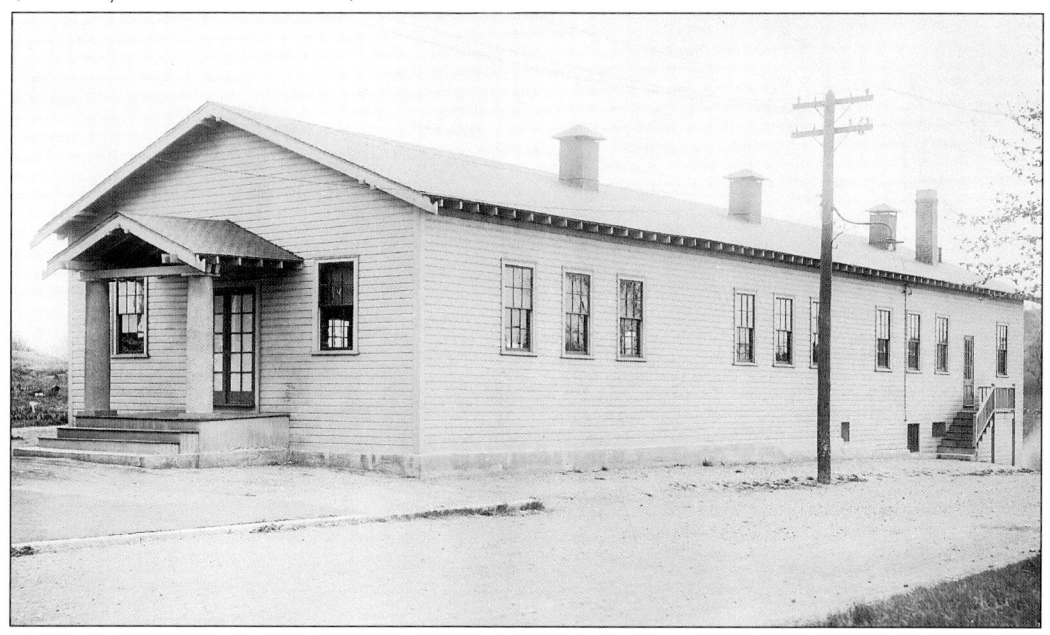

The sturdy brick-built rectory for Saint Anne's parish on Jefferson Avenue, built in 1921. (Courtesy D. Michel Michaud.)

The single-story, clapboard-covered, wood-framed hall of Saint Anne's parish, located on Cleveland Street, built in 1920. The building was razed to build Saint Anne's School, which opened in 1957. (Courtesy D. Michel Michaud.)

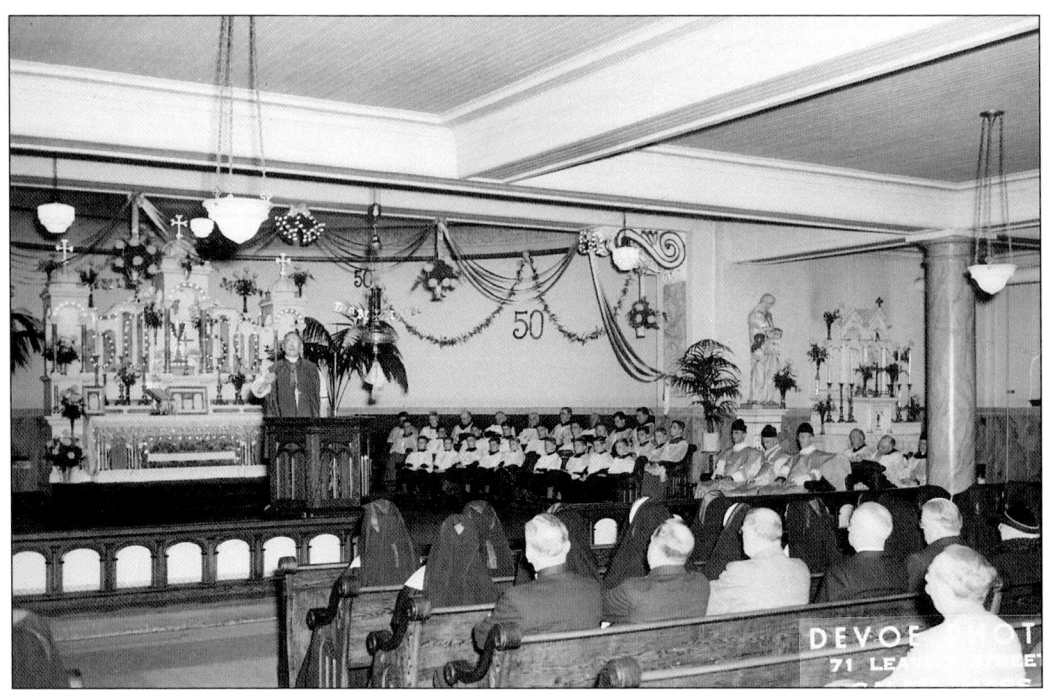

Interior of Saint Joseph's Church. In 1939, Monsignor Jean Baptiste Labossiere celebrated fifty years in the priesthood. A special service was given by Monsignor Alfred Peltier. (Courtesy D. Michel Michaud.)

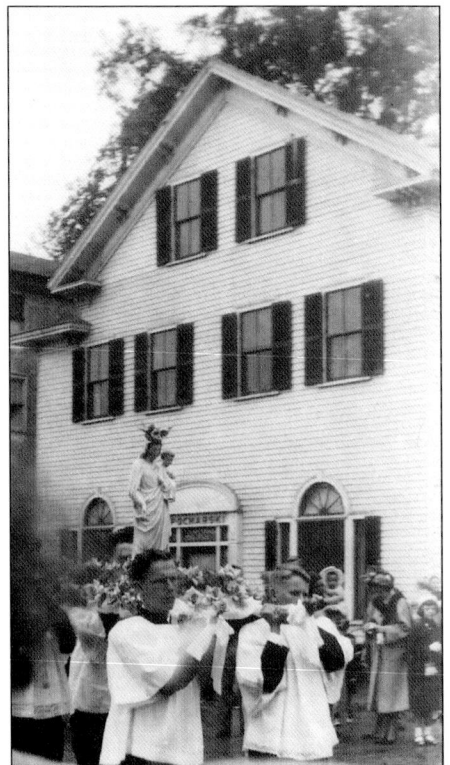

A procession organized by the Immaculate Conception Roman Catholic Church on Hawthorne Boulevard, c. 1940. (Courtesy Ben and Sally Mathias.)

# Six

# Salem Businesses

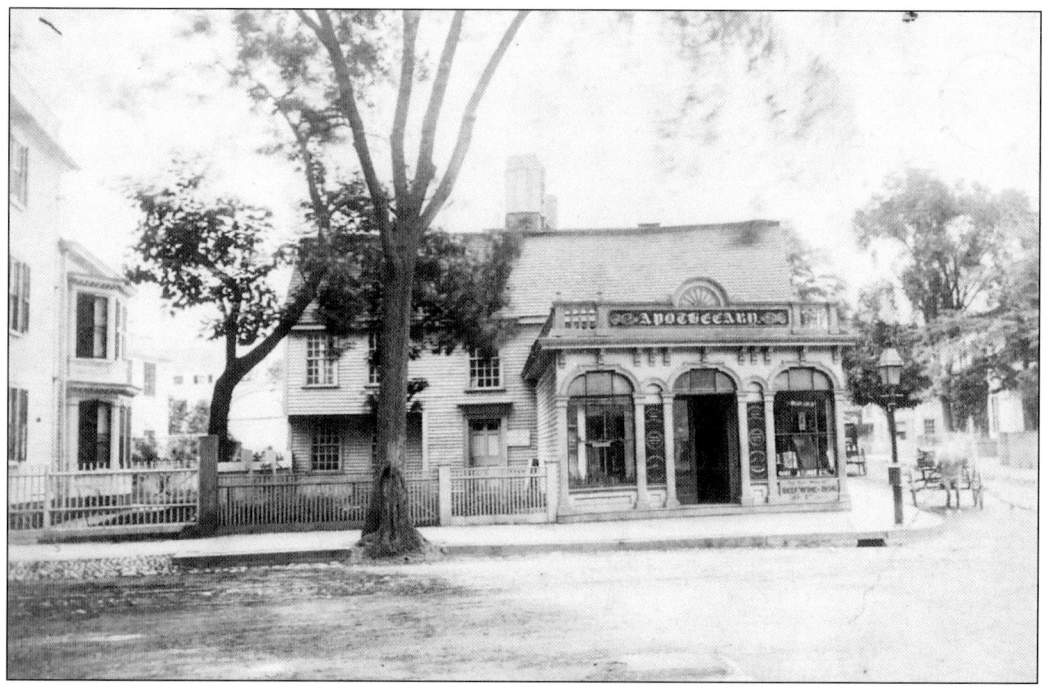

The Jonathan Corwin House, built c. 1675. This structure is known as the "Witch House," and is located at the corner of North and Essex Streets. The apothecary shop was added in 1856 and remodeled in 1885 by the proprietor, George P. Farrington.

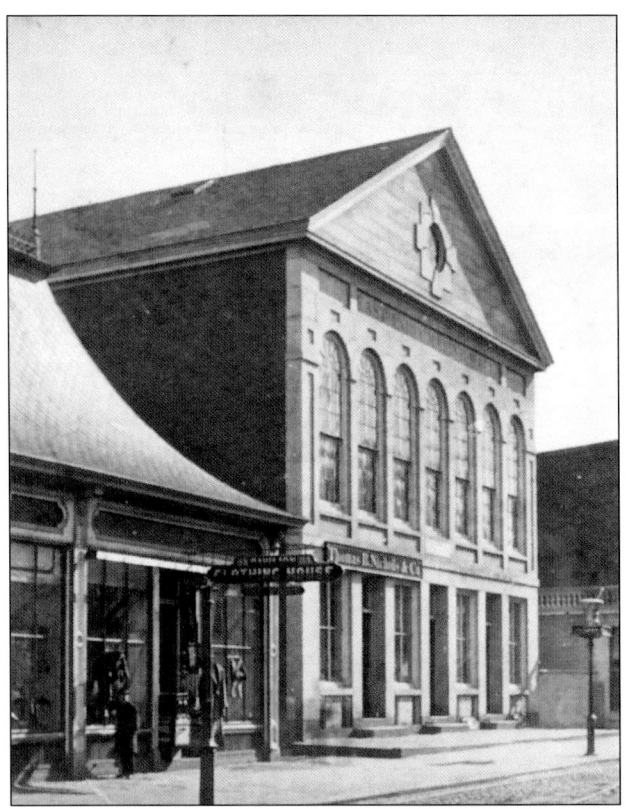

The Pavillion. The pagoda-roofed building to the left of the former Peabody Museum was built c. 1870. It was known as "the Pavilion," and originally sold "millinery finery." In 1967 the quaint Chinese-style building was removed for museum expansion. This photograph dates from 1876. (Courtesy D. Michel Michaud.)

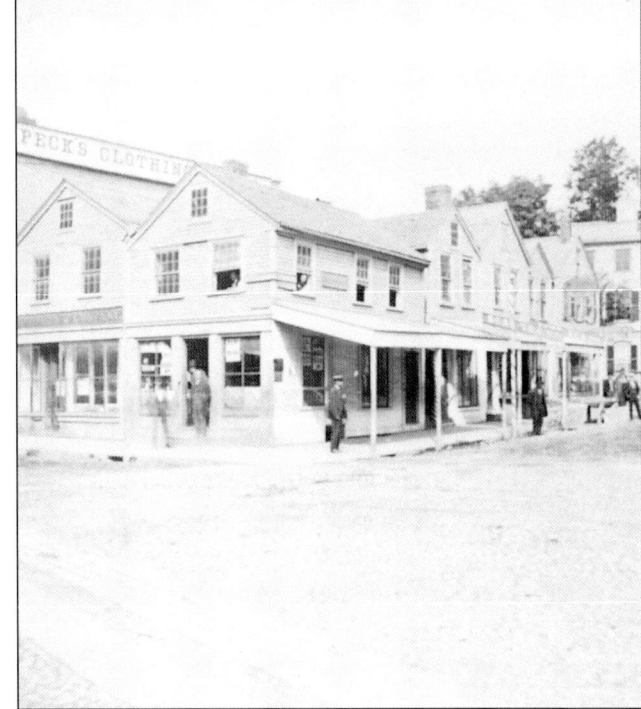

An early stereoscope view, c. 1870, showing the corner of Essex and Washington Streets. Today this would be diagonally across from Daniel Low & Company. (Courtesy D. Michel Michaud.)

Washington Street, c. 1880. This view shows the Salem Savings Bank, the Odd Fellows Hall (on the upper level), and the First Unitarian Church. (Courtesy D. Michel Michaud.)

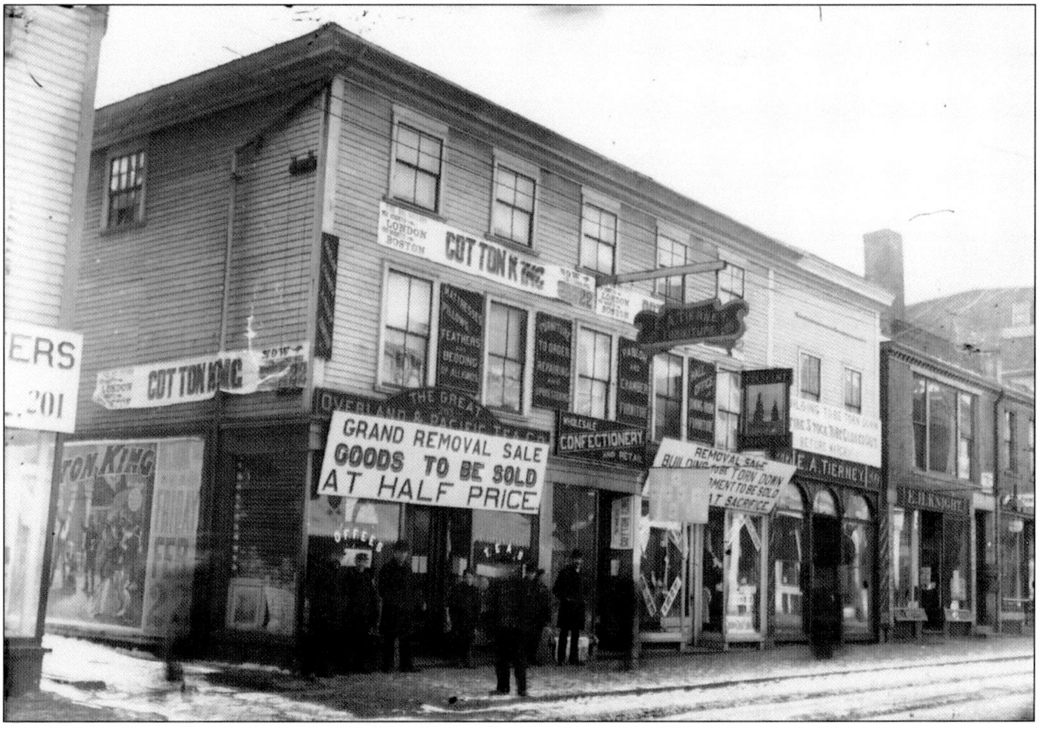

The Norris Building, 203–209 Essex Street, razed March 1895. The right-hand portion of the building (#209), built in 1730, was originally the home of Captain Ebenezer Bowditch. After 1829, the building was remodeled to house businesses, and an addition (#203–207) was added. The structure was first called the Holyoke Block. When it was purchased by the Norris brothers, it became known as the Norris Block. This photograph was taken in February 1895. (Courtesy Bodin Historic Photo, Gloucester, MA.)

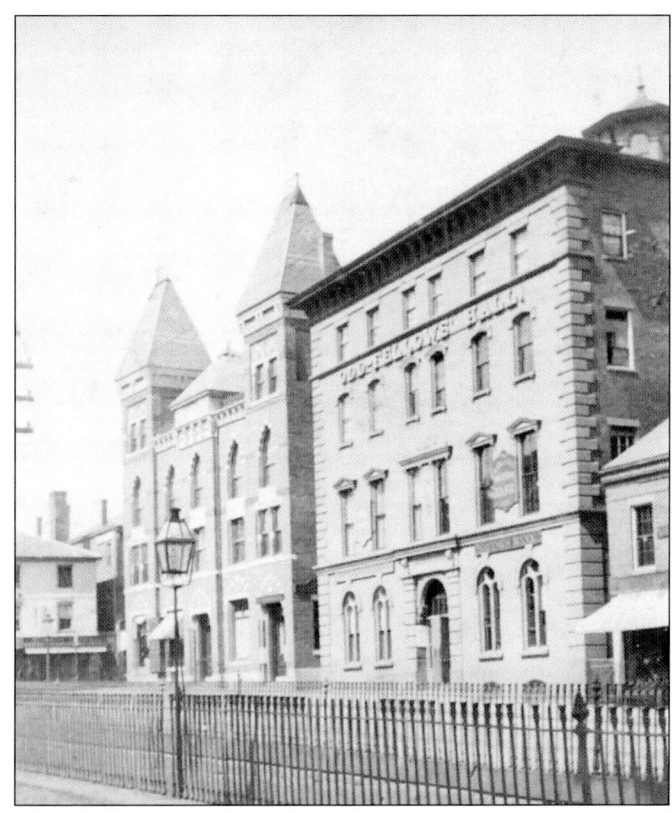

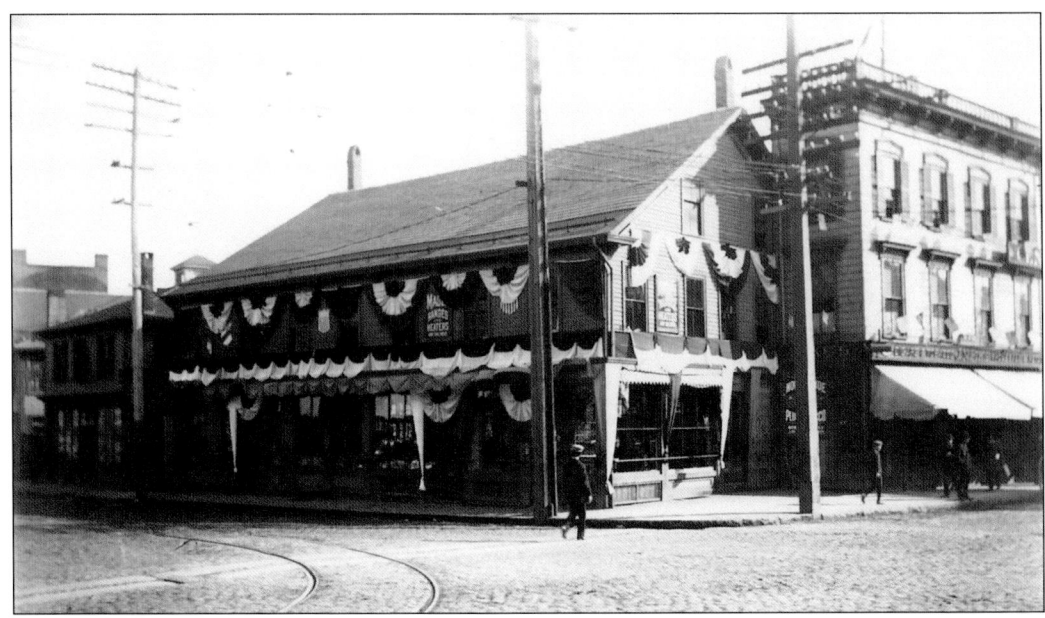

The corner of Front and Washington Streets, the present location of the *Salem Evening News*, c. 1897. The building on the right at 159–161 Washington Street was the Central House Hotel. That building contained several shops on the first floor, including the shop of J.N. Pike & Company, a tobacconist. The building at 39–43 Front Street housed the shop of Fifield & Page, dealers in stoves. (Courtesy Bodin Historic Photo, Gloucester, MA.)

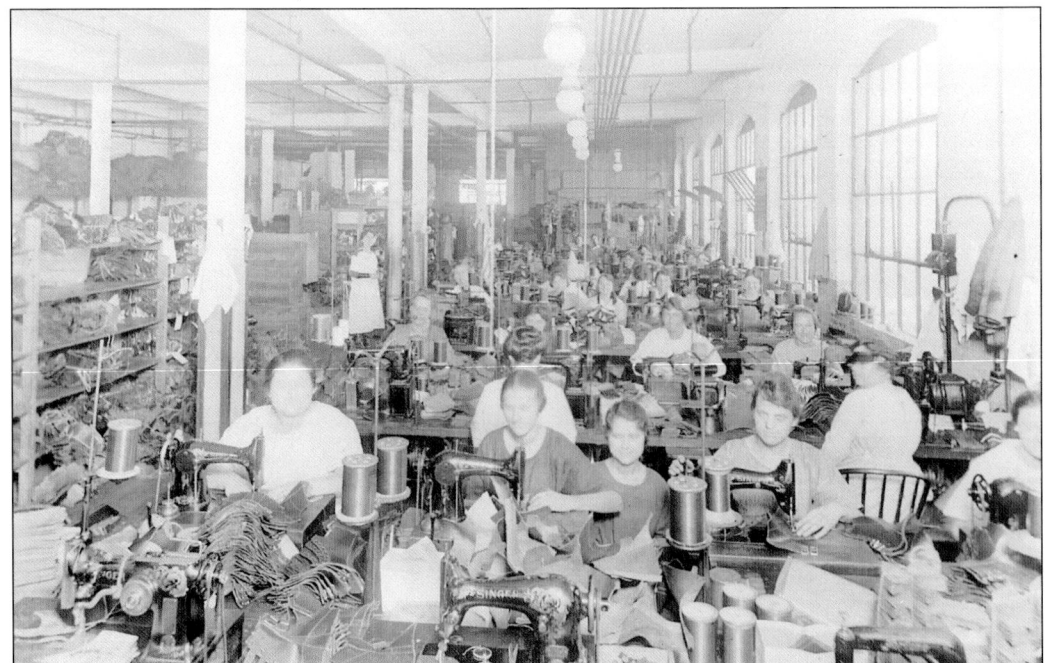

The Daniel Glover & Son Shoe Company, located at 3 New Derby Street in 1919. Shoe manufacturing—with Lynn as its center—was one of Essex County's main industries. In this view of the busy stitching room, Rose and Marie-Laure Michaud can be seen in the front row, second from the left and to the right respectively. (Courtesy D. Michel Michaud.)

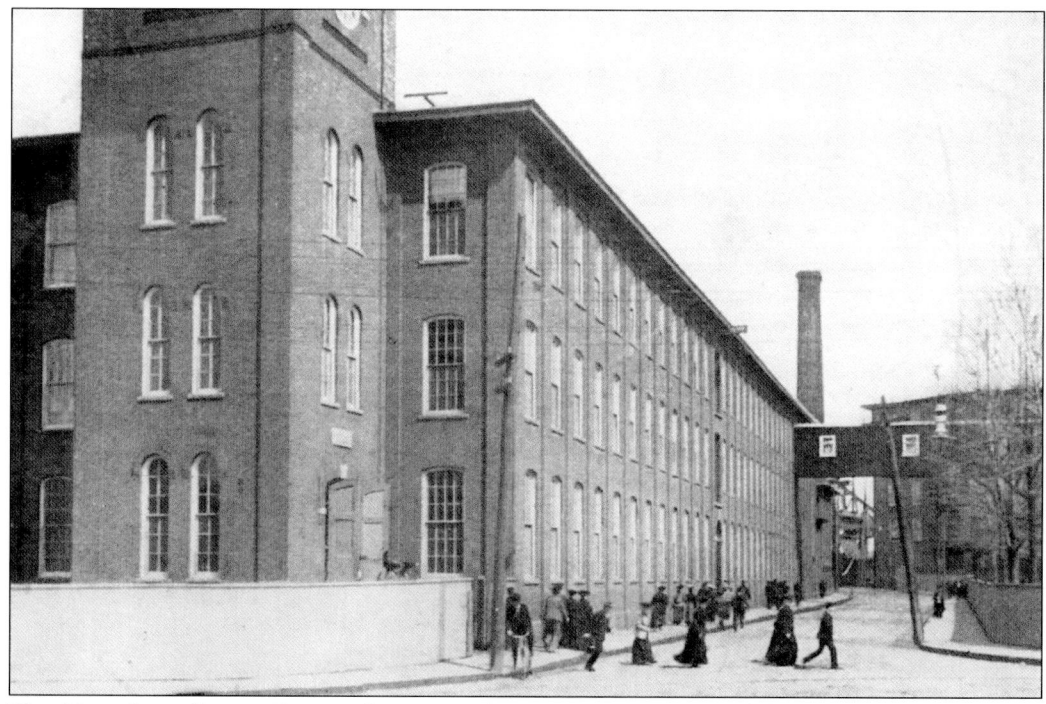

The Naumkeag Steam Cotton Company, Congress Street. One of the principal industries of Salem, Naumkeag Steam Cotton was incorporated in 1839. These buildings were constructed c. 1845. The company made the famous "Pequot" sheets and pillowcases. The entire mill complex was destroyed in the 1914 fire. (Courtesy D. Michel Michaud.)

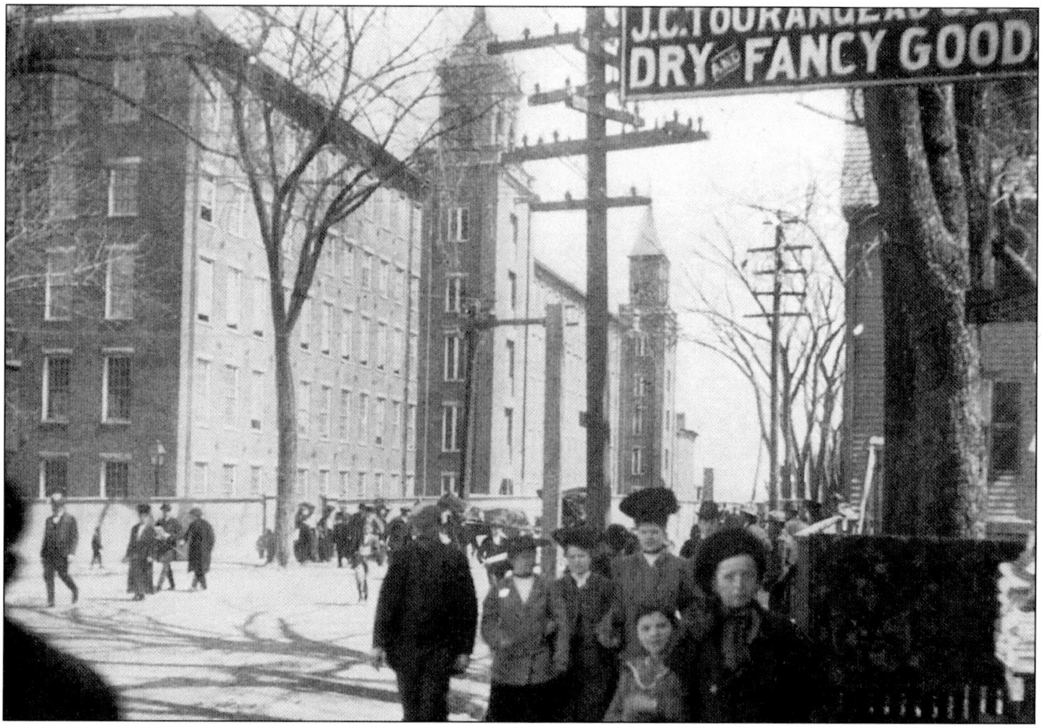

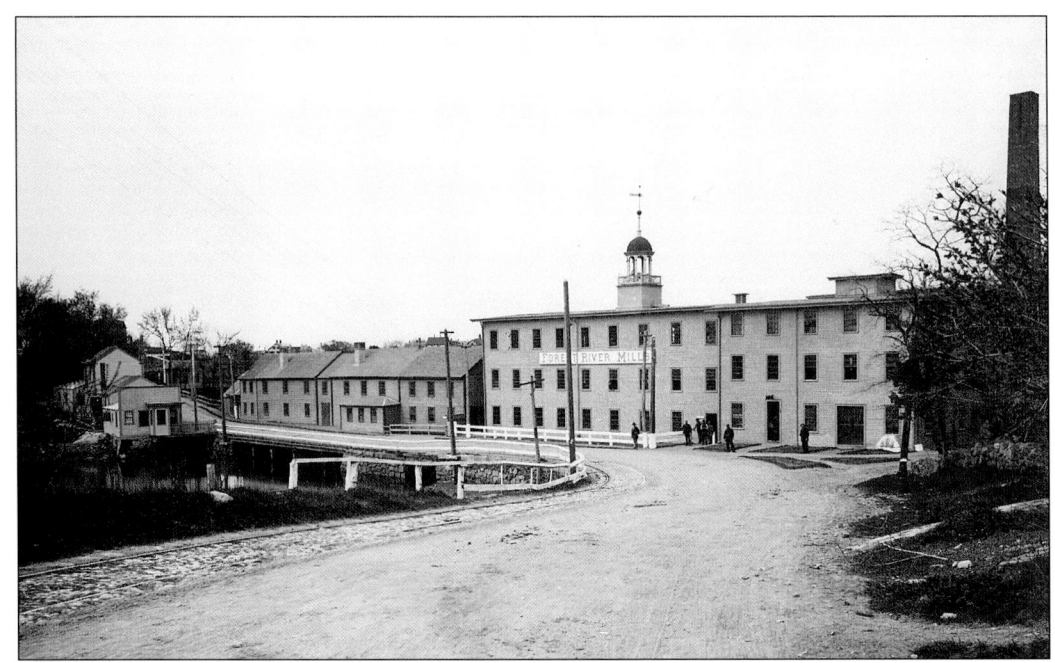

Two views of the Lead Mills at Forest River. The mills were located at 485 Lafayette Street at the Salem/Marblehead line. Lead mills in Salem date back to the late 1820s when Colonel Francis Peabody opened a white lead business in South Salem. The property shown here was vacated by the mid-1930s; it housed the Associated Grocers' Co-operative (wholesale grocers) by the mid-1940s, and burned in 1968. (Courtesy D. Michel Michaud.)

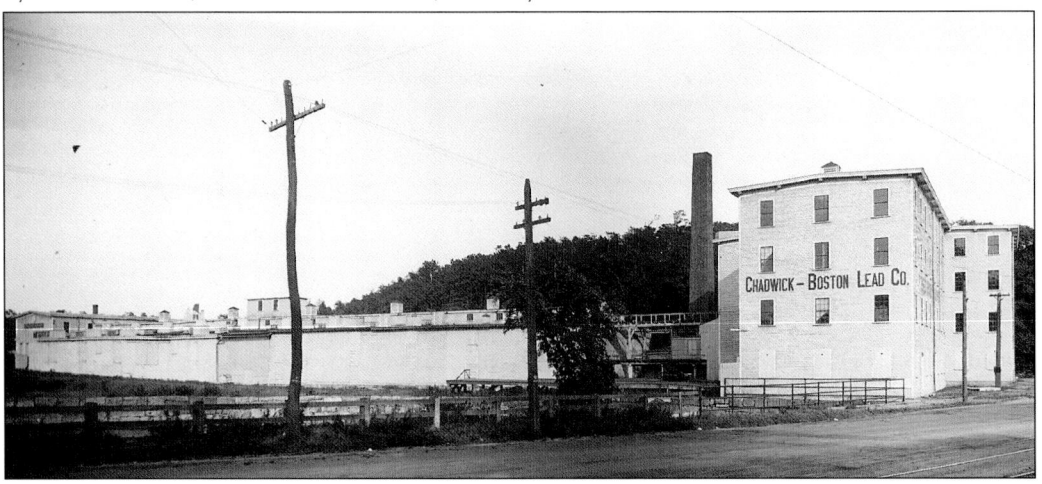

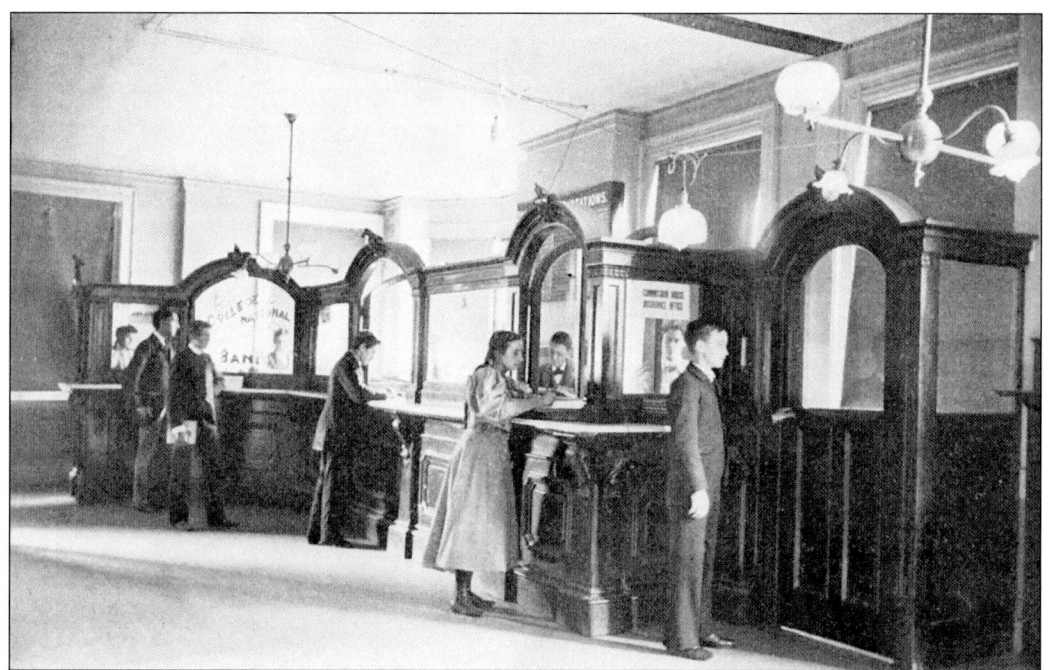

The Spence & Peaslee Business College, 210 Essex Street, 1897. The school dates from 1891 and prided itself on a practical curriculum: "Nothing is so useful to young ladies and gentleman . . . as a thorough business training and a practical acquaintance with commercial methods and office work."

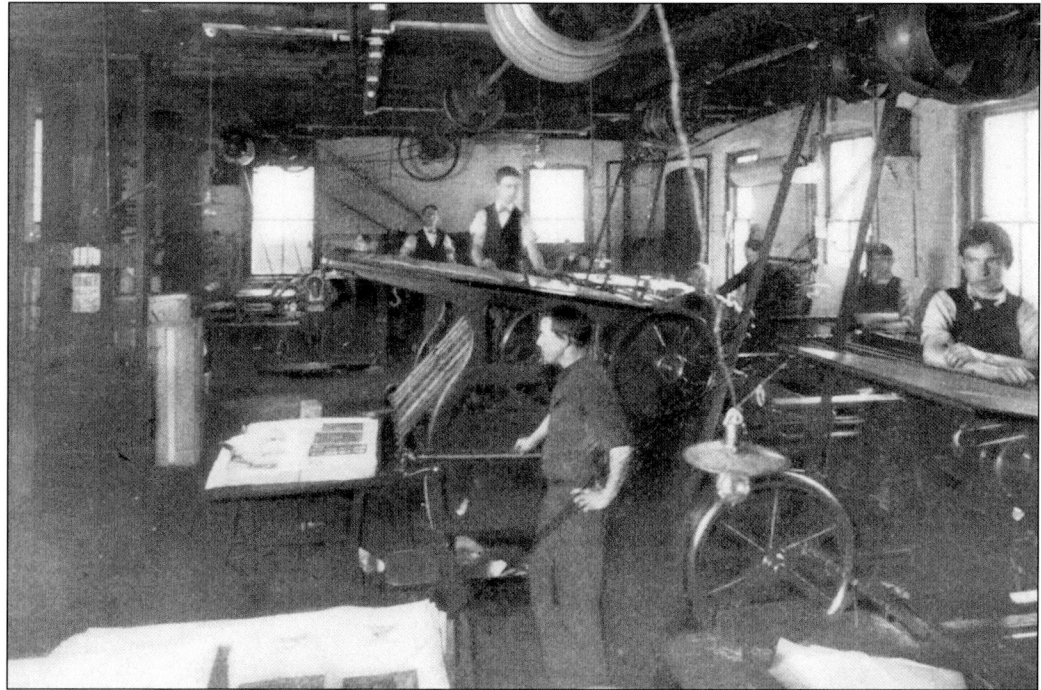

Newcomb & Gauss, printers, 1897. This is an interior view of the press room, located next to city hall on Washington Street.

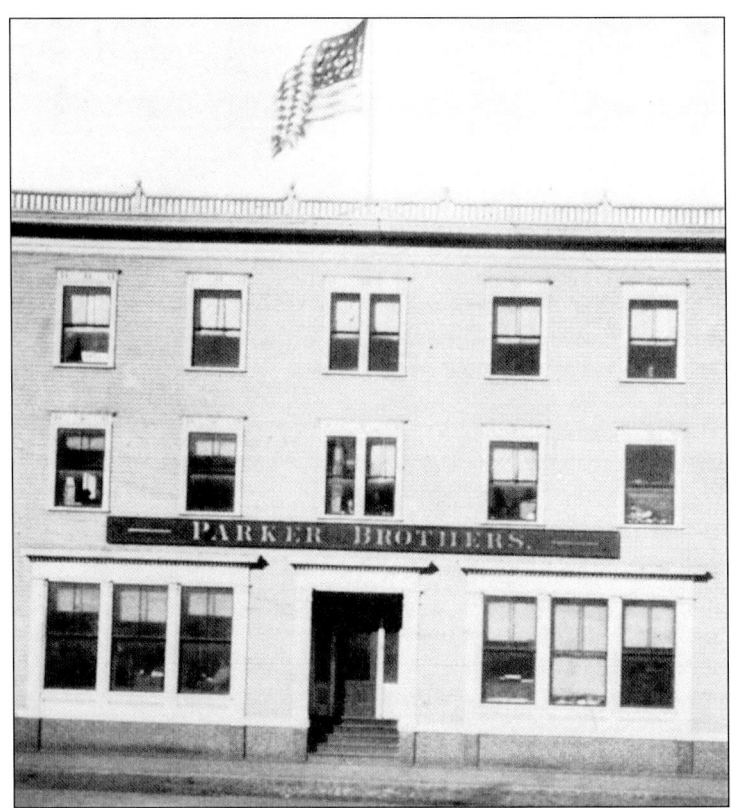

The Parker Brothers Factory, Bridge Street, 1897. George S. Parker founded the nationally known company, originally called George S. Parker Company, on the corner of Washington Square. When Charles H. Parker joined the firm in 1888, it became known as Parker Brothers.

Sheplee & Etheridge Undertakers, organized in 1896 at 64 Washington Street. An 1897 description states: "They make a specialty of embalming and possess the necessary natural endowments as well as the technical knowledge so peculiarly needful in this business."

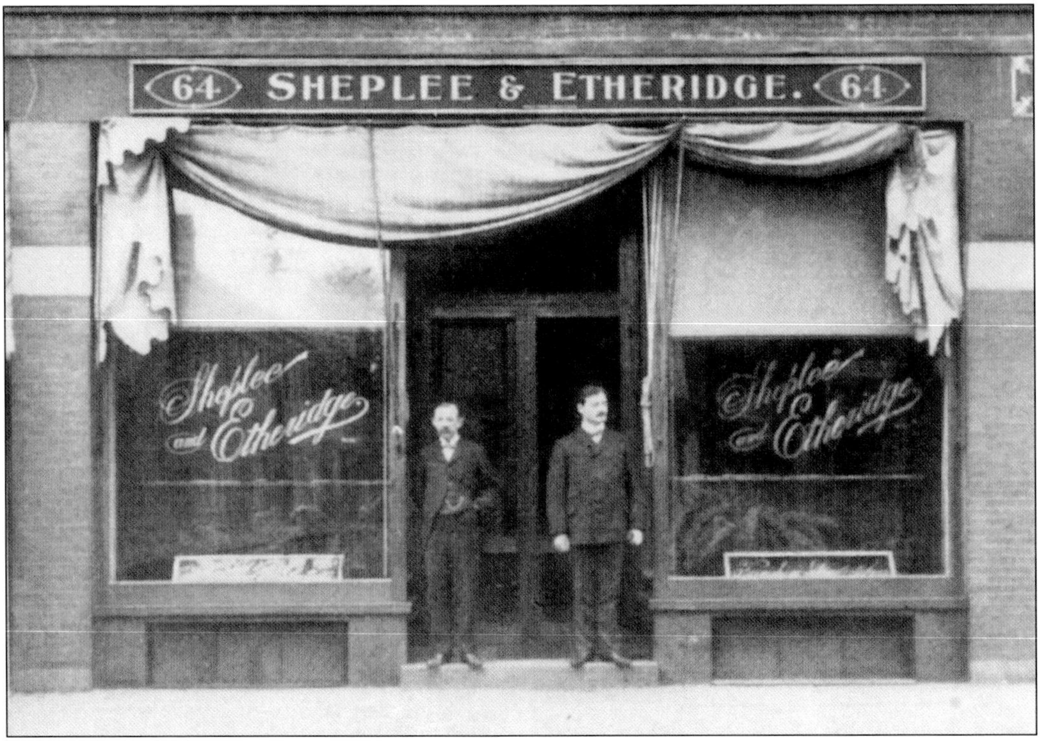

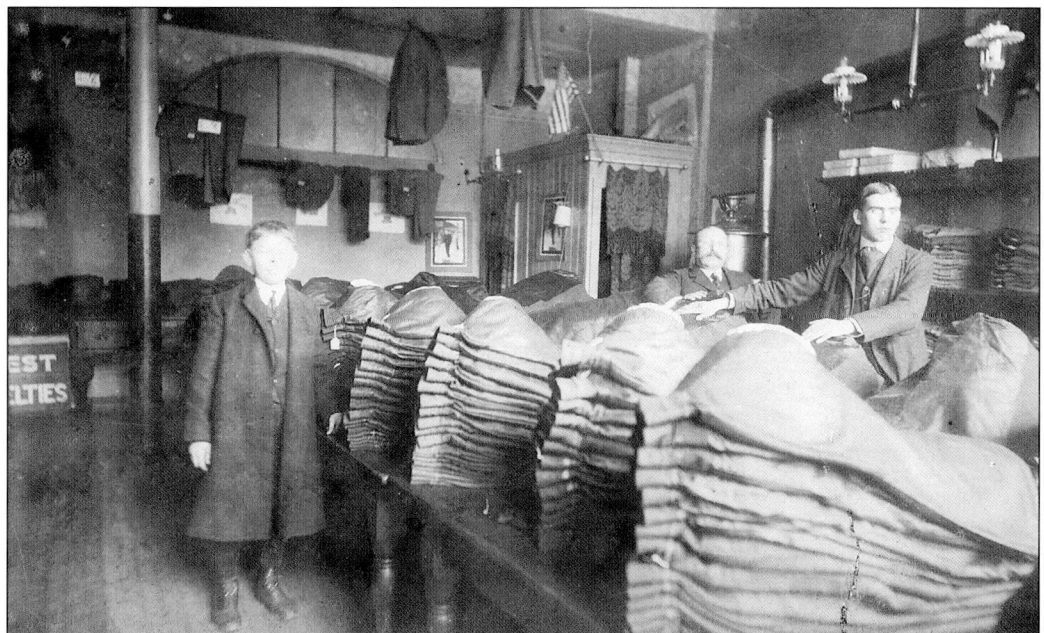

The New England Supply Company, 1897. Max Winer (in background) and family arrived in Salem in 1885 when there was no organized Jewish community. His clothing store, the New England Supply Company (later known as Winer's Specialty Shop), opened in 1895 and is shown here in 1897 at 243 Essex Street. In 1919, a local advertisement for Winer's offered "the people of Greater Salem the benefits of a selling-out sale with every garment in the store at a ridiculously low price." (Courtesy North Shore Jewish Historical Society.)

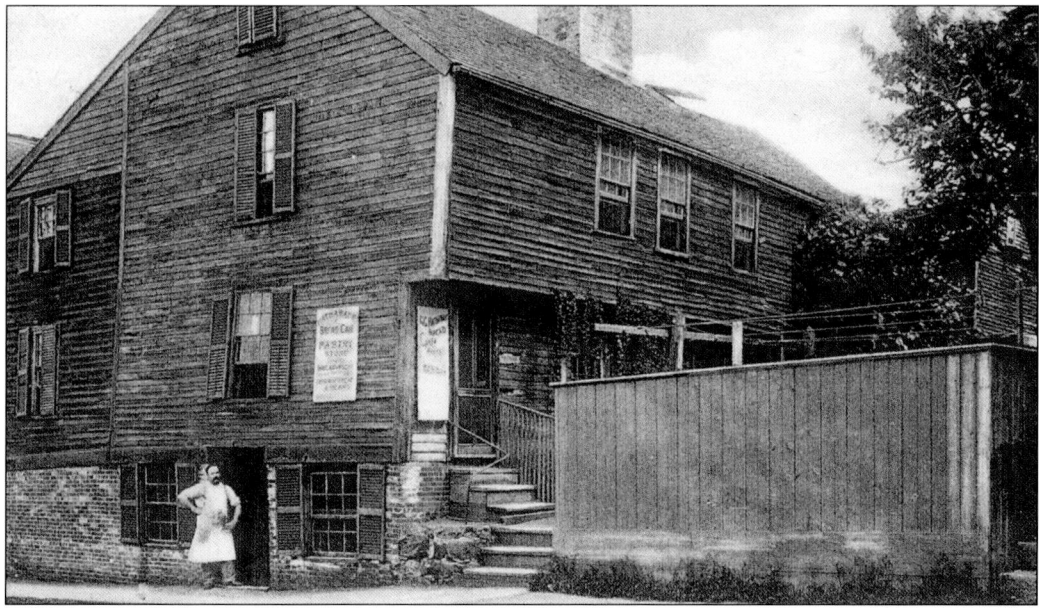

The Old Bakery, located at 23 Washington Street, was built c. 1682 as a private home. Around 1864 the Hathaway family purchased the house and established a bakery. By 1911 the ancient dwelling had fallen into disrepair. Miss Caroline O. Emmerton purchased the house and moved it to the grounds of The House of Seven Gables.

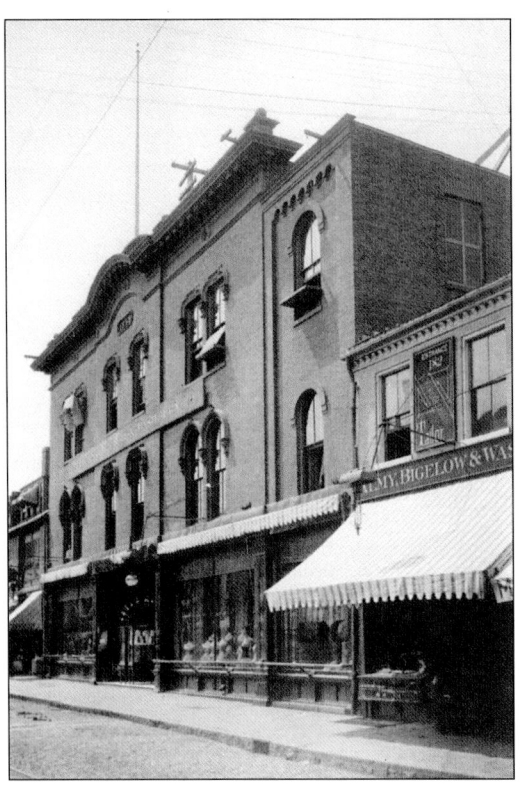

The department store of Almy, Bigelow, and Washburn, established in 1858 in a small room at 156 Essex Street. This building on Essex Street was built in the late 1890s. The business continued to flourish and expand with outlets in neighboring cities and towns. Its demise came in the early 1980s; the building was torn down and replaced by luxury condominiums.

Merchants National Bank in 1908. When the bank was being formed in 1811, the *Salem Gazette* reported that "it cannot be considered as an institution for the common benefit of our citizens, but on the contrary for the purpose of unblushing political corruption."

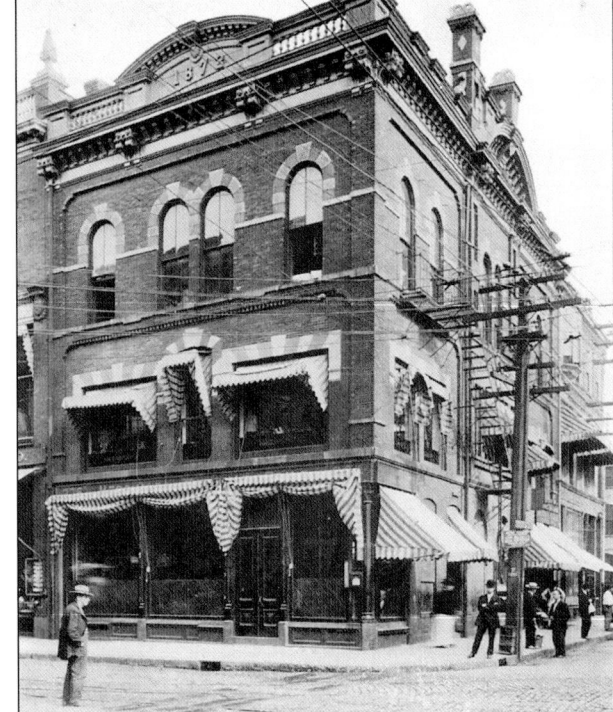

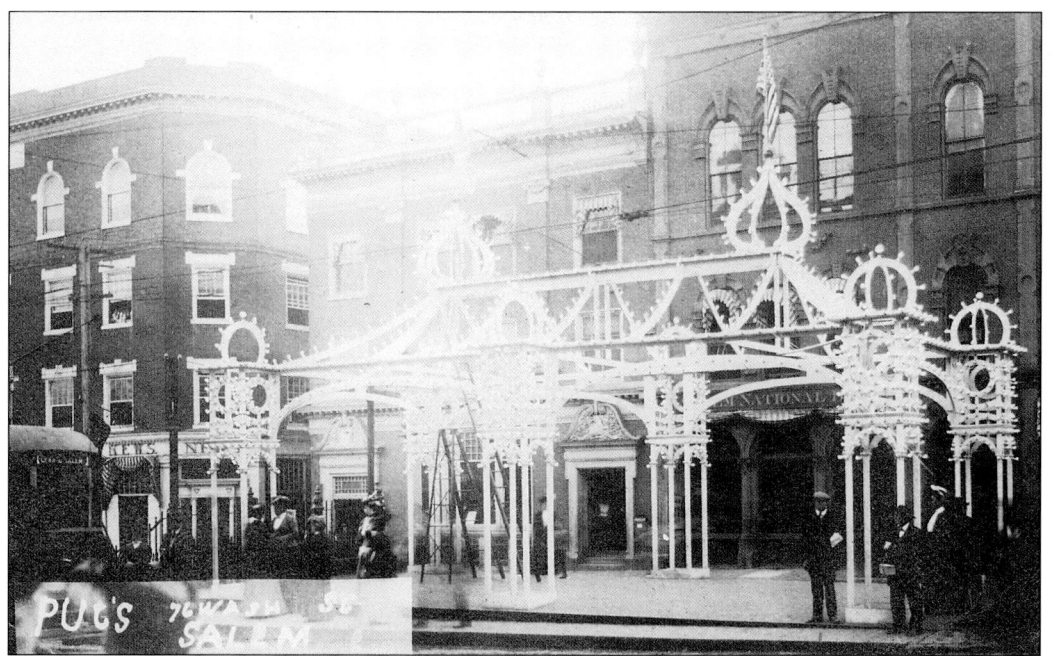

Put's, 76 Washington Street. The pagoda was erected for Merchants Week, October 1906. (Courtesy D. Michel Michaud.)

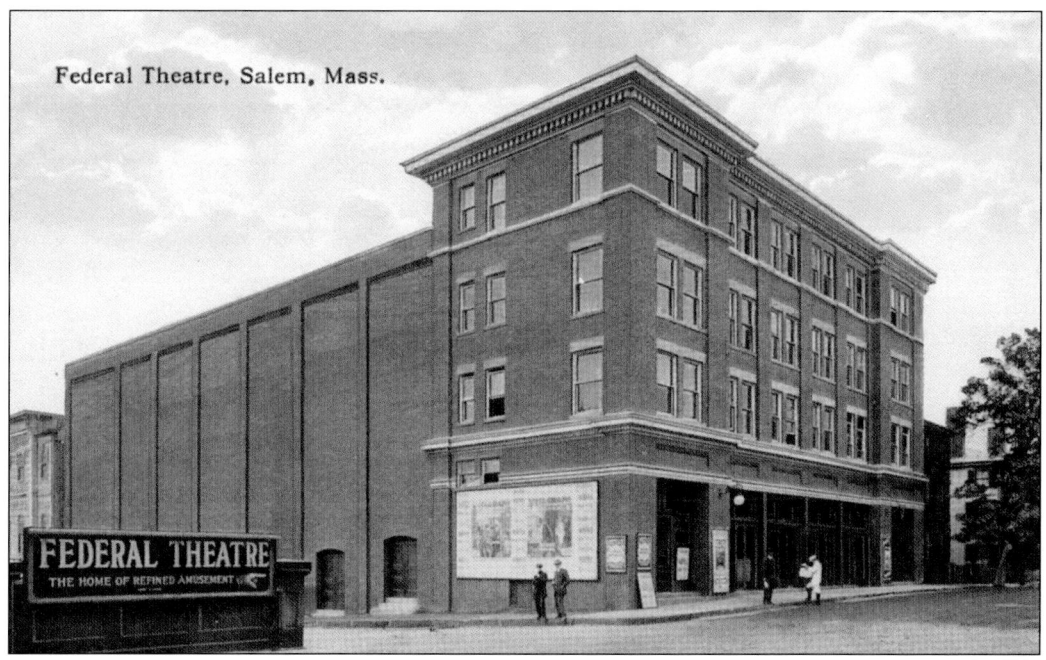

The Federal Theatre, located at the corner of Washington and Federal Streets. It opened in 1913 and closed in 1936. The building then housed an A & P supermarket in 1937 with the Salem Bowling Center located in the basement. The A & P closed in 1966 and the bowling lanes later in the 1970s. Condominiums were built on the site in 1978 on land acquired by the Salem Redevelopment Authority. (Courtesy D. Michel Michaud.)

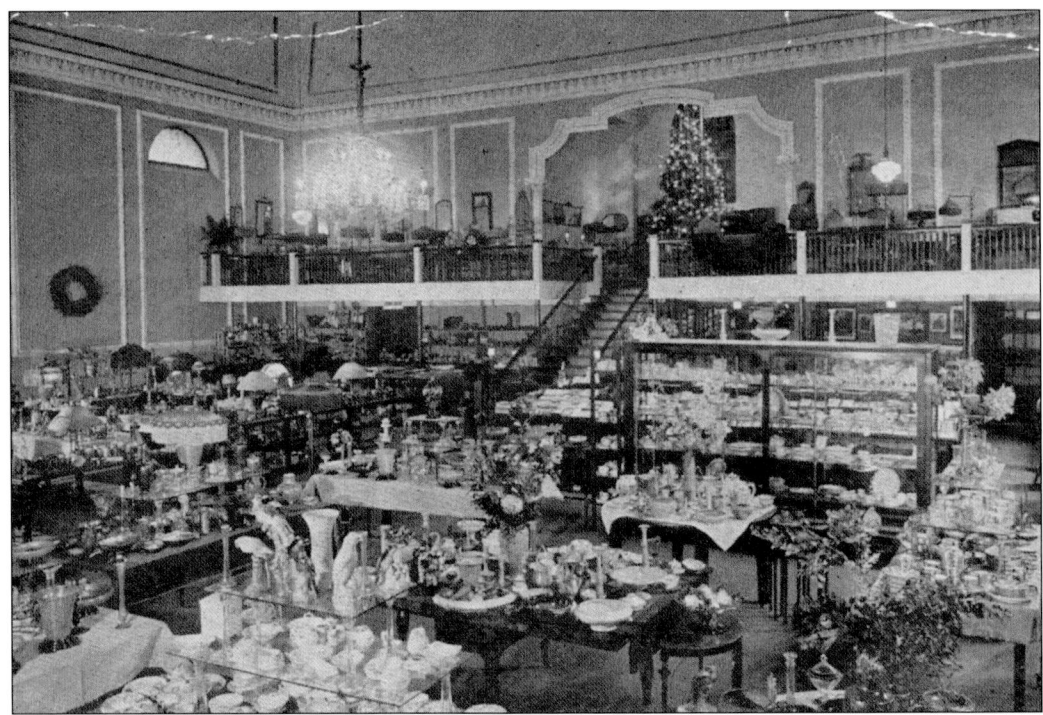

An interior view of Colonial Hall at Daniel Low & Company during a past Christmas season. (Courtesy D. Michel Michaud.)

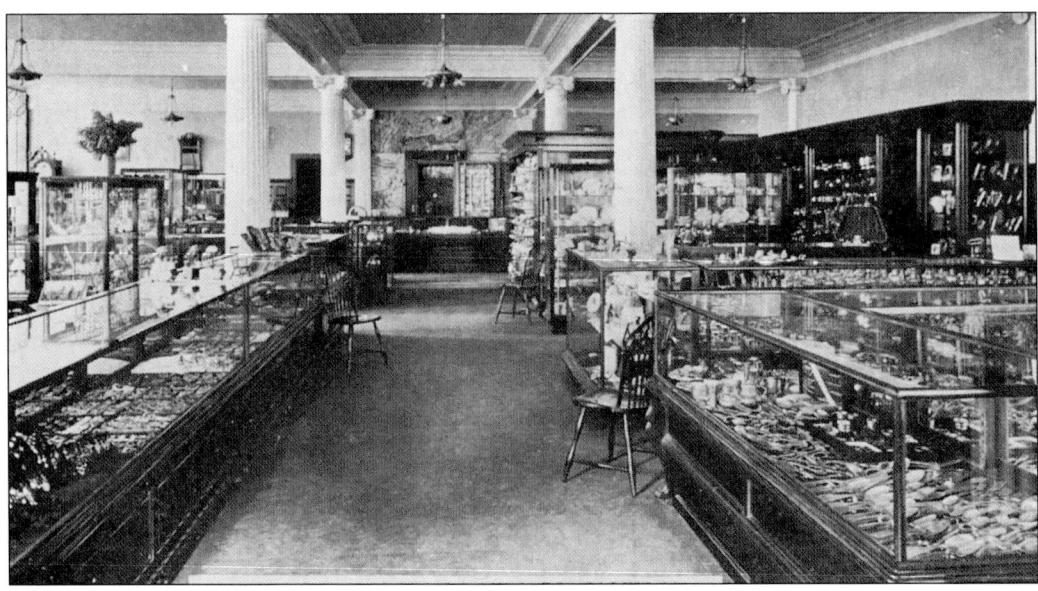

The ground-floor interior of Daniel Low & Company at the beginning of this century. The company was located at the corner of Washington and Essex Streets; the wide variety of goods available is clearly shown.

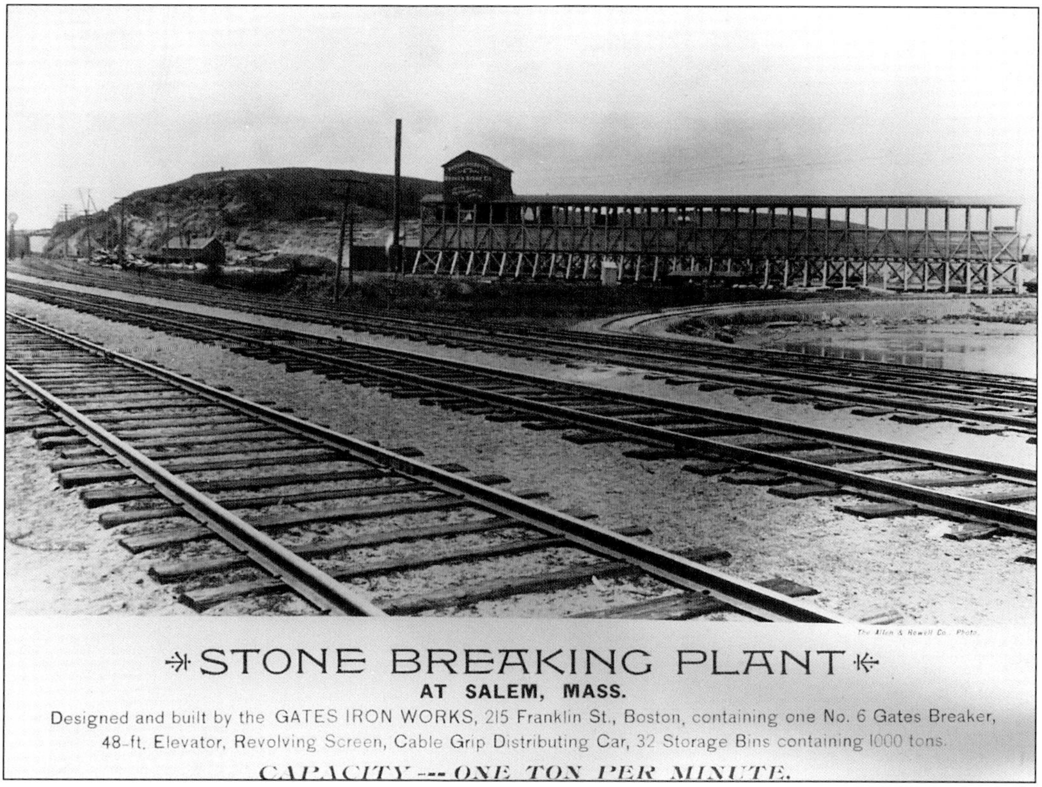

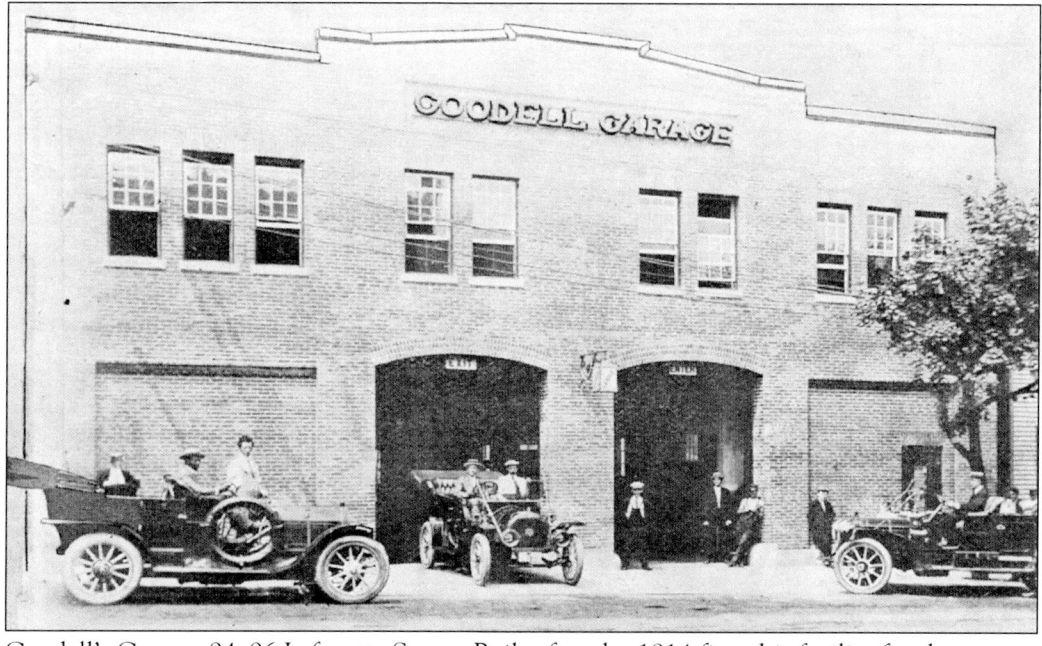

**STONE BREAKING PLANT AT SALEM, MASS.**
Designed and built by the GATES IRON WORKS, 215 Franklin St., Boston, containing one No. 6 Gates Breaker, 48-ft. Elevator, Revolving Screen, Cable Grip Distributing Car, 32 Storage Bins containing 1000 tons.
CAPACITY --- ONE TON PER MINUTE.

Today the name Castle Hill survives as a part of Salem, but the hill was leveled by the Massachusetts Broken Stone Company in the 1890s. (Courtesy D. Michel Michaud.)

Goodell's Garage, 94–96 Lafayette Street. Built after the 1914 fire, this facility for the storage and repair of cars was open twenty-four hours a day. (Courtesy D. Michel Michaud.)

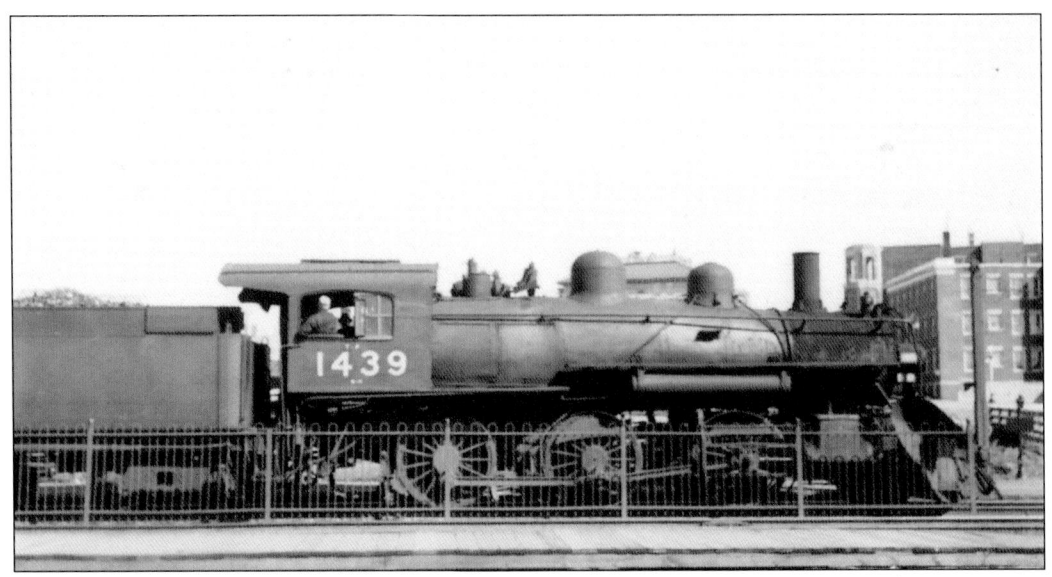

A B&M locomotive. The Boston & Maine Railroad, which began operating in the 1830s, was important to Salem's business interests after the decline of maritime trade. By the time of this c. 1915 picture, the B&M's passenger service had greatly expanded. A typical locomotive, No. 1439, is shown here Boston-bound at Salem Station. (Courtesy Lynn Historical Society.)

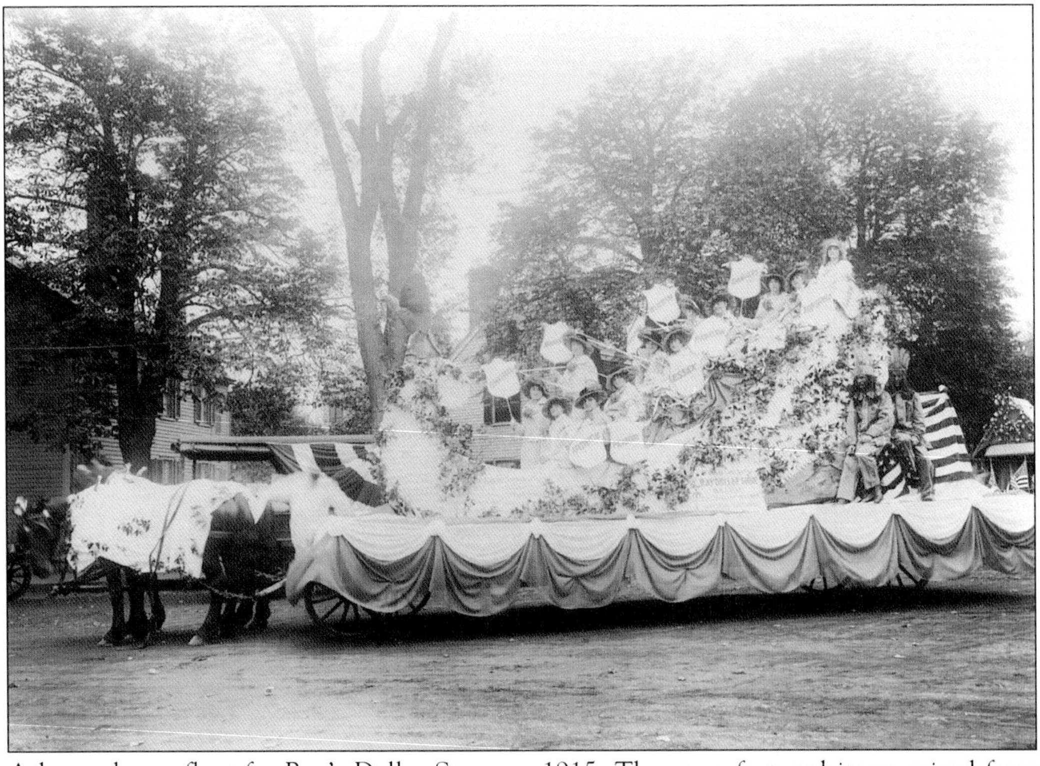

A horse-drawn float for Ray's Dollar Store, c. 1915. The store featured items priced from 1¢ to $1. As the sign states: "All Roads Lead to the Ray Dollar Store." (Courtesy D. Michel Michaud.)

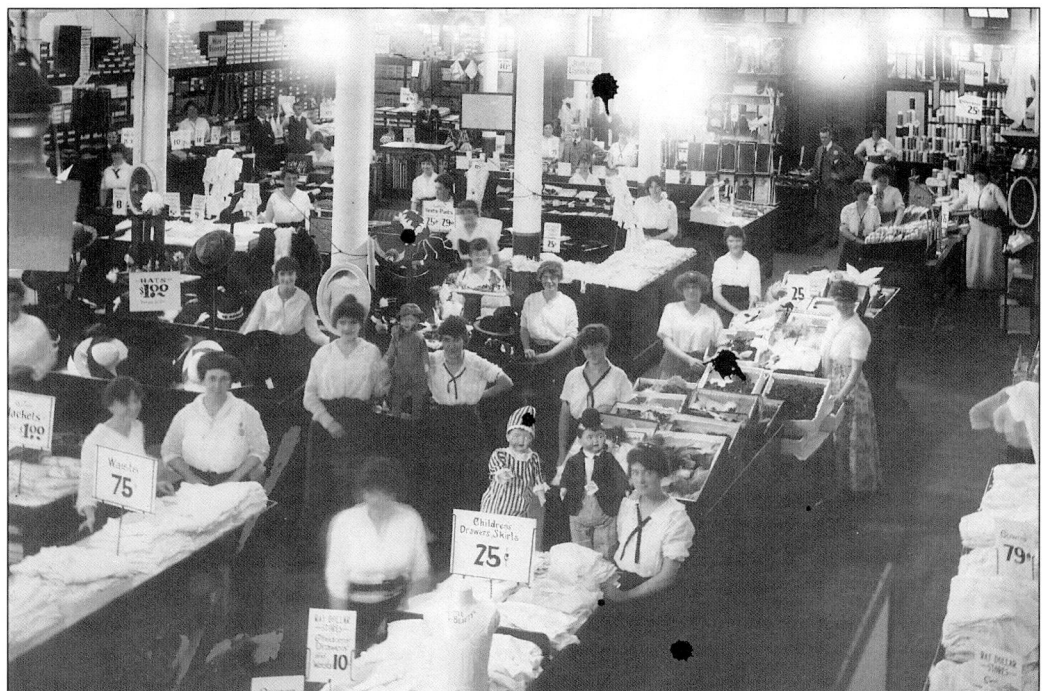

Ray's Dollar Store, 174–176 Essex Street in the Donahue Building, c. 1920. This photograph depicts the staff of the store proudly showing the wide range of inexpensive clothing available to customers. (Courtesy D. Michel Michaud.)

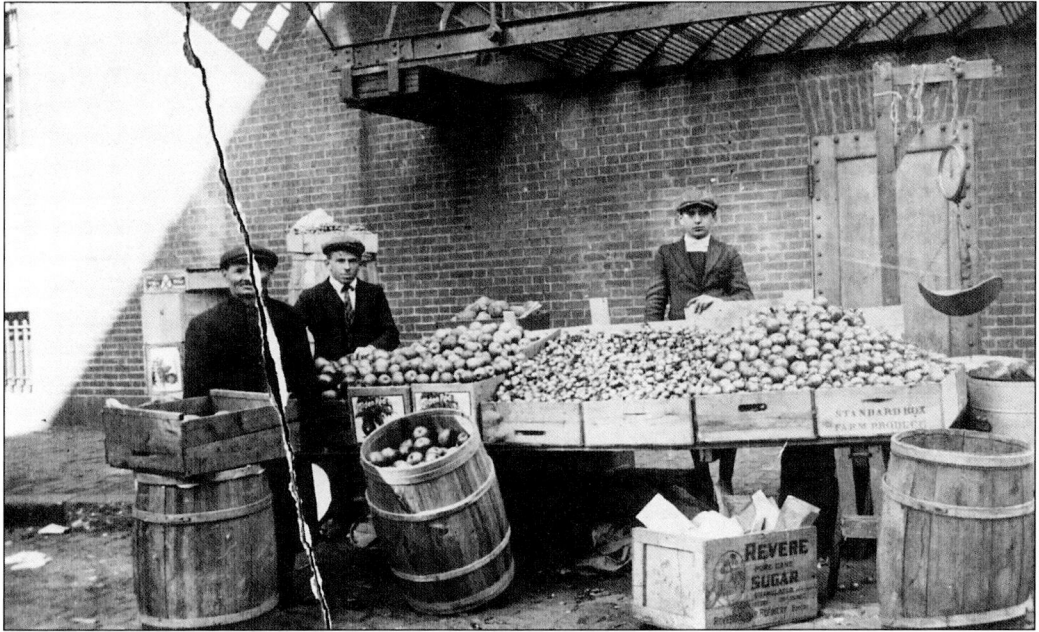

The Salem Market Place. For many years the Salem Market Place, located at the Market House, was a popular spot to buy groceries. In 1920 Zundel Lampert (left) and his son, Hyman Lampert (center), took a minute to pose for this photograph. By this time Salem's Jewish community had grown to over four hundred families. (Courtesy North Shore Jewish Historical Society.)

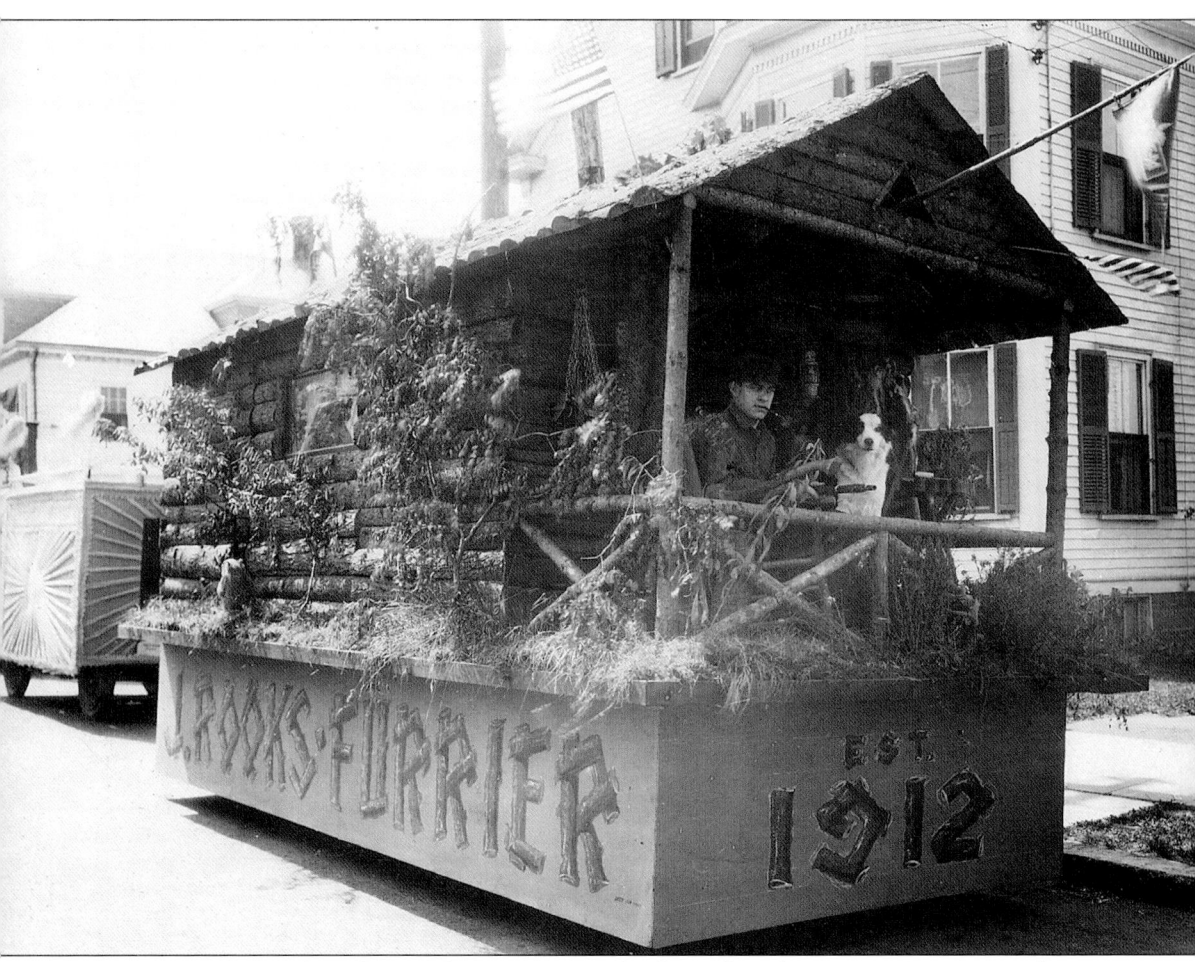

A prominent retailer. The 300th anniversary of Salem's founding in 1926 was cause for major celebration. One highlight was a massive parade in which J. Rooks, furrier, participated. Founded in 1912, the Rooks company was one of the North Shore's leading retailers in women's apparel. There were eleven Rooks stores in Massachusetts and New Hampshire at the peak of their business. (Courtesy North Shore Jewish Historical Society.)

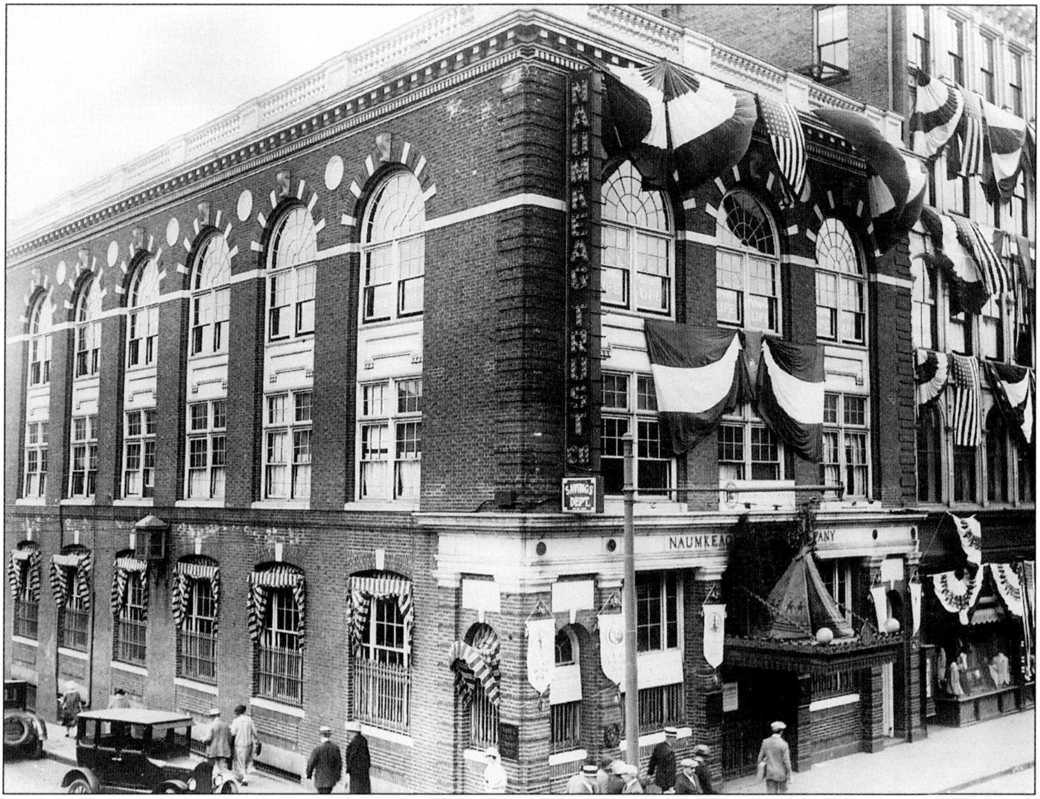

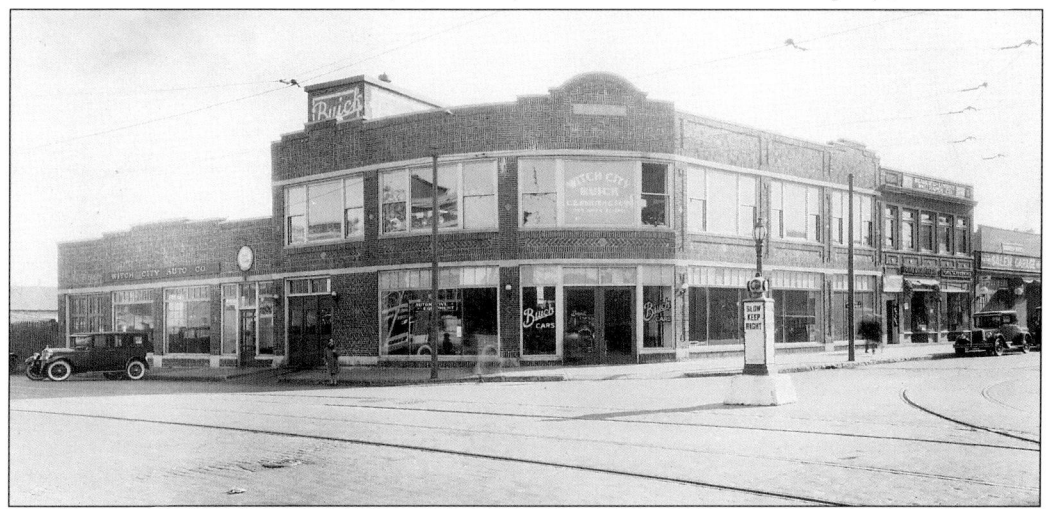

The Naumkeag Trust Company building, 217 Essex Street. This building dates to 1900, when it housed the W.E. Hoyt Company, clothiers and furnishers. The Naumkeag Trust Company purchased the building in 1910–11 and had it remodeled. This 1926 view shows the building at the time of the Salem Tercentenary. (Courtesy Eastern Bank & Trust Company.)

The Witch City Auto Company, located in the Goldberg Building, c. 1920. Note the early traffic signal in front of the building. One of several Buick dealerships owned by C.E. Whitten of Lynn was located here. Whitten began his business in 1883 selling bicycles. (Courtesy Lynn Historical Society.)

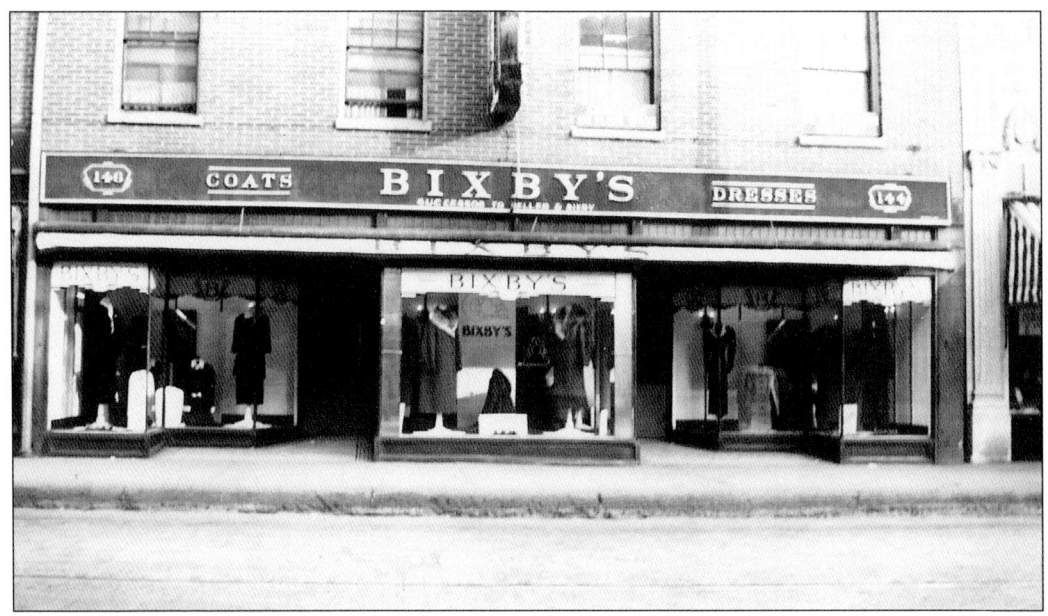

Direct mail advertising, c. 1940. In June 1937, Bixby's, a fashionable ladies' clothier at 144–146 Essex Street, sent this photographic postcard to a Miss Francisca of Salem. The card read: "We have many beautiful white coats—white suits dressed—cottons beachwear for your vacation wardrobe." (Courtesy D. Michel Michaud.)

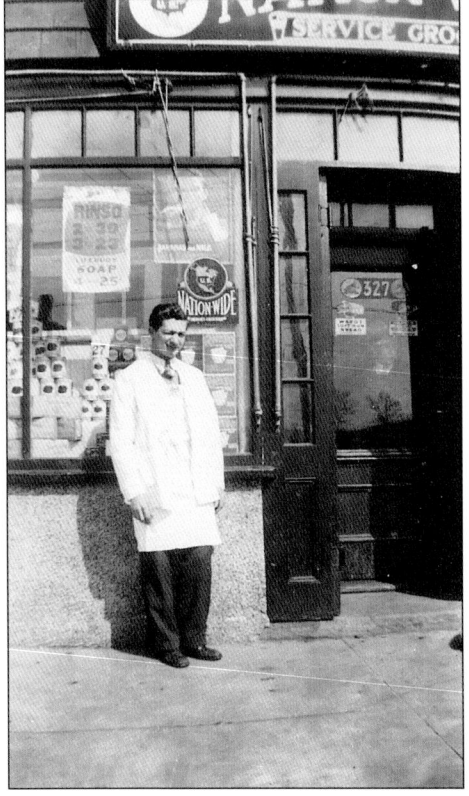

Fontaine's Grocery, 327 Jefferson Avenue, founded by Napoleon Fontaine, c. 1935. This was the first of five Fontaine grocery stores opened in Salem and Lynn. Emile Fontaine is shown here. The family lived above this store. (Courtesy D. Michel Michaud.)

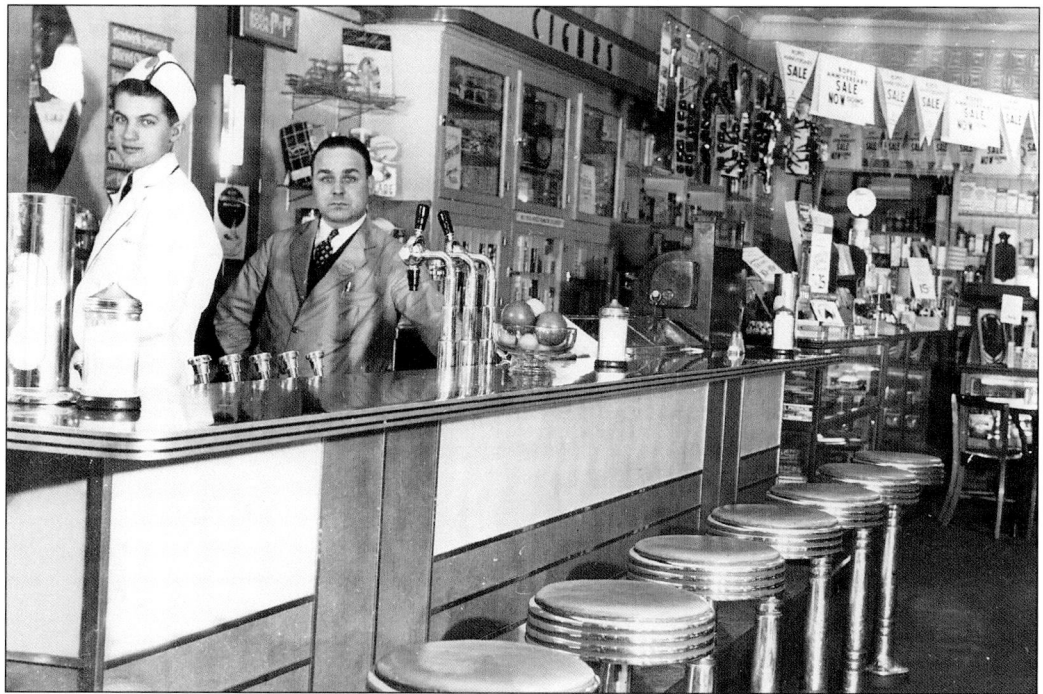

The Soda Fountain, Ropes Drug Company, 1940. Alfred Kobuszewski is pictured on the left. Ropes Drug Company had three locations in Salem at this time: 123 Lafayette Street, 107 Bridge Street, and 93 North Street. (Courtesy John M. Kobuszewski.)

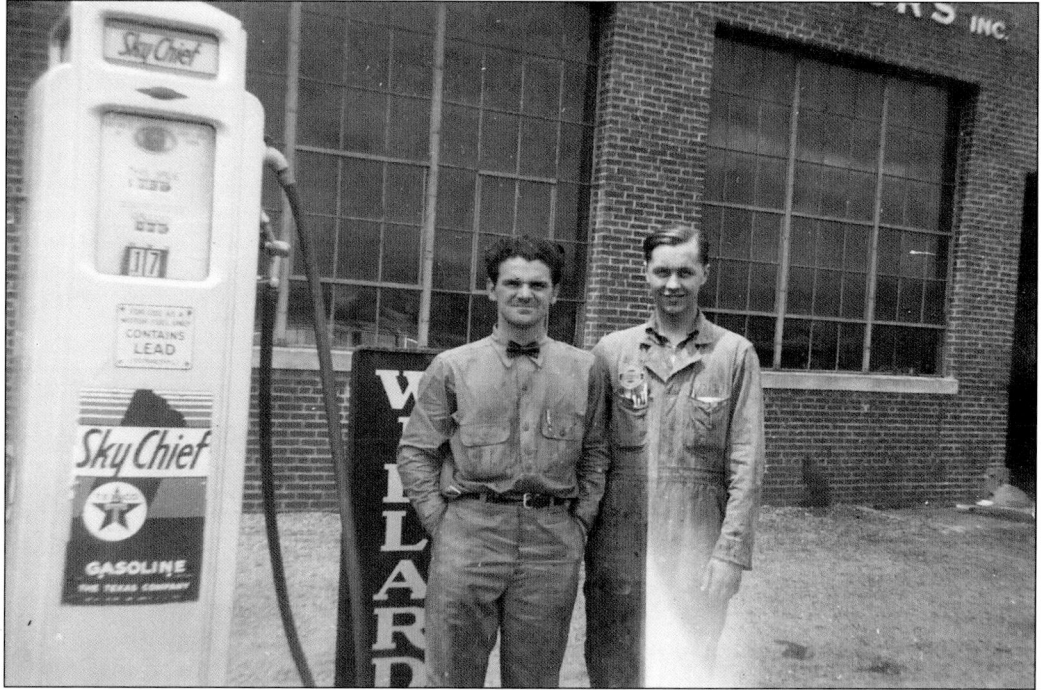

Loring Motors, Canal Street, c. 1940s. Shown here are Henri Michaud and Lucien Berube. Note the price of gasoline—17¢ per gallon. (Courtesy D. Michel Michaud.)

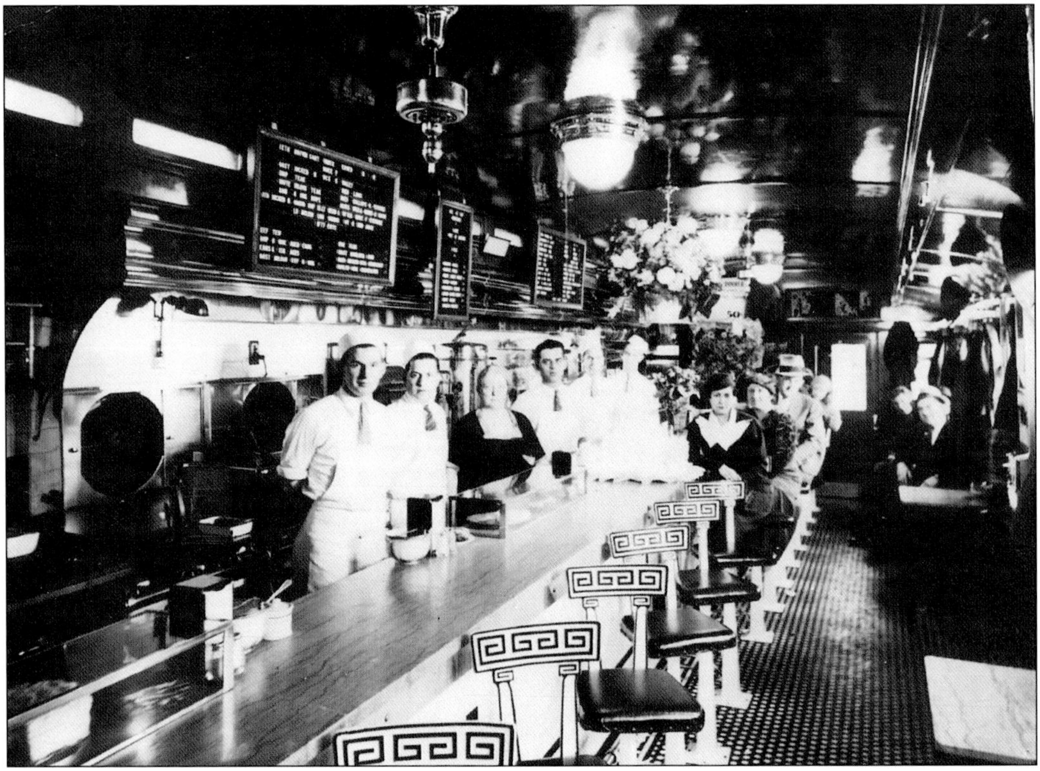

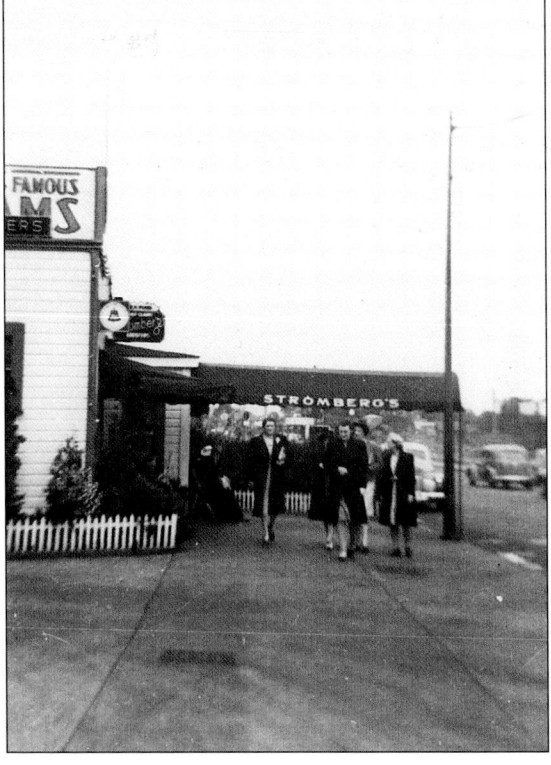

Holt's Diner, 22 Washington Street, c. 1940. Holt's was one of several popular Salem diners. The stylish interior shows that this diner, a Worcester Lunch Car from 1928, was the top of the line. Here the staff proudly pose for a photograph. (Courtesy Joe Jalbert.)

Stromberg's Restaurant, Bridge Street, 1941. Stromberg's has been a Salem landmark for generations and is famous for its seafood. (Courtesy Christopher Mathias.)

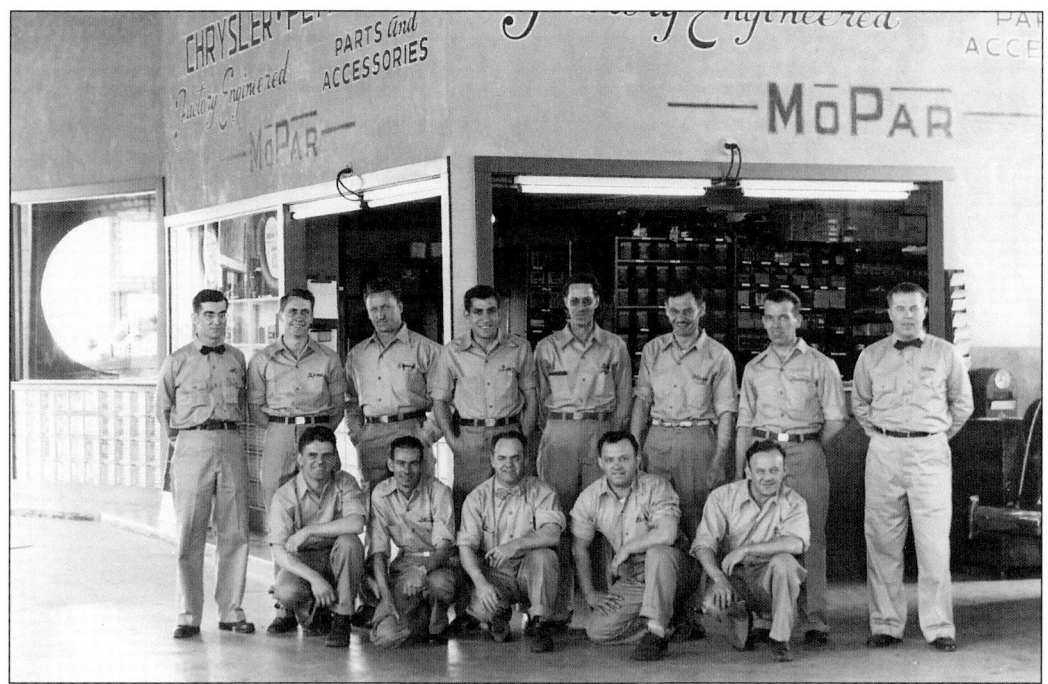

Loring Motors, 282 Canal Street, 1952. From left to right are: (front row) Henri Michaud, unknown, "Scoop" Roulier, Dick Berube, and unknown; (back row) Albert Pelletier, Leon Fontaine, Frank Whalen, Albert Ciprioni, "Babe" Morin, Harold Wain, Henry Cloutier, and Harold Van Horn. (Courtesy Henri Michaud.)

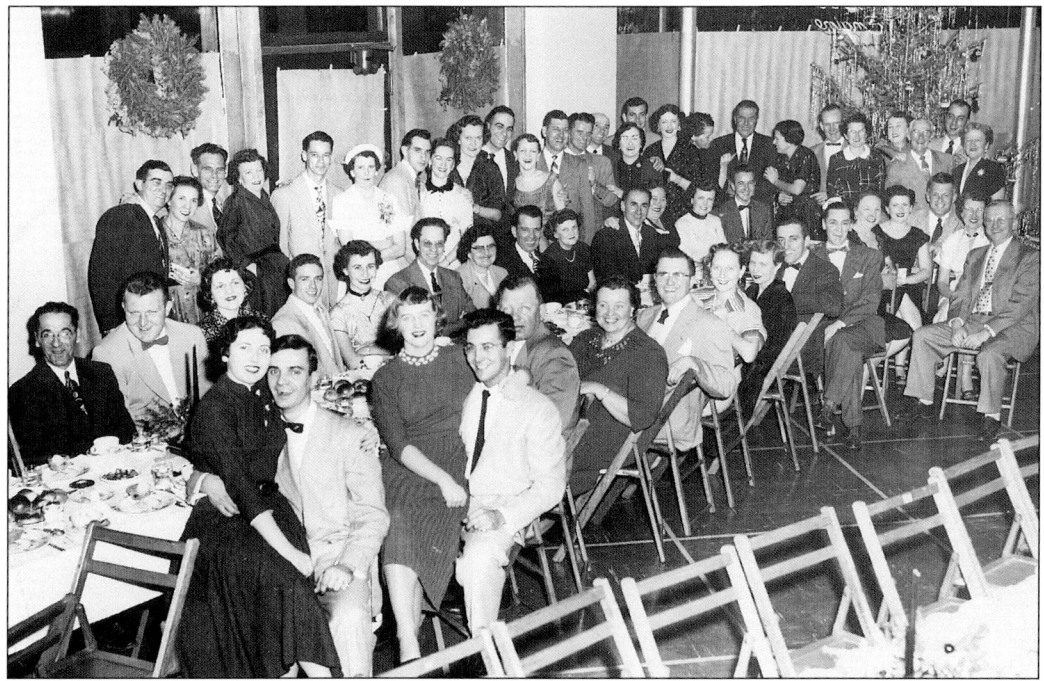

The Loring Motors showroom, the site of the company Christmas party in 1952. (Courtesy Henri Michaud.)

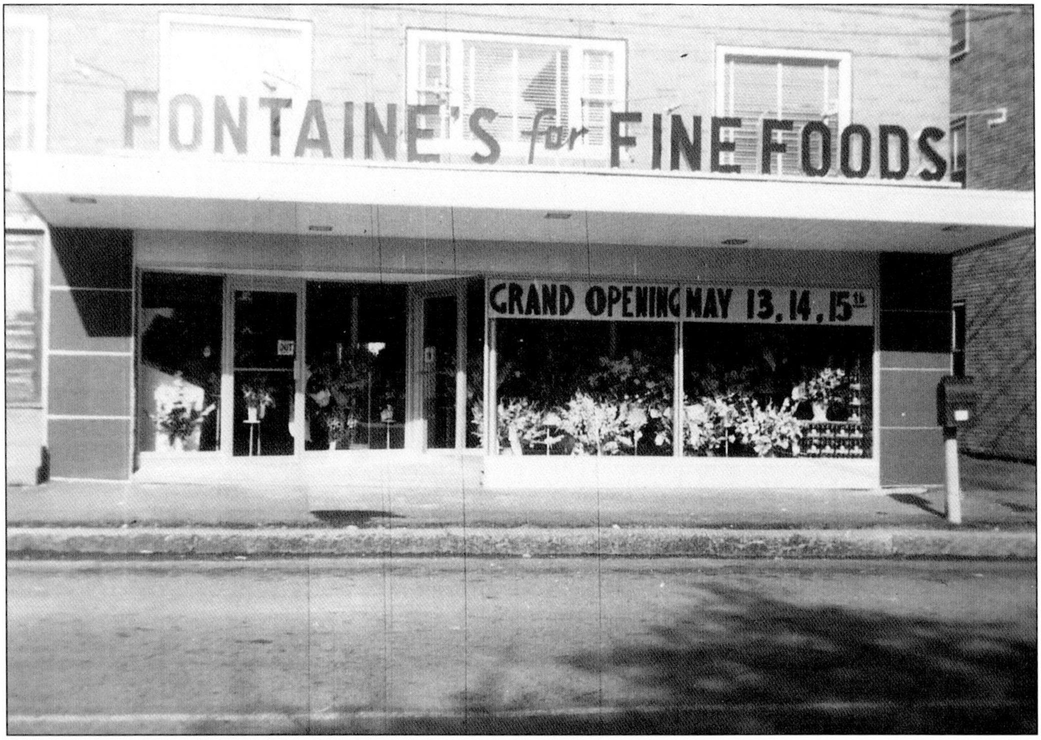

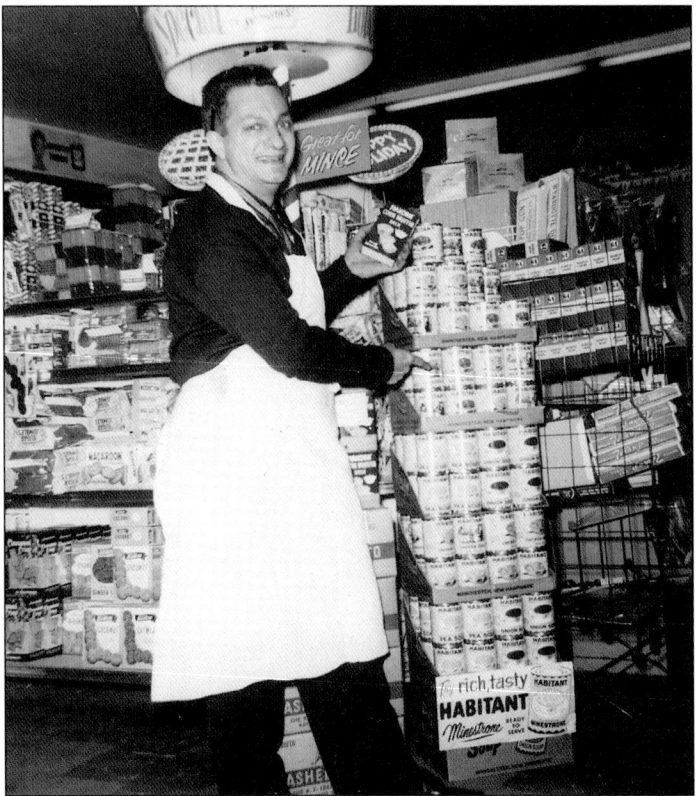

Fontaine's Grocery at 271 Jefferson Avenue, 1954. The store windows are filled with flowers to celebrate the grand opening of another store. Pictured is owner Emile Fontaine, touting his merchandise. (Courtesy D. Michel Michaud.)

# *Seven*
# Fires and Firefighting

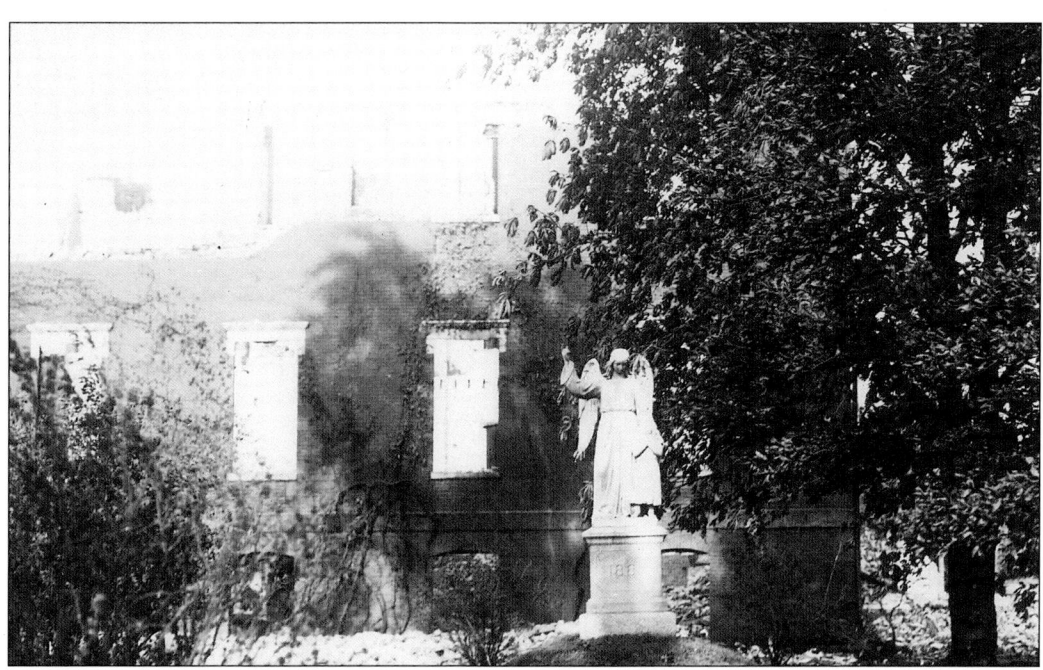

The ruins of the city orphan asylum on Lafayette Street. The angel statue seems to have escaped the great fire of June 25, 1914, unscathed. (Courtesy D. Michel Michaud.)

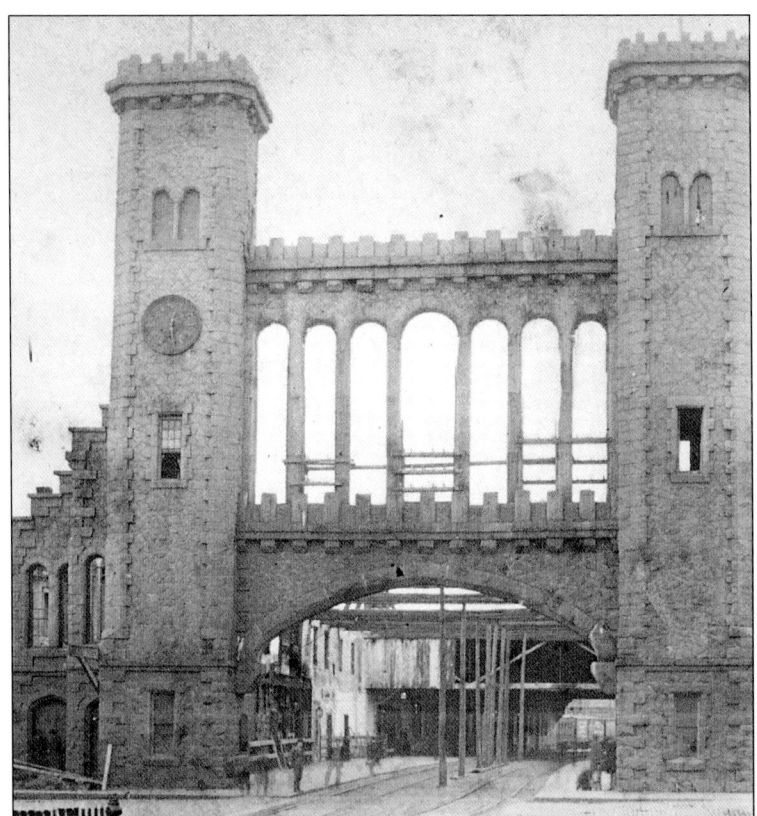

The depot destroyed, 1882. Over the years firefighting and fires have played an important role in Salem's history; here the wooden superstructure surrounding the granite facade of the Eastern Railroad Depot was destroyed by fire on April 7, 1882. (Courtesy of D. Michel Michaud.)

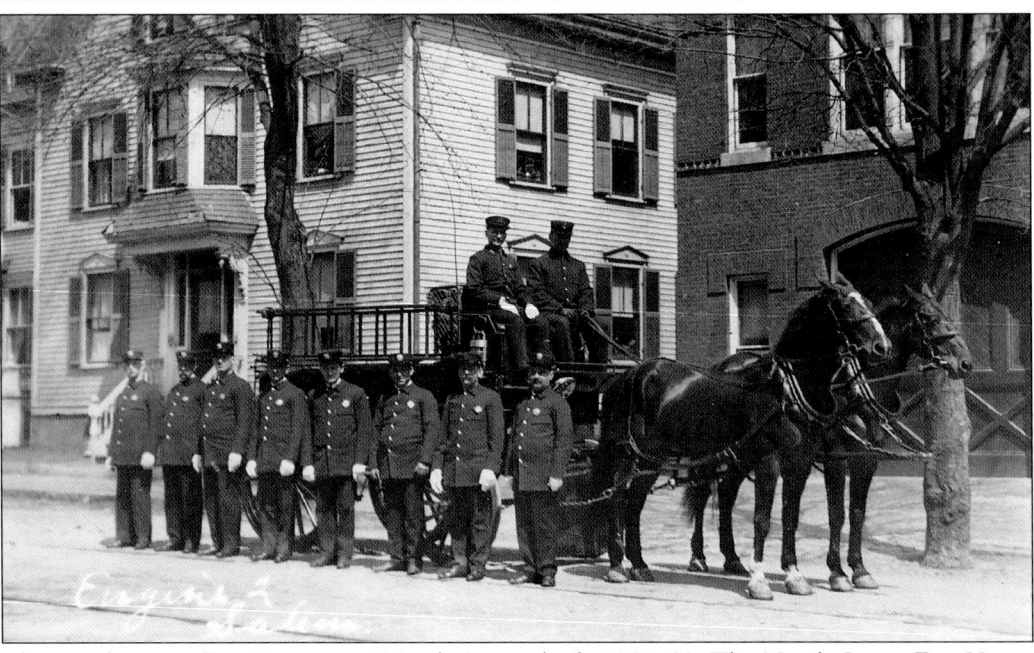

The North Street Fire House, 142 North Street, built 1881–82. The North Street Fire House was originally called Hose Company Number 6. Shown here are the men of Engine 2. This is the oldest continuously operating fire station in Salem. (Courtesy D. Michel Michaud.)

A Chestnut Street resident preparing to evacuate her home during the great fire. The house at 37 Chestnut Street was built for Captain Thomas Sanders in 1805. In 1893 it was remodeled in the Colonial Revival style by Boston architect Arthur Little. Fortunately, Chestnut Street was spared in 1914.

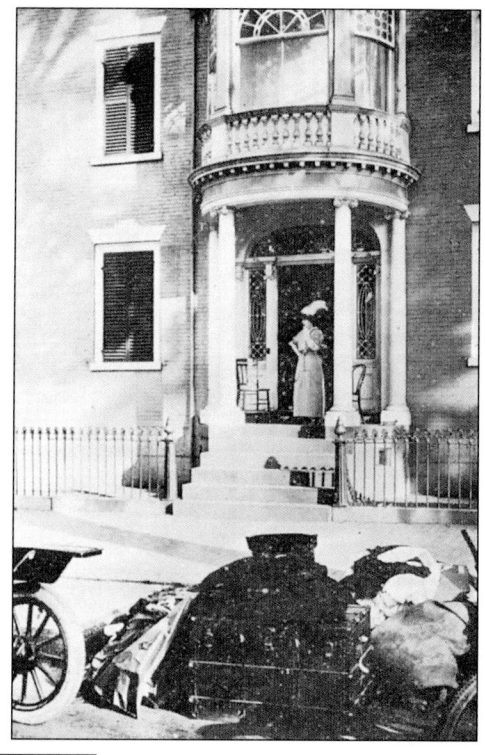

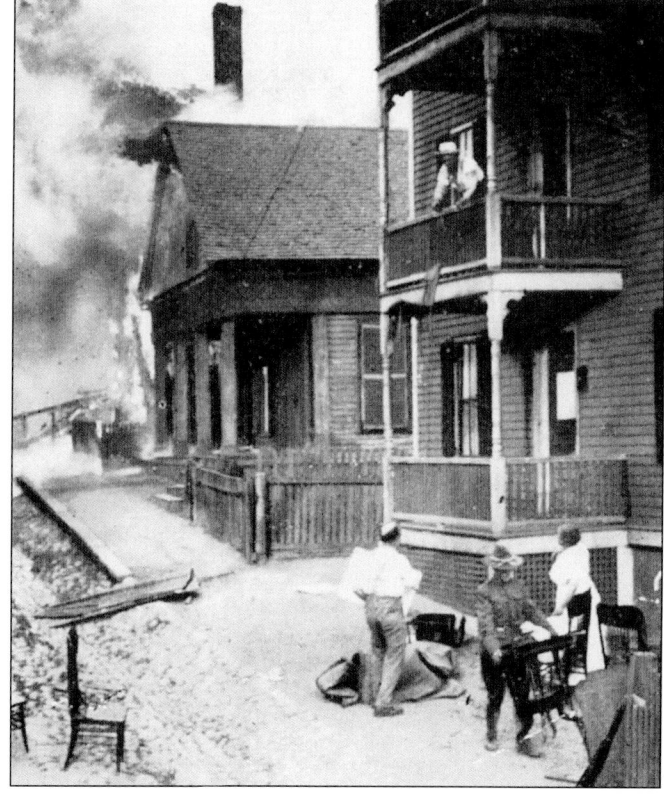

Calling in the troops. When the fire began to rage out of control, the city called in the military. Here, militiamen are helping remove household goods during the 1914 fire.

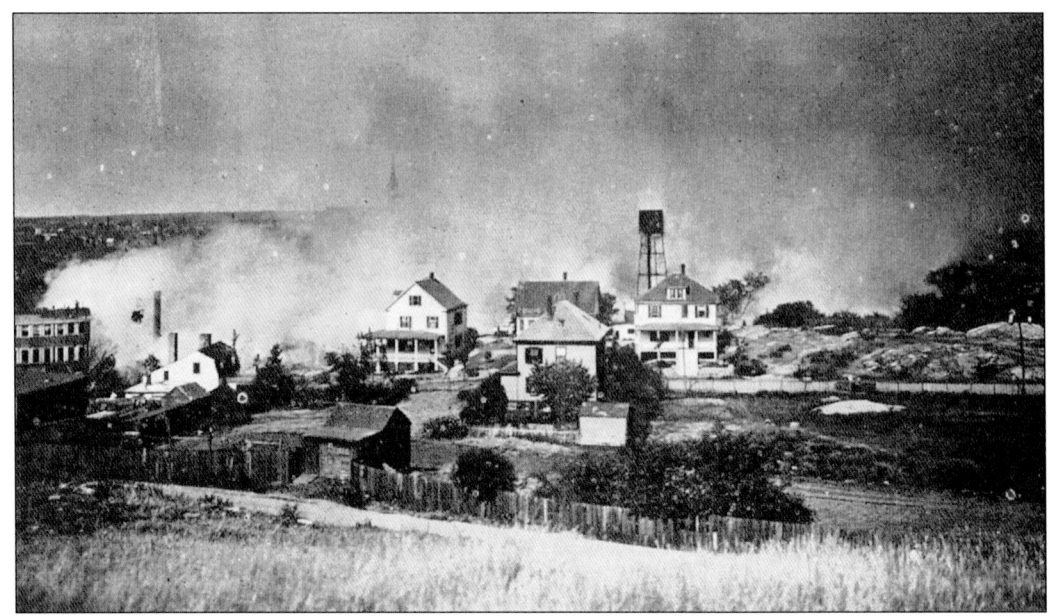

The conflagration of 1914 as seen from Gallows Hill. Firemen from twenty-two cities were called in to battle the blaze.

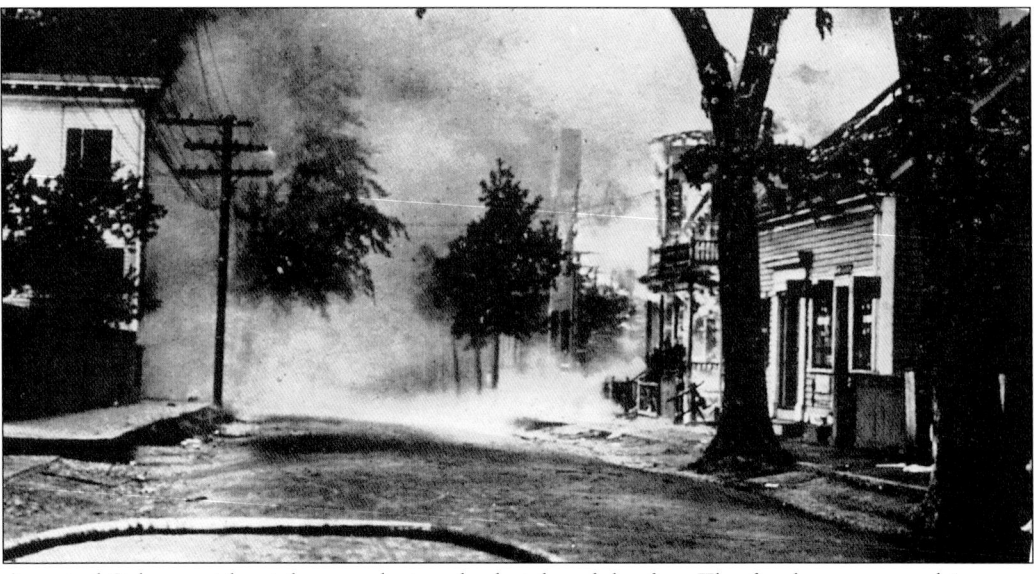

A typical Salem residential street during the height of the fire. The fire began around 1 pm at Blubber Hollow; a general alarm sounded at 1:41 pm.

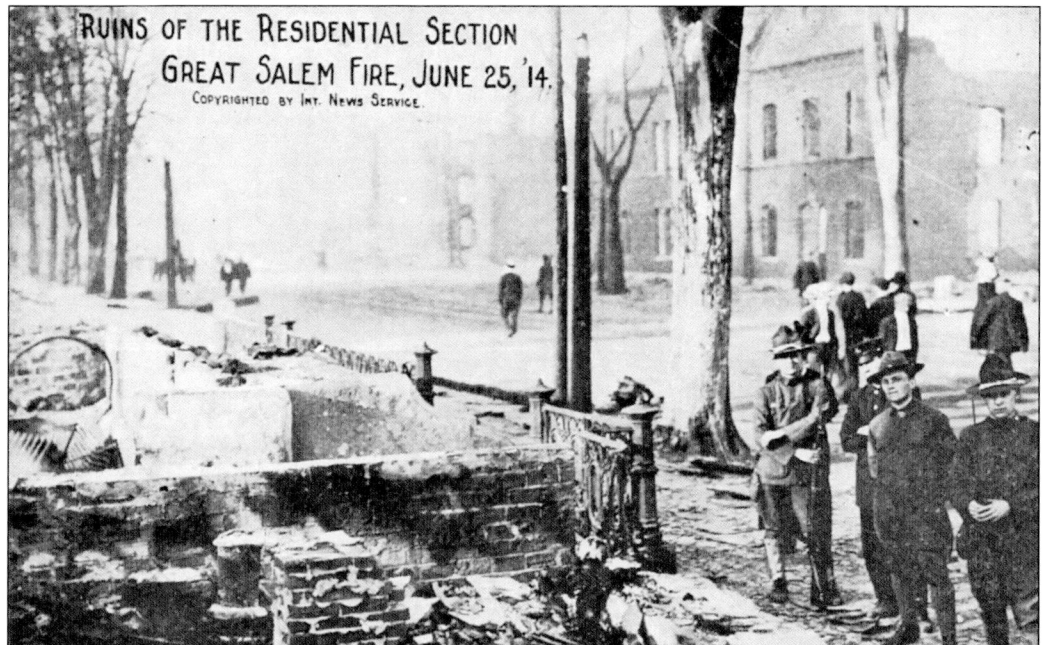

A disaster area. The militia were summoned from every part of the city and surrounding areas; they reported and equipped themselves for service at the Salem Armory. The National Guard protected and secured the areas devastated by the disaster. After twelve days of active service, the guardsmen were relieved of duty on July 7. (Courtesy Pickering Foundation.)

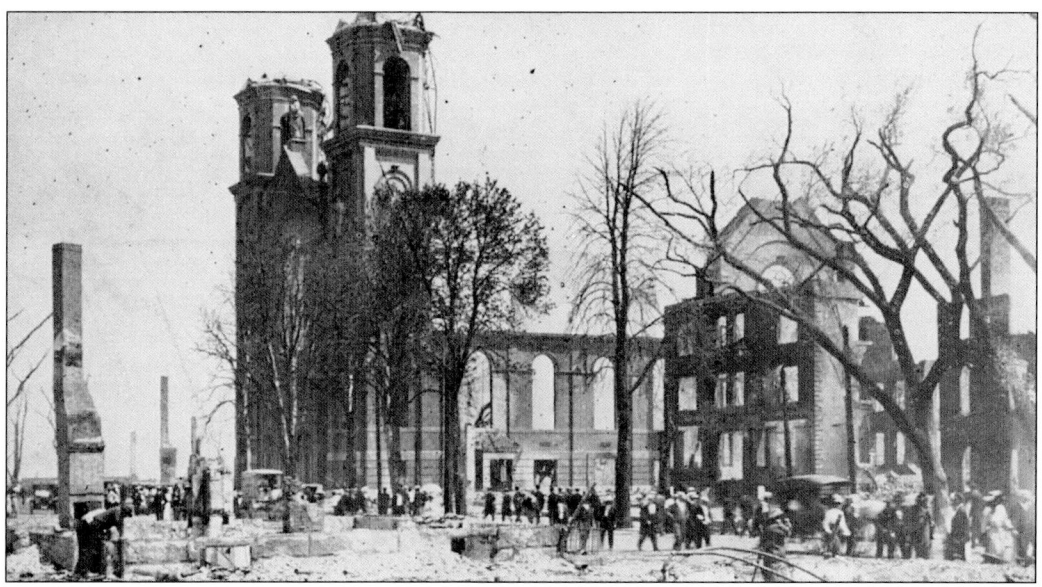

Saint Joseph's Roman Catholic Church, 133 Lafayette Street, built in 1910–11. The church was dedicated on September 7, 1913, and destroyed in 1914 by the fire.

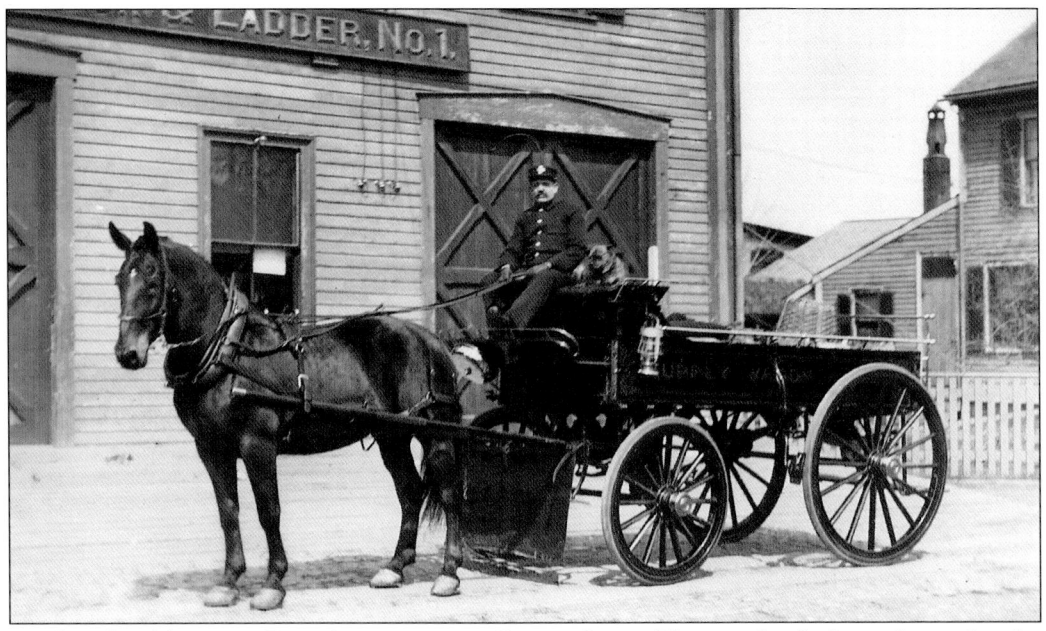

Hook and Ladder No. 1, Essex Street, opposite Boston Street. The wooden firehouse burned in the 1914 fire. The site is the location of the present fire station. (Courtesy D. Michel Michaud.)

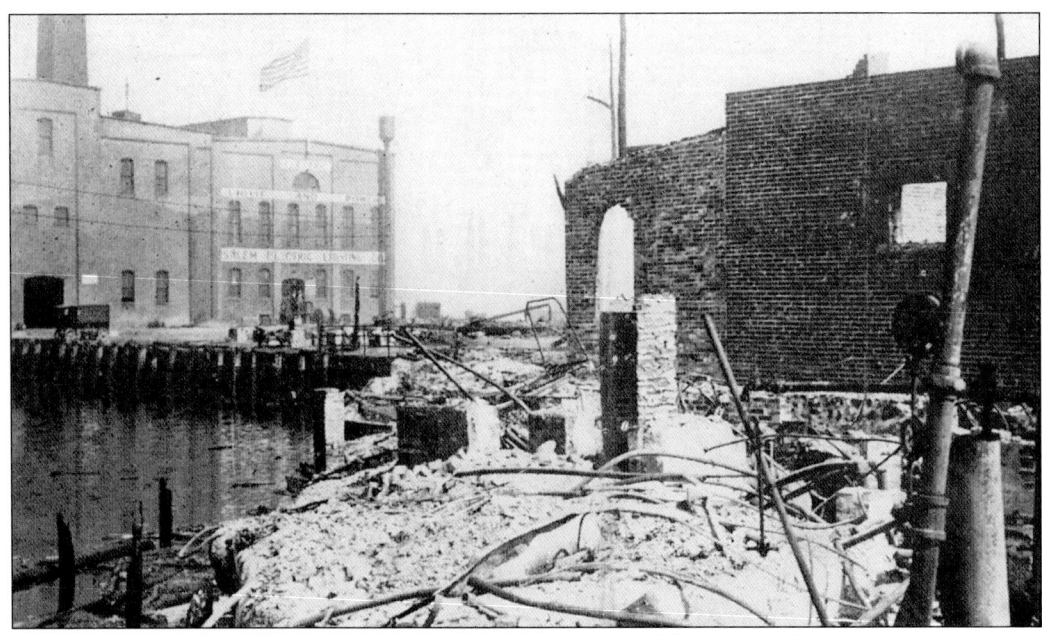

Ruins near the Salem Electric Company on Peabody Street. The electric light and power station survived the fire. Officials fearing that a fire might break out in this congested area had spent a great deal of money fireproofing the complex. (Courtesy Pickering Foundation.)

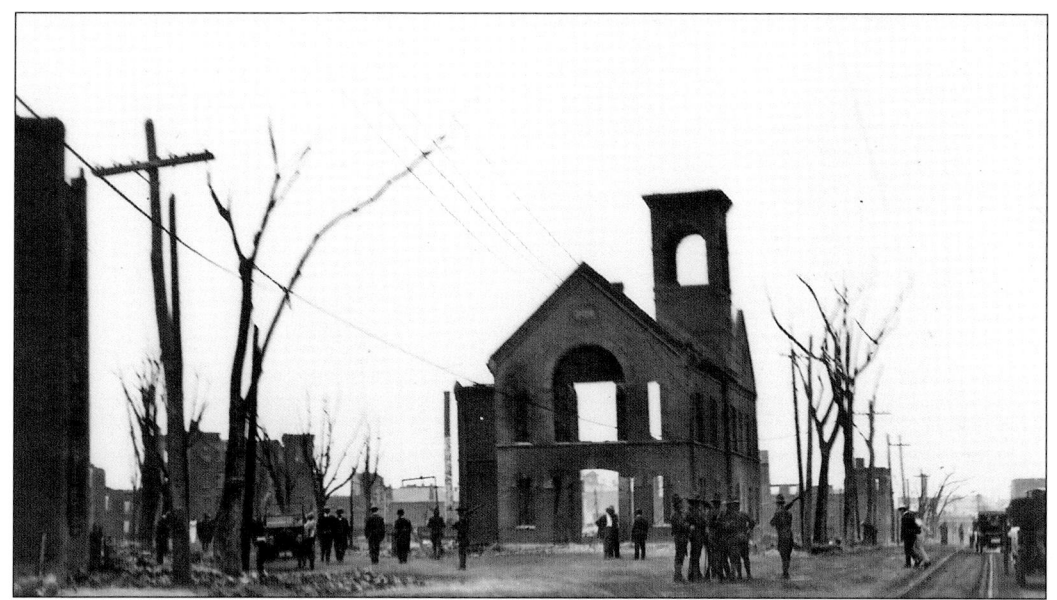

The brick firehouse, c. 1890, destroyed. Not even this brick structure on the corner of Washington and Lafayette Streets was spared when the titanic fire raged uncontrolled. (Courtesy D. Michel Michaud.)

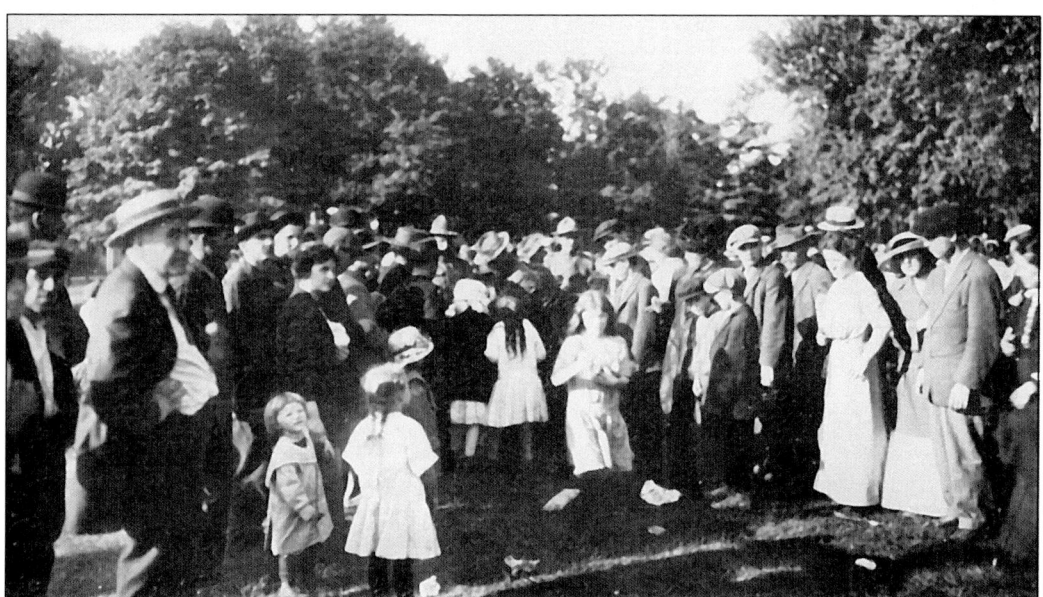

The bread line after the Salem fire, in a photograph taken at either Forest River or Highland Park. At the armory the day after the fire, twenty-five hundred people were given provisions. After a few days, all food was distributed at the refugee camps. (Courtesy D. Michel Michaud.)

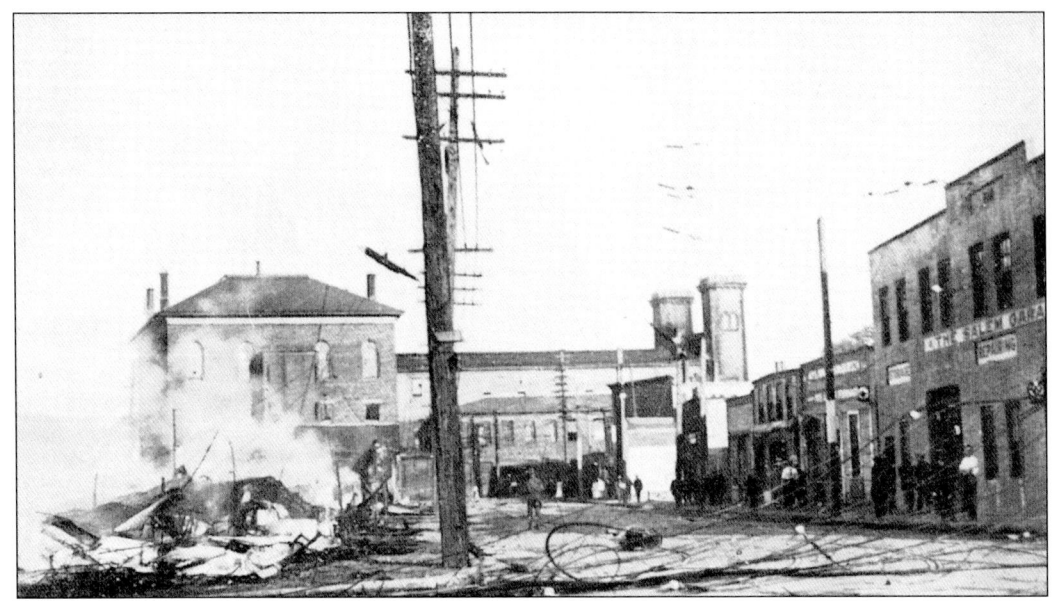
The smoldering ruins of New Derby Street. The railroad depot was spared by the fire of 1914.

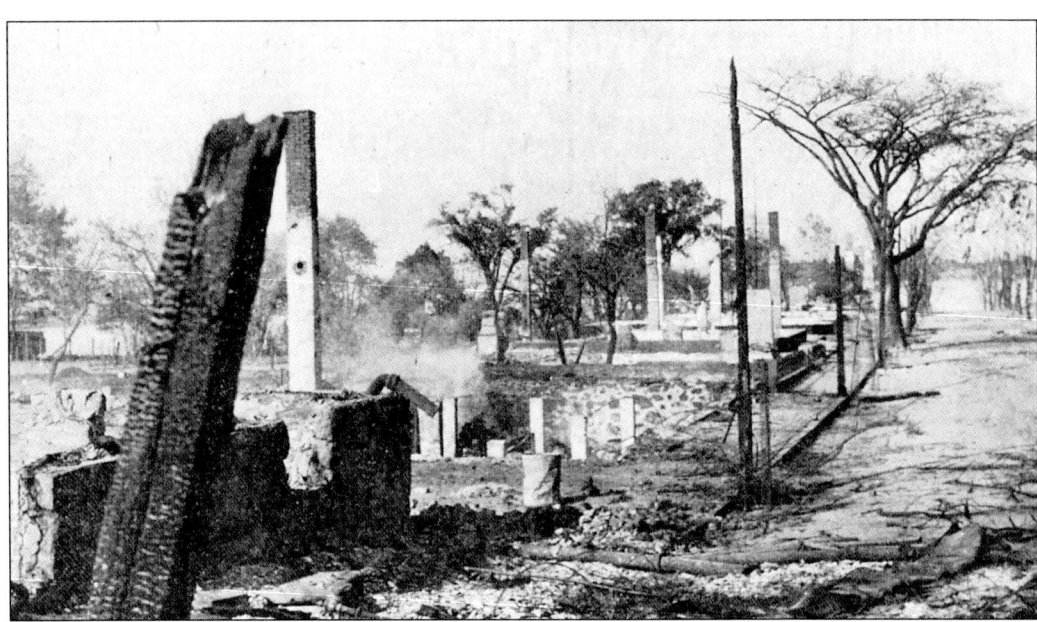
Ruins on Leach and Lafayette Streets, a scene repeated throughout Salem. The devastating fire consumed 252 acres and 1,376 buildings. Property loss was valued at close to fifteen million dollars. (Courtesy Pickering Foundation.)

The tower of the Naumkeag Steam Cotton Company on Congress Street. Only the tower remained standing after the fire of 1914 destroyed the brick building, built in 1845.

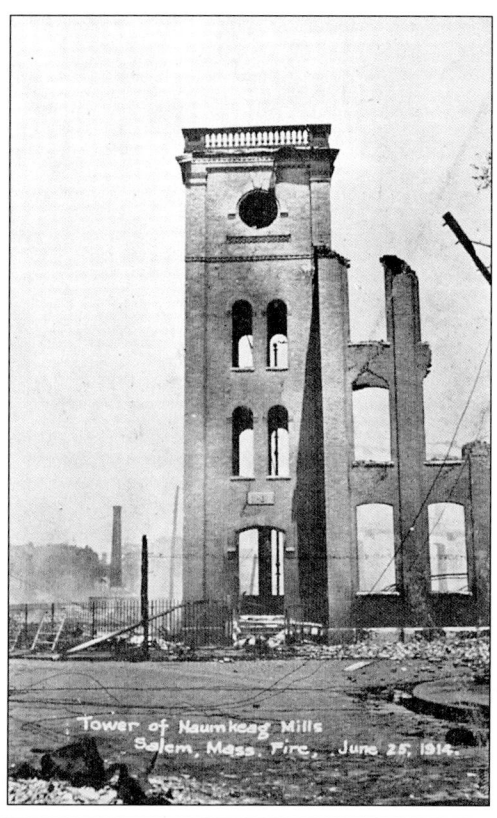

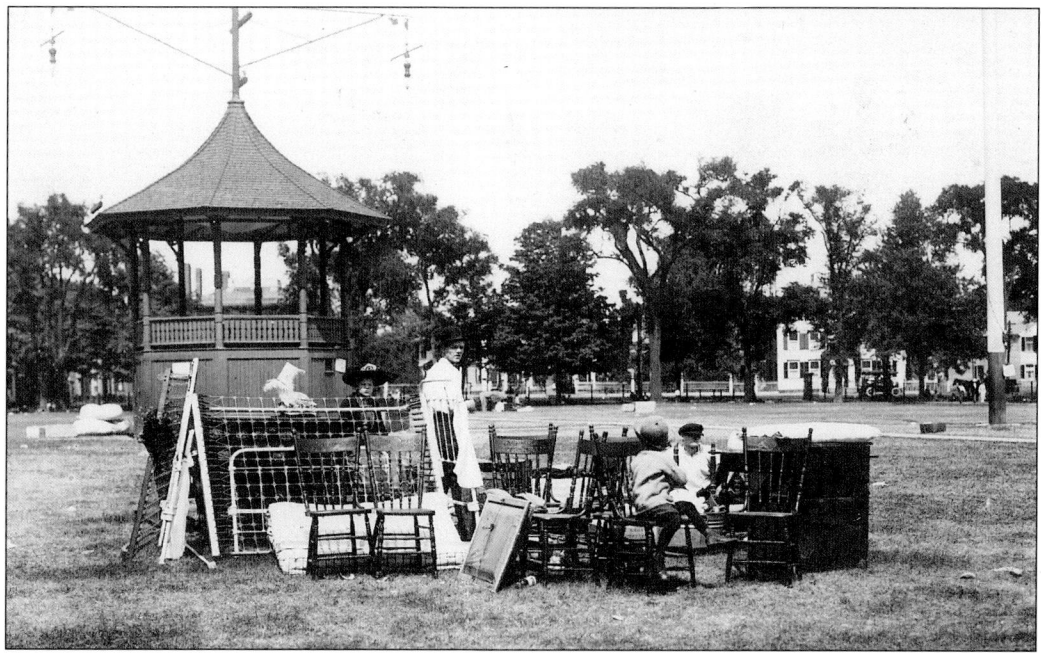

A devastating loss. Many of the refugees of the Salem fire gathered on Salem Common with all their belongings. Although the fire devastated a large section of the city, Salem had a speedy recovery. (Courtesy D. Michel Michaud.)

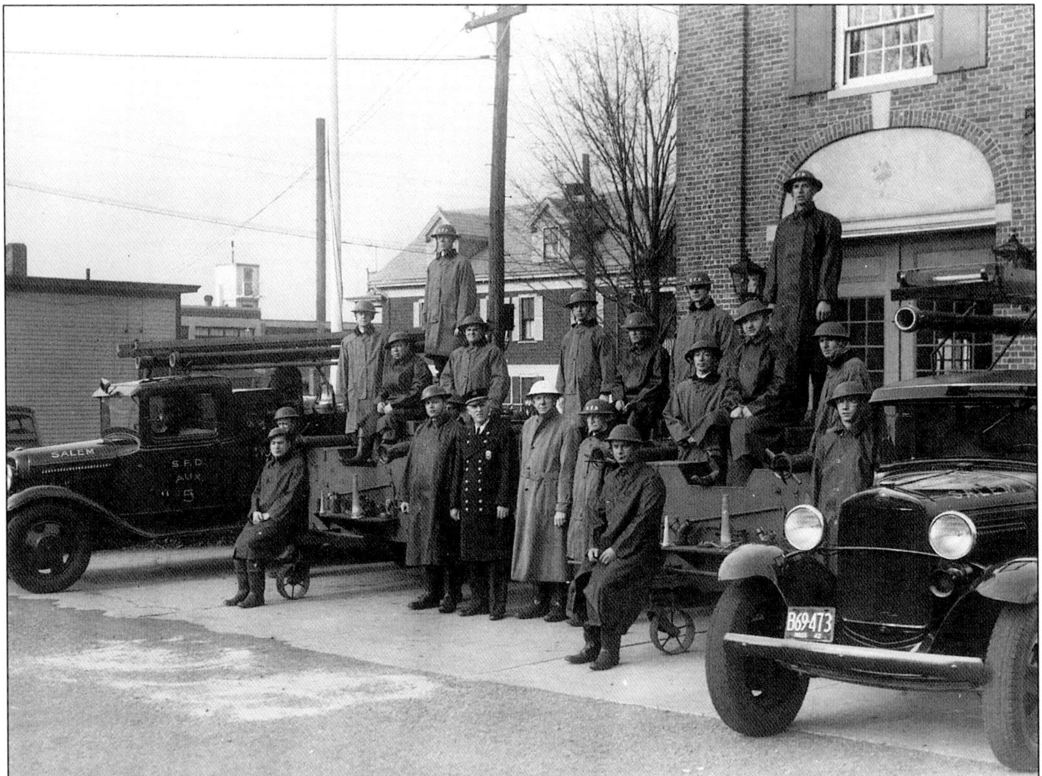

Members of the Salem Fire Department Engine No. 5, 64 Loring Avenue at Broadway. The men proudly pose with Captain Edward W. Flynn and Lieutenant Terence Nolan, c. 1942. (Courtesy D. Michel Michaud.)

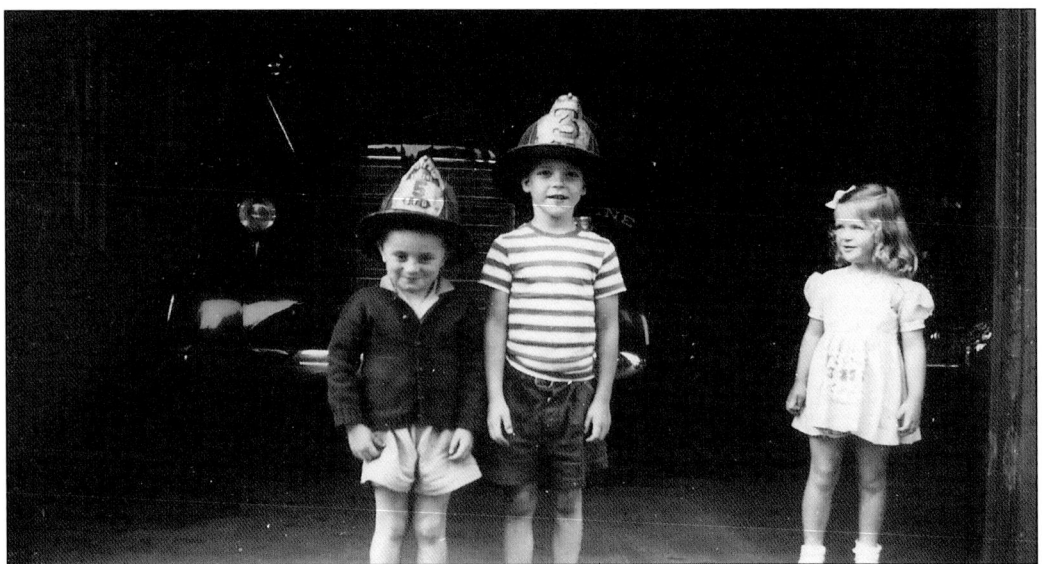

Junior Salem firefighters dressed and ready for action, c. 1940. (Courtesy Ben and Sally Mathias.)

# *Eight*
# Salem Willows and Surrounding Areas

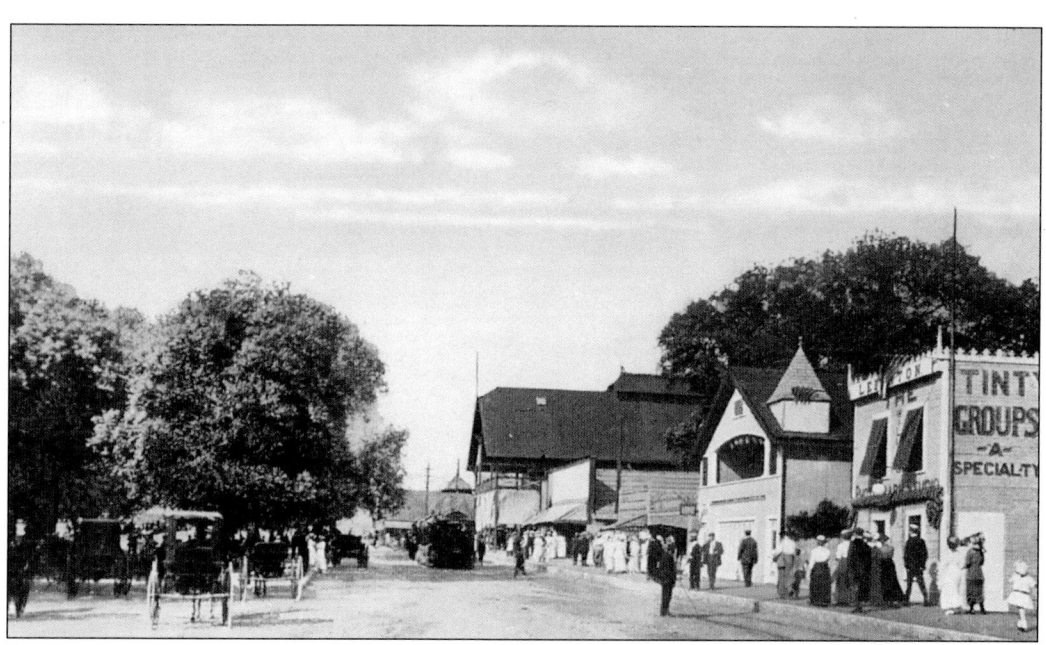

A street scene at Salem Willows, c. 1915. Horse-drawn carriages, the trolley, and people dressed in their best outfits mingle happily together.

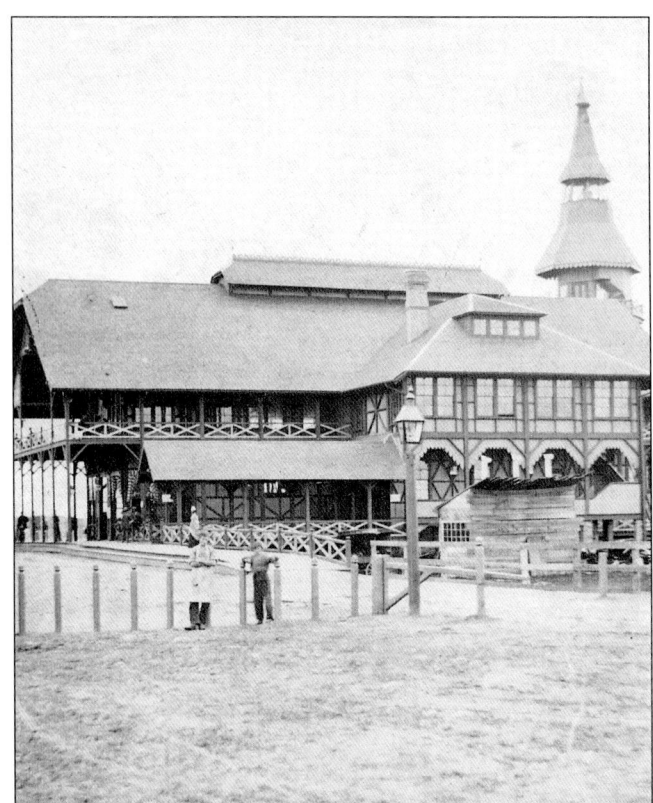

The Pavilion and Restaurant at Salem Willows, c. 1885. First opened on June 17, 1880, the restaurant had a commanding view of the shoreline. (Courtesy D. Michel Michaud.)

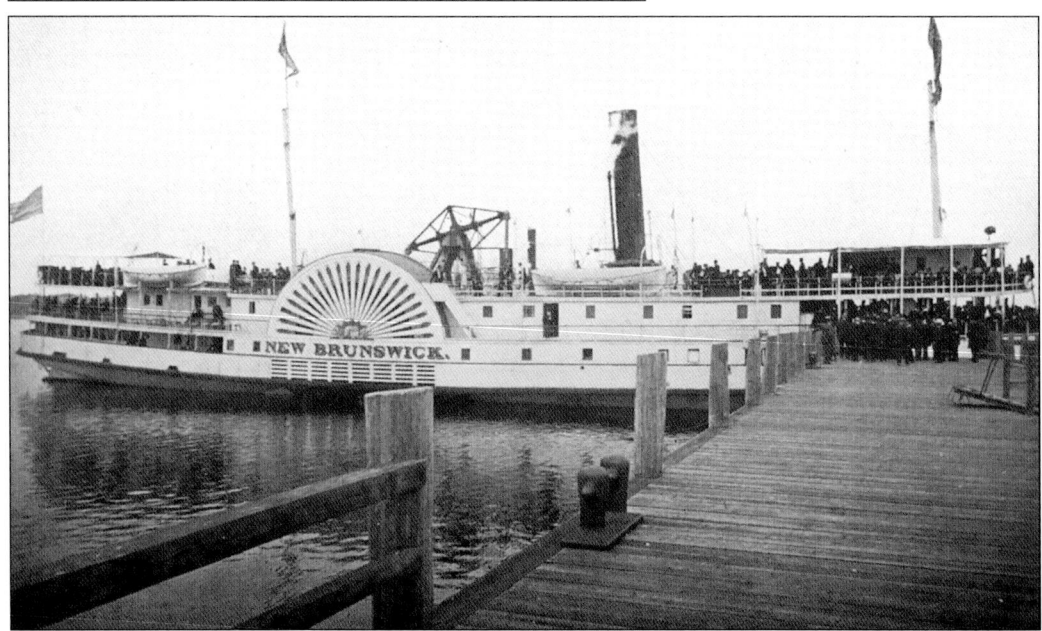

The Willows pier, c. 1904. During the summer season on hot, sultry days, hundreds of people would come to Salem Willows for the cool, ocean breezes, the fine restaurants, and various amusements. They would arrive by land and water transport. Pictured here is the Boston steamer *New Brunswick* at the Willows pier picking up passengers for their return voyage home.

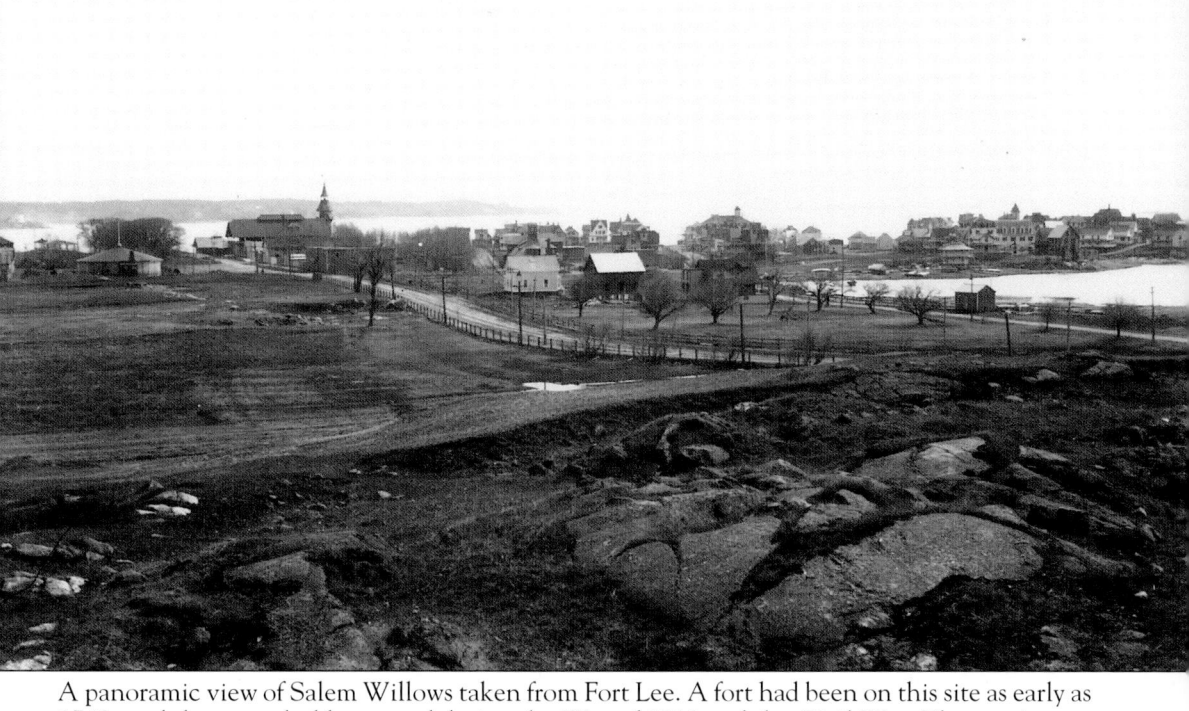

A panoramic view of Salem Willows taken from Fort Lee. A fort had been on this site as early as 1742, and the stronghold was used during the War of 1812 and the Civil War. The scenic area is also known as Cannon Hill because four Civil War cannons were at one time located on the embankment. (Courtesy Bodin Historic Photo, Gloucester, MA.)

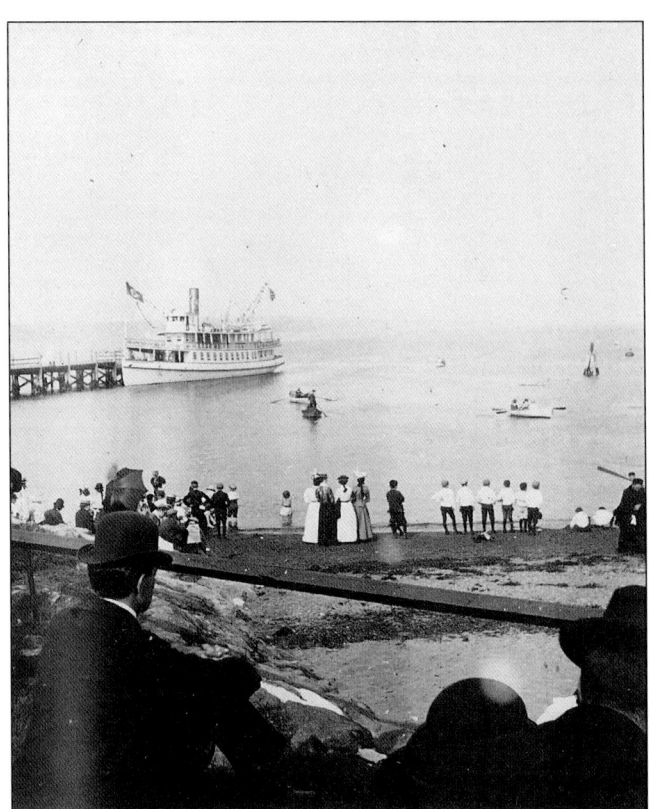

A Boston steamer at the Salem Willows pier, *c.* 1895. The spectators on shore appear to be watching rowboat races on the placid water. (Courtesy D. Michel Michaud.)

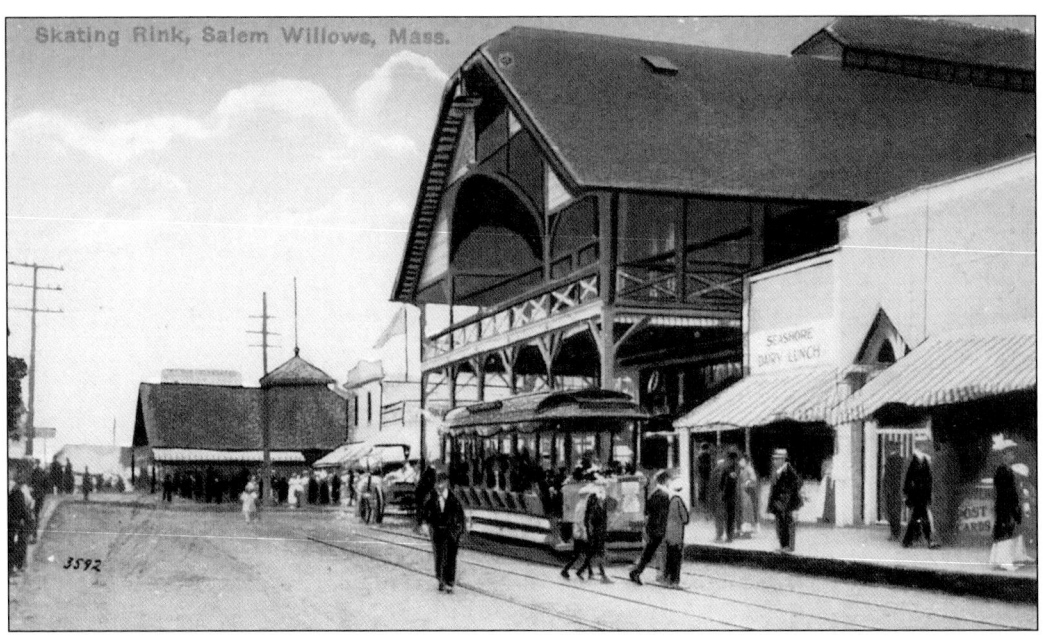

The roller skating rink at Salem Willows, *c.* 1915.

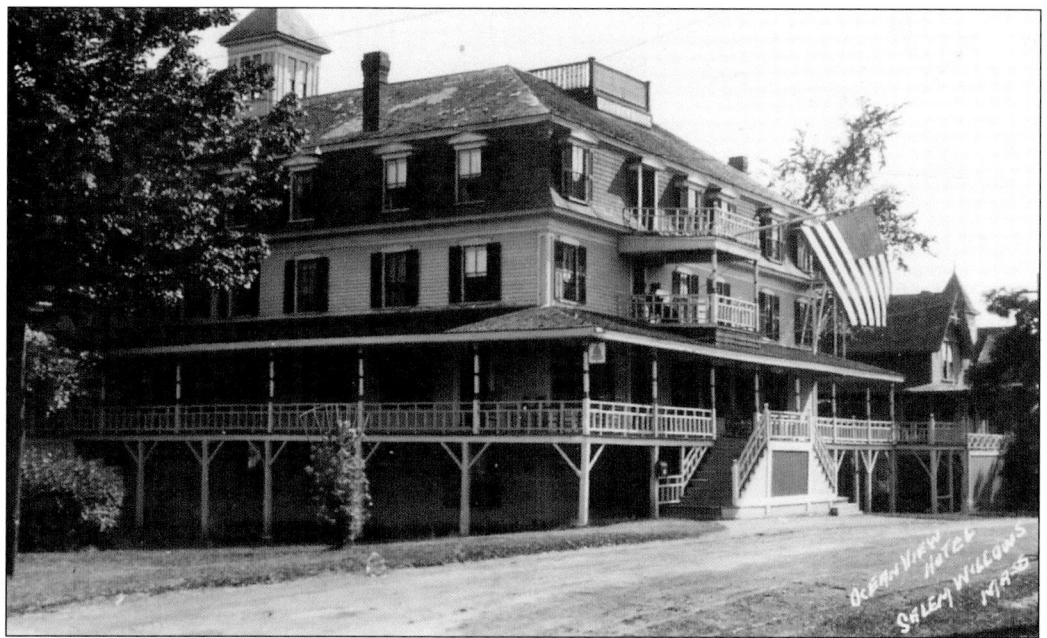

The Ocean View House, c. 1910. This large wooden structure with a view of Massachusetts Bay and the islands was built on Columbus Avenue in 1876. The popular hotel became the Juniper Point Inn in 1912; it closed in 1935 and was razed in 1938.

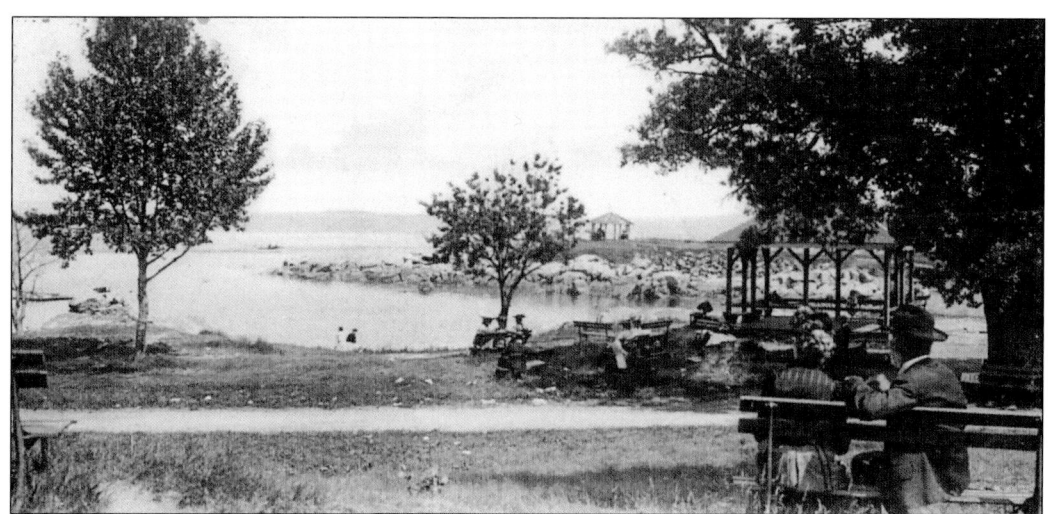

People enjoying halcyon summer days at Salem Willows.

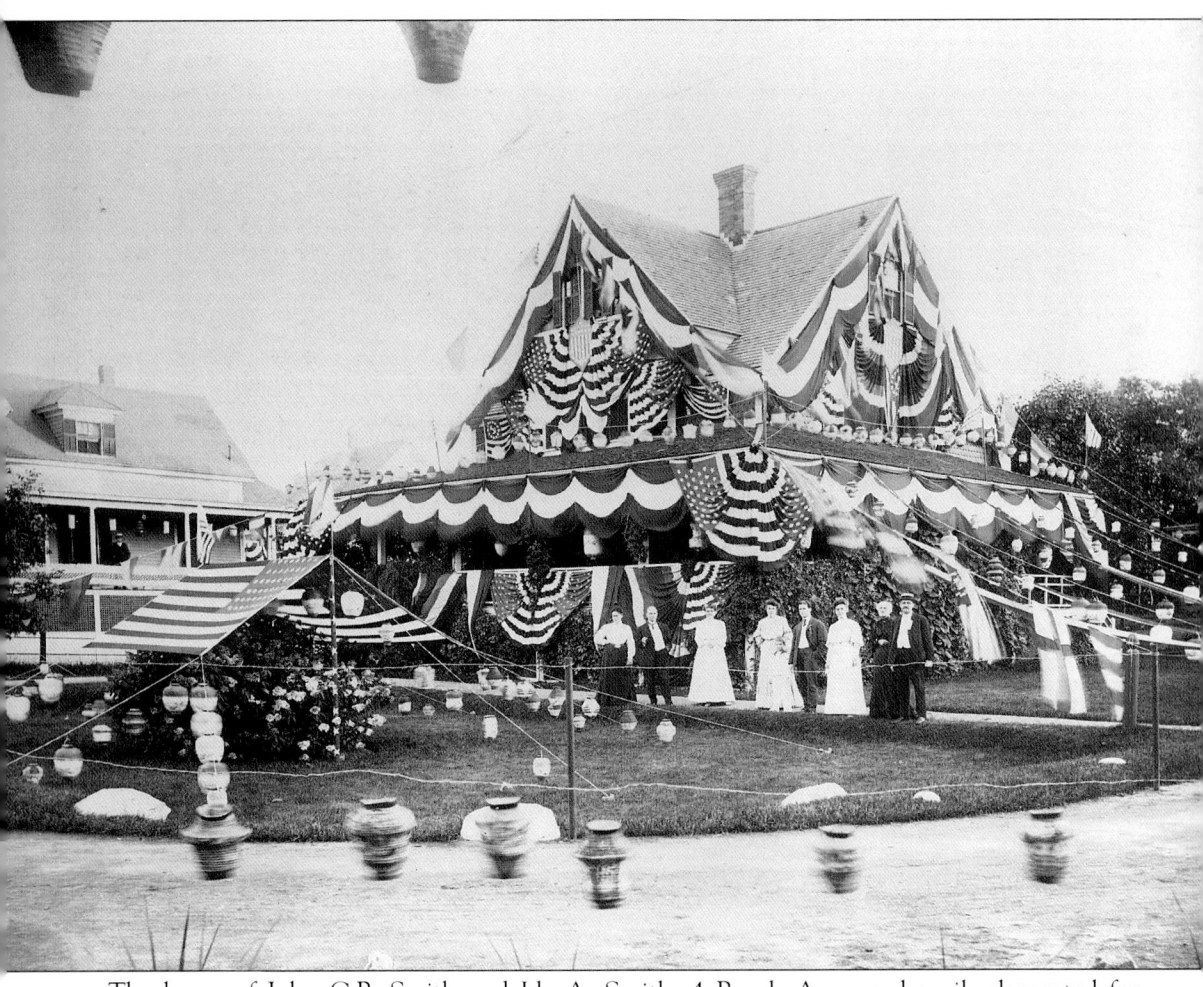

The home of John C.B. Smith and Ida A. Smith, 4 Beach Avenue, heavily decorated for Carnival Week at Salem Willows and Juniper Point, August 14, 1905. The Smith Taylor Company of Boston held its annual employee outing during Carnival Week at Salem Willows. Mr. J.C.B. Smith was a member of this firm. The house is decorated for the "illumination fireworks." (Courtesy D. Michel Michaud.)

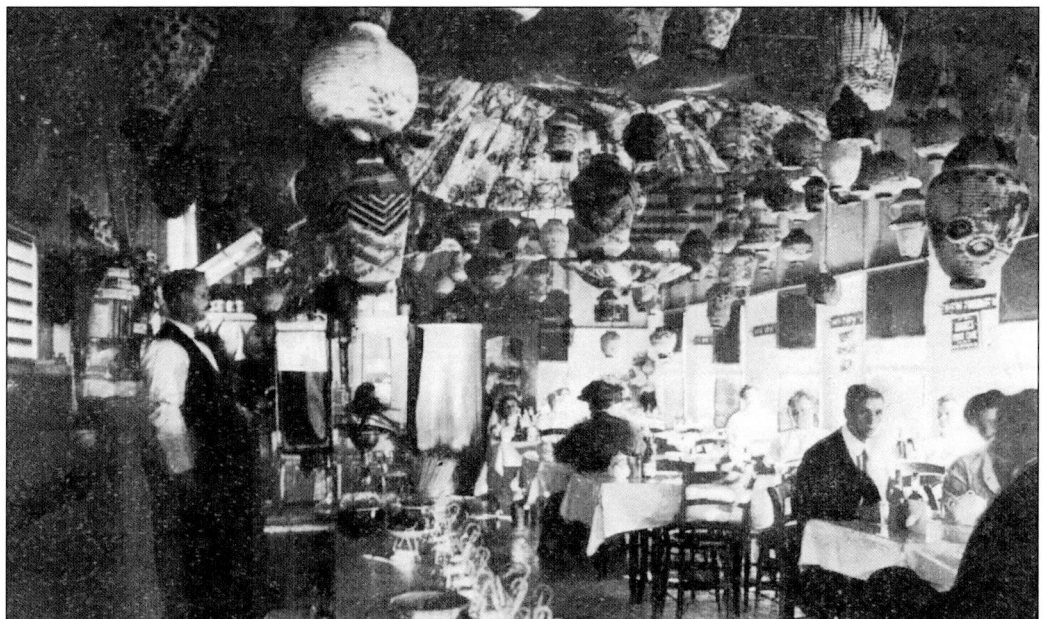
J.C. Downing's, c. 1915. The interior of this restaurant at Salem Willows had an oriental flair. (Courtesy D. Michel Michaud.)

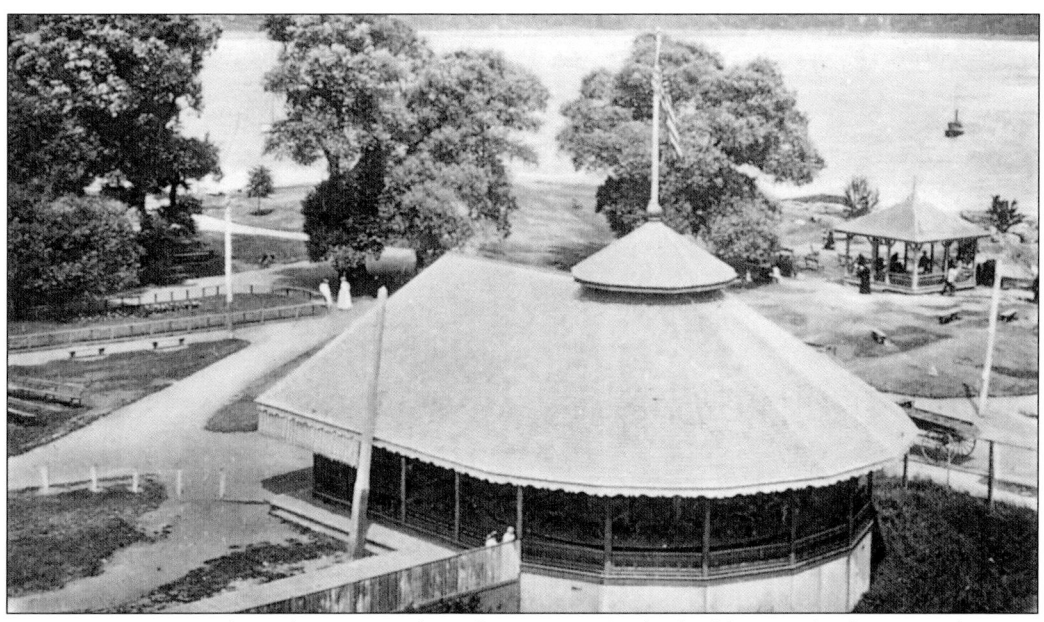
A picturesque view from the Tower of Pavilion, c. 1905. The building in the foreground is now the Hobbs Ice Cream concession stand. The trees are European white willows, from which the park gets its name. Across the water is the Beverly shoreline.

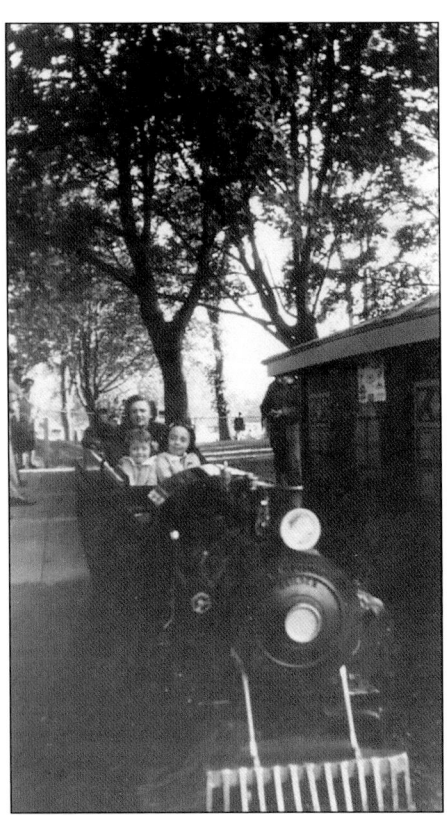

The miniature train. One of the more popular amusement rides was this miniature-scale model train, c. 1950. (Courtesy Ben and Sally Mathias.)

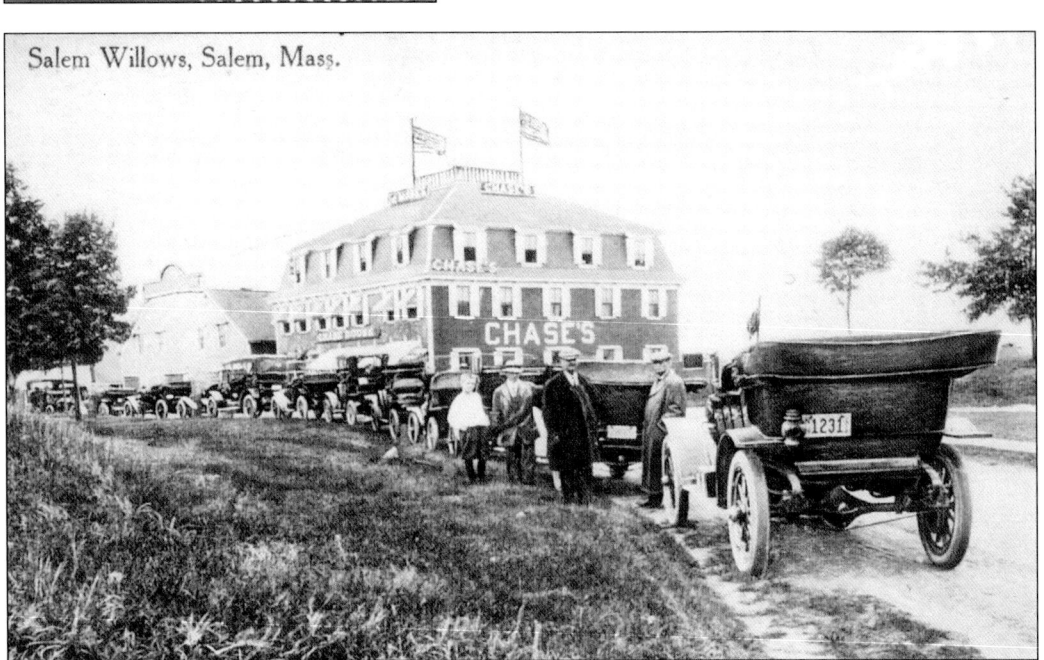

The Chase House, c. 1920. A popular destination for Salem residents in the summer season was Salem Willows, and the Chase House was one of the park's landmark restaurants. The restaurant opened in 1874 and closed in 1957. (Courtesy D. Michel Michaud.)

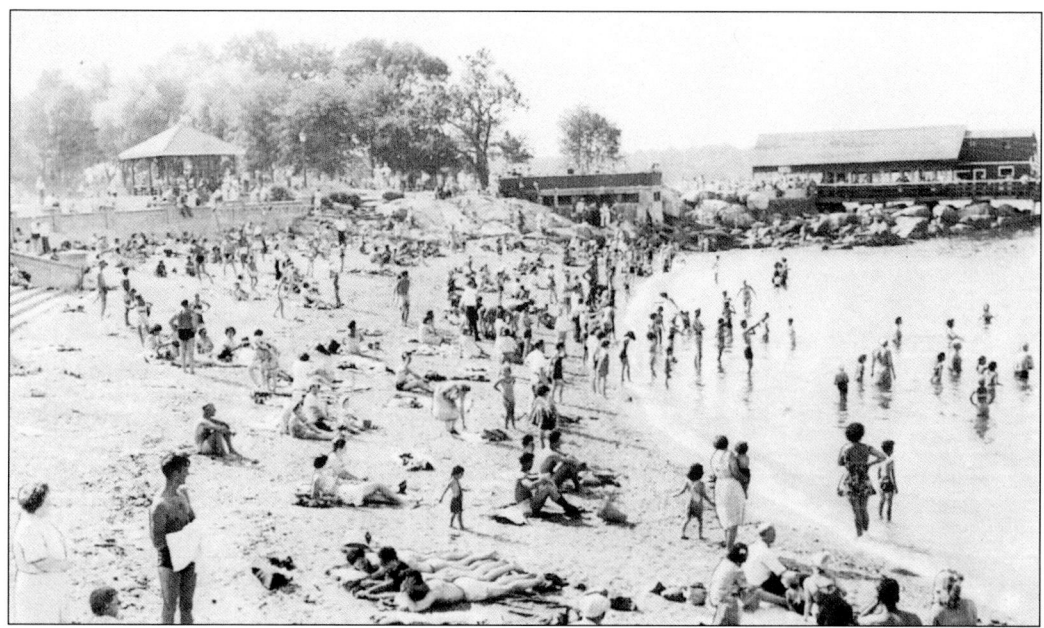

The crowded, sandy beach at Salem Willows, c. 1940, always a favorite spot for young and old alike. The chilly Salem waters bring cooling relief during the proverbial dog days of summer. (Courtesy Borinous Schier.)

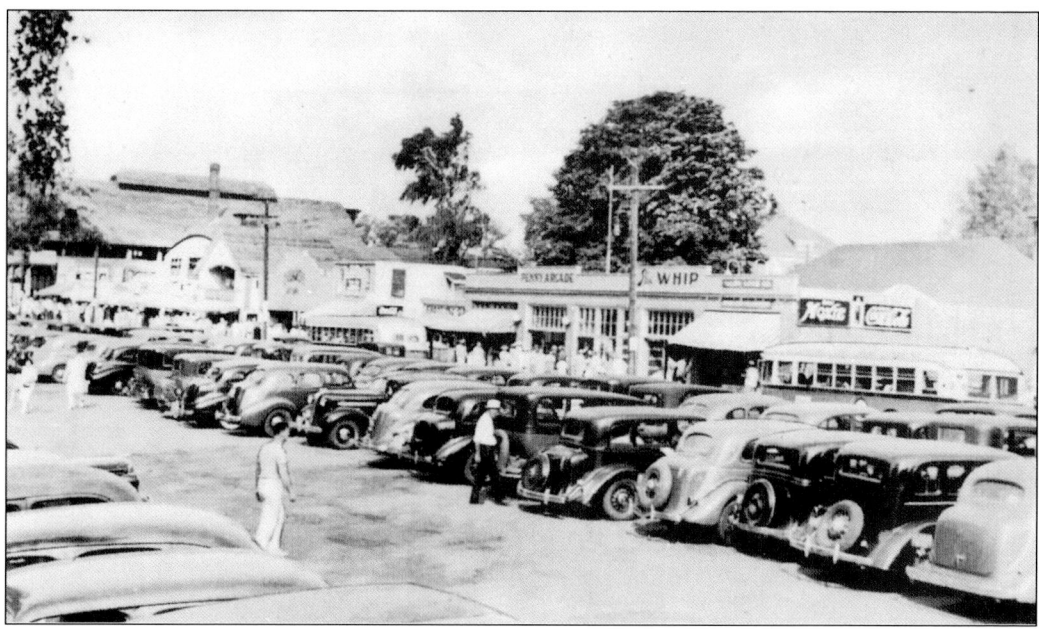

Throughout the decades the popularity of this seaside park never seems to wane. During the summer the parking lot is always full. Buses and trolleys made it their destination, c. 1940. (Courtesy Borinous Schier.)

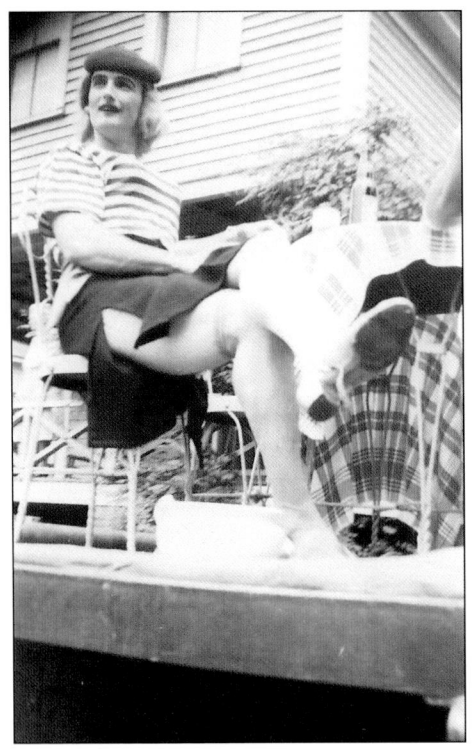

The Horribles. This parade has been a Fourth of July tradition at the Willows for many years. Two comic scenes from the 1950s are shown here.

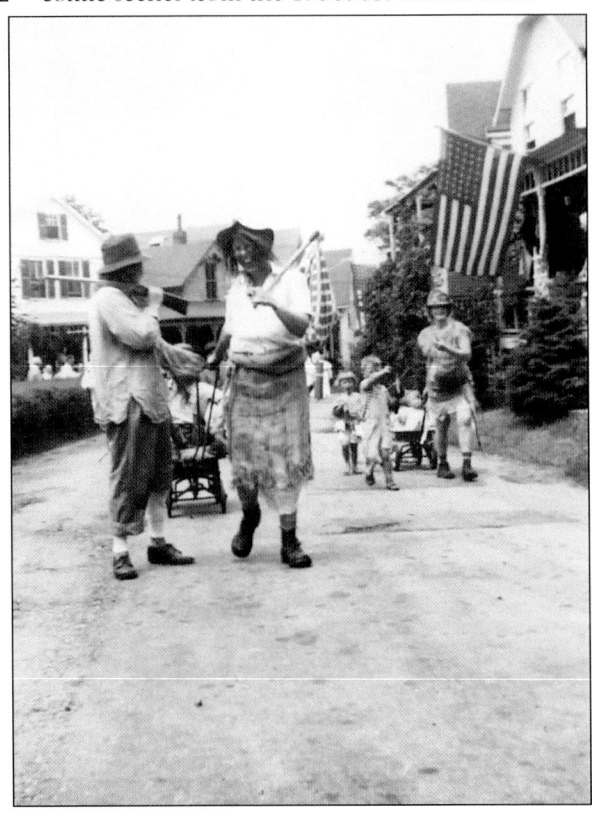

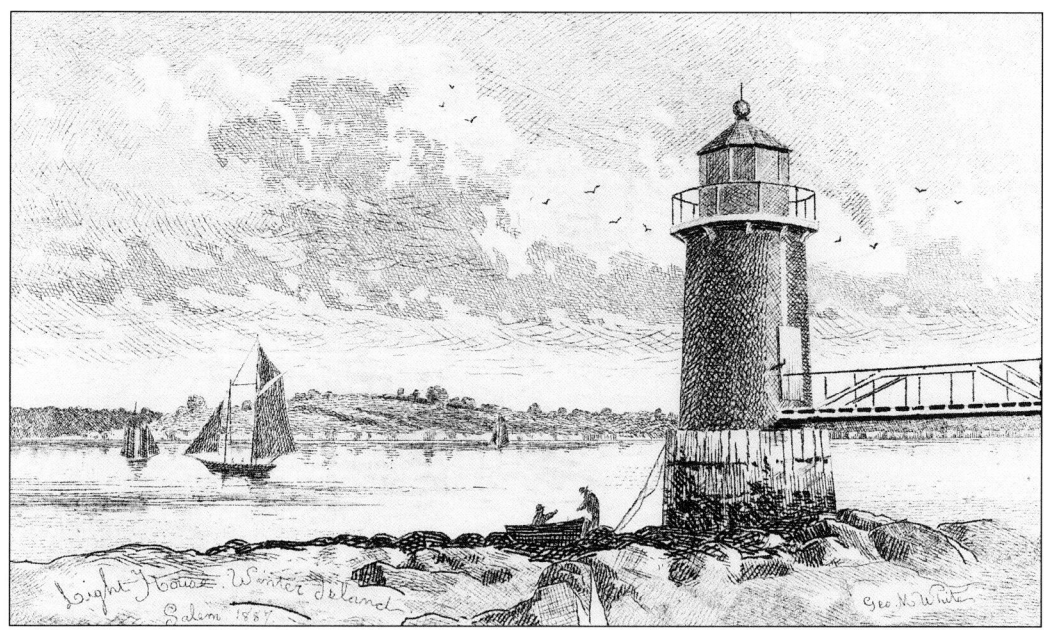

A copper plate engraving of the Winter Island Lighthouse, dated 1887, by Salem artist George Merwanjee White (1849–1915). (Courtesy John Hardy Wright.)

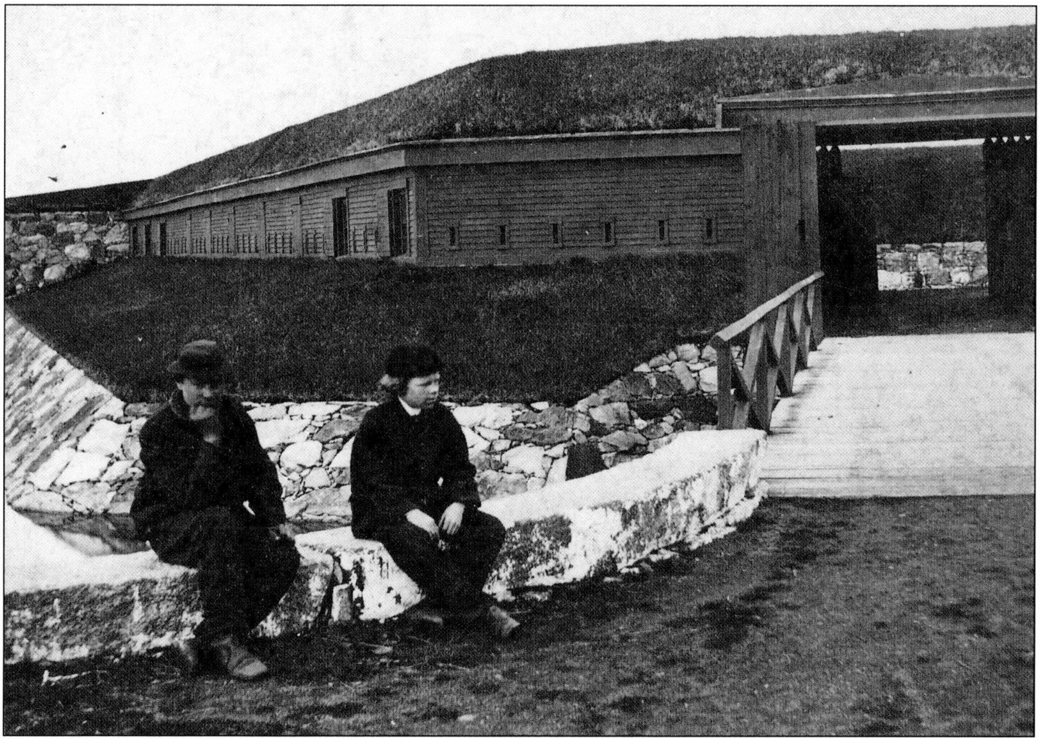

Fort Pickering at Winter Island, c. 1880. For over three hundred years, Winter Island was a site of military activity. In the late seventeenth century it was known as Fort William. In 1799 it was renamed in honor of Colonel Timothy Pickering, who was secretary of war under George Washington. (Courtesy D. Michel Michaud.)

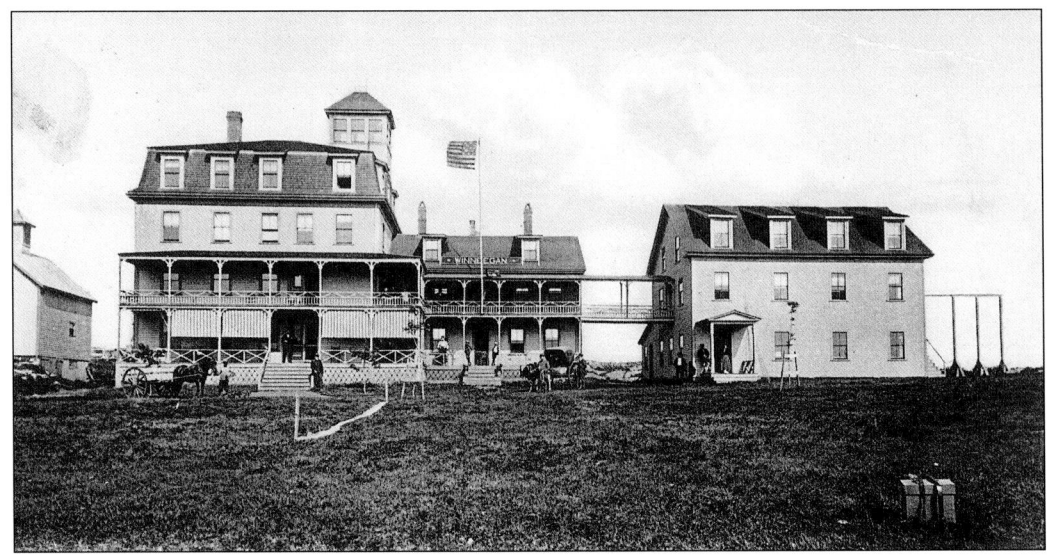

The Hotel Winneegan, Baker's Island. Dr. Nathan R. Morse purchased the island in 1887 and began construction on the wood-framed building; through the years additions were added. It probably opened for business during the 1888 season. The name means "beautiful expanse of water." The popular hotel's demise came in 1906 when it was consumed by fire before the start of the season.

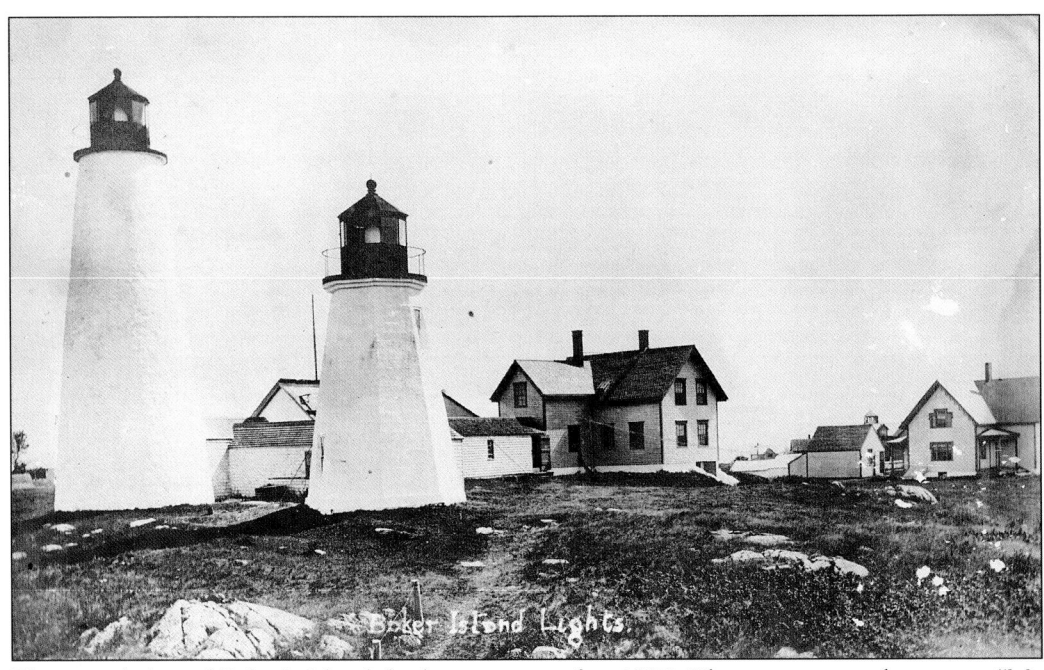

The twin lights of Baker's Island, built sometime after 1820. The towers were known as "Ma and Pa Baker." The smaller lighthouse was removed in 1926. (Courtesy D. Michel Michaud.)

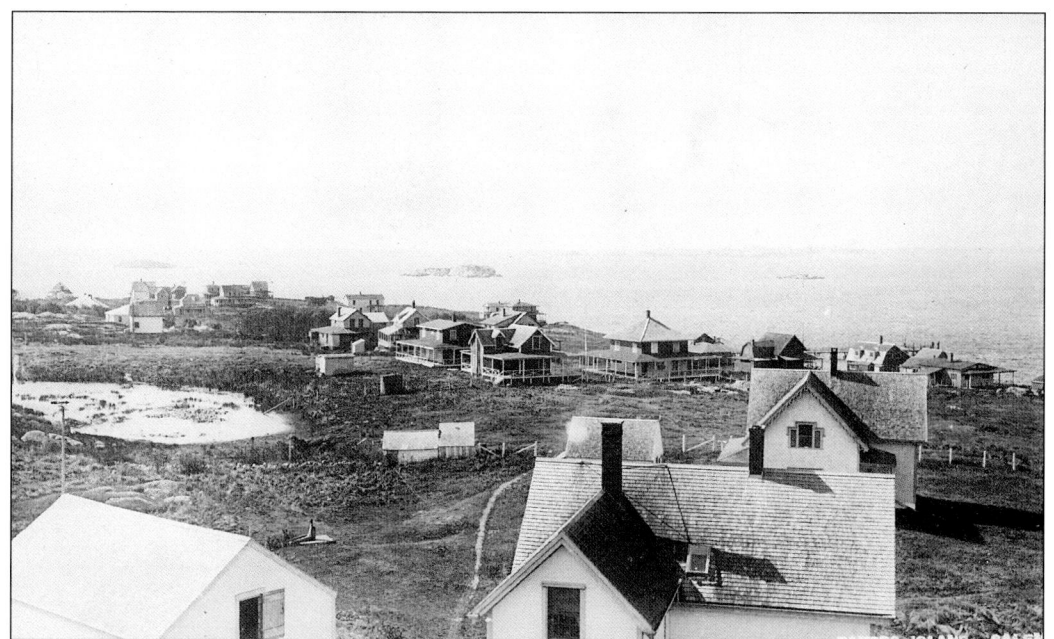

A bird's eye view of some of the summer cottages of Baker's Island, c. 1910. Baker's Island has been a select island retreat for North Shore residents for many years. (Courtesy D. Michel Michaud.)

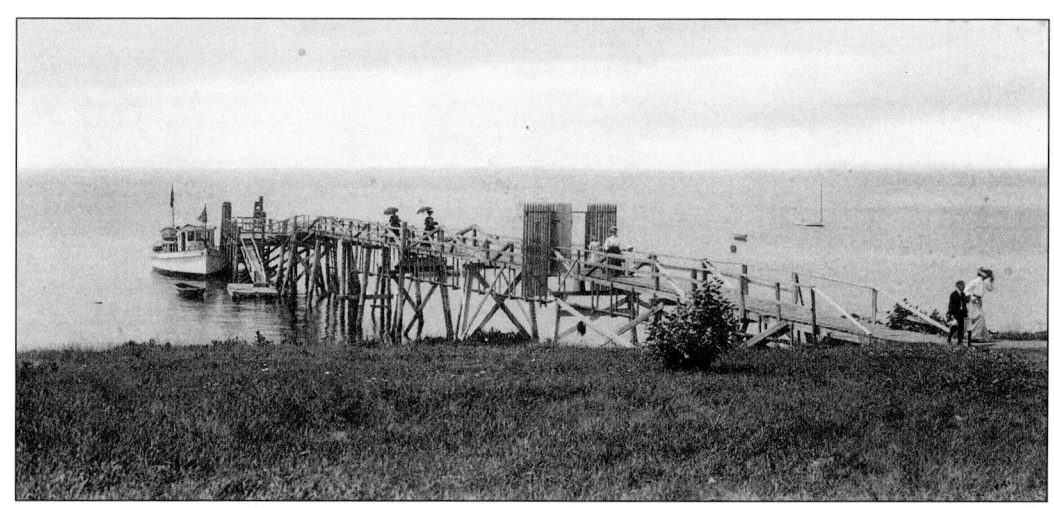

The pier at Baker's Island, c. 1905, originally built by an early summer resident, George P. Woodbury. Woodbury built the pier to discharge ferry passengers bound for the Hotel Winneegan.

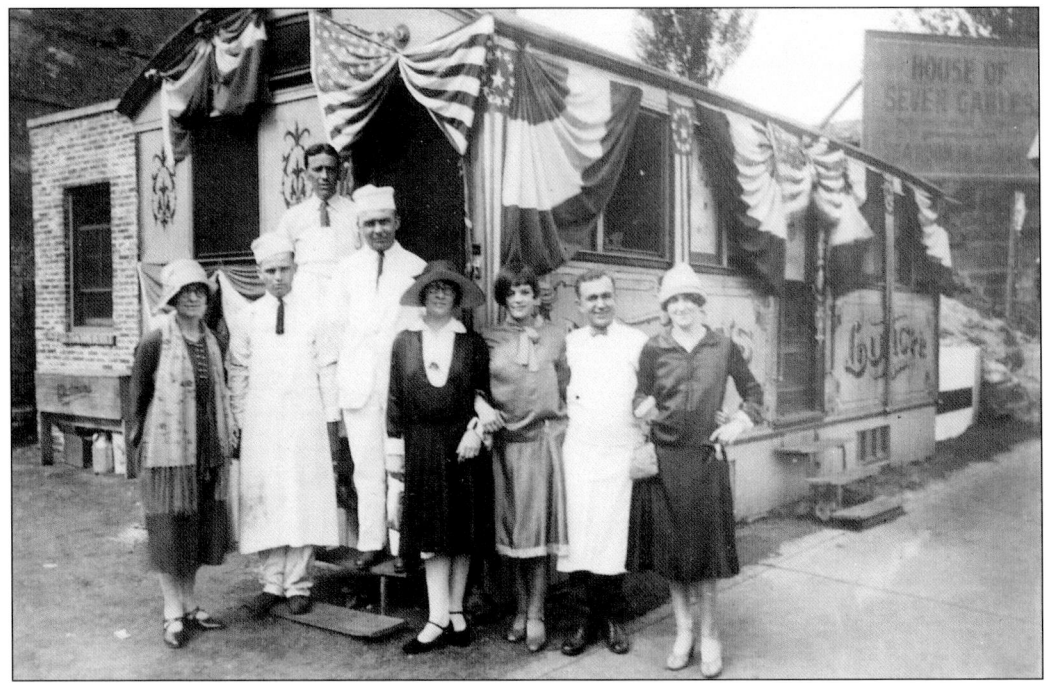

Mother's Lunch, located at 288 Derby Street, draped in flags and bunting for Salem's Tercentenary in 1926. (Courtesy Armand Martel.)

# ACKNOWLEDGMENTS

The authors wish to thank the kind people who made this pictorial history of Salem, Massachusetts, possible. Particular thanks must go to D. Michel Michaud who generously allowed the authors to select photographs from what is surely one of the finest private collections of Salem memorabilia, and who also provided much needed historical information. Several historical museums kindly loaned images for the book: the Danvers Historical Society; the Lynn Historical Society; the North Shore Jewish Historical Society; and the Pickering Foundation (Sarah C. Pickering was especially helpful). Other lenders included Bodin Historic Photo of Gloucester, MA, Joe Jalbert, John Kobuszewski, Marblehead Antiques, Armand Martel, Ben and Sally Mathias, Henri Michaud, Gary Peterson of the Eastern Bank and Trust Company, Borinous Schier, Gary Thomas, and John Hardy Wright. Fay Greenleaf processed the manuscript and offered editorial assistance, as did John Hardy Wright, Lee Oestriecher, and Christopher Mathias.